AF575915

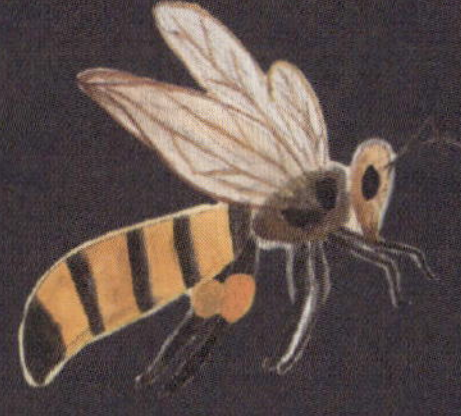

PAUL J. STANKARD

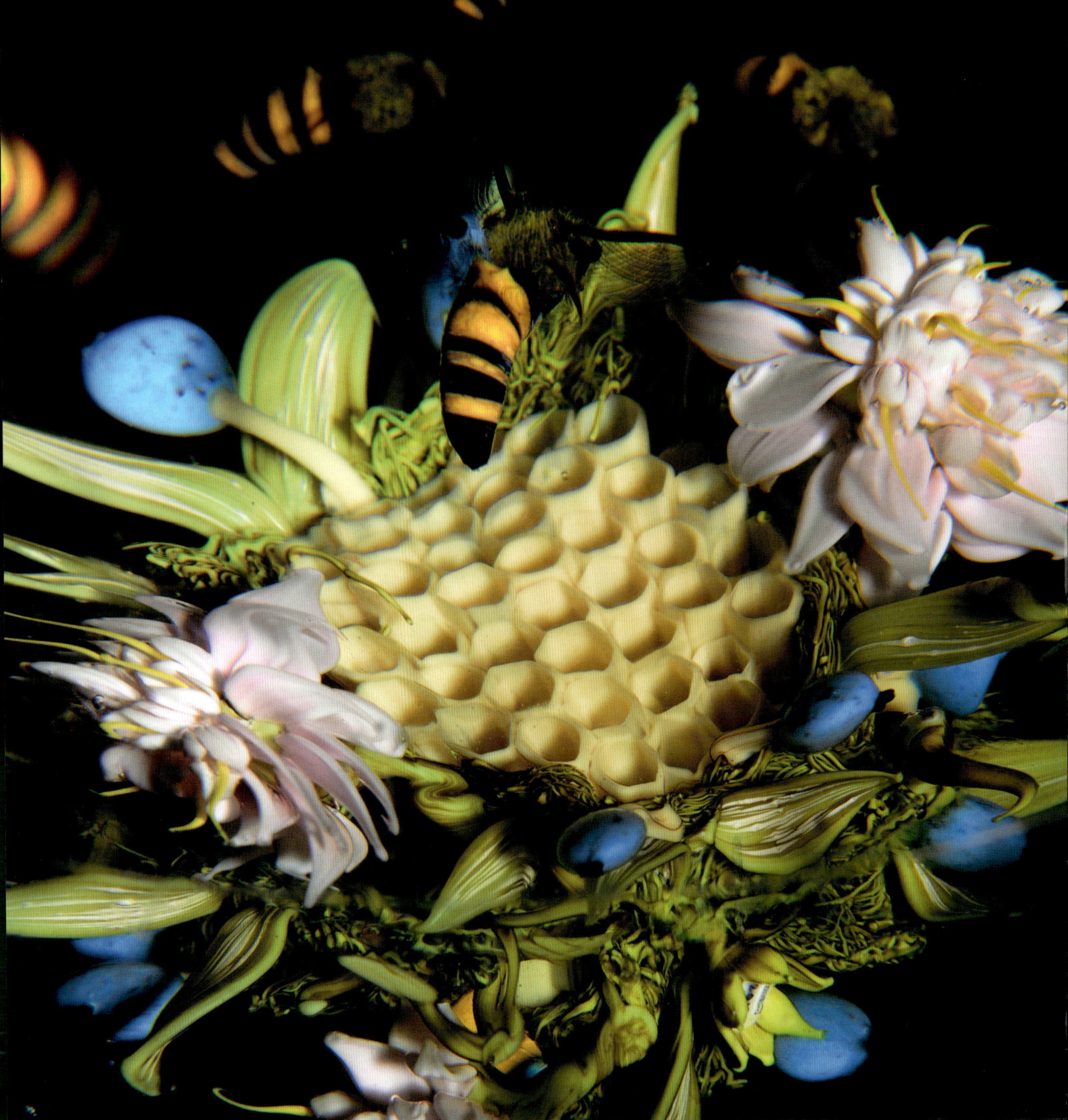

Inspiration from the Art of

PAUL J. STANKARD

A Window into My Studio and Soul

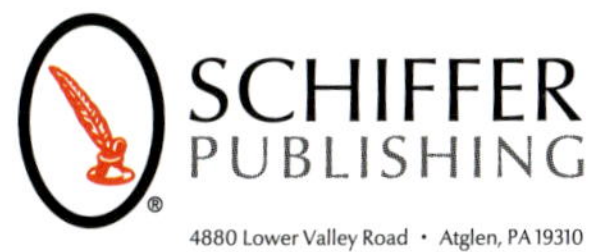

4880 Lower Valley Road • Atglen, PA 19310

Library of Congress Control Number: 2020952778

Designed by Ashley Millhouse
Type set in Granville/Muli

ISBN: 978-0-7643-6257-6
Printed in Serbia

Published by Schiffer Publishing, Ltd.
4880 Lower Valley Road
Atglen, PA 19310
Phone: (610) 593-1777; Fax: (610) 593-2002
Email: Info@schifferbooks.com
Web: www.schifferbooks.com

For our complete selection of fine books on this and related subjects, please visit our website at www.schifferbooks.com. You may also write for a free catalog.

Schiffer Publishing's titles are available at special discounts for bulk purchases for sales promotions or premiums. Special editions, including personalized covers, corporate imprints, and excerpts, can be created in large quantities for special needs. For more information, contact the publisher.

We are always looking for people to write books on new and related subjects. If you have an idea for a book, please contact us at proposals@schifferbooks.com.

Other Schiffer Books by the Author:

Studio Craft as Career,
ISBN 978-0-7643-5252-2

When the work is completed, I think of it as my prayer traveling into the future, my soul connected to time, space, and beauty.

—Paul J. Stankard

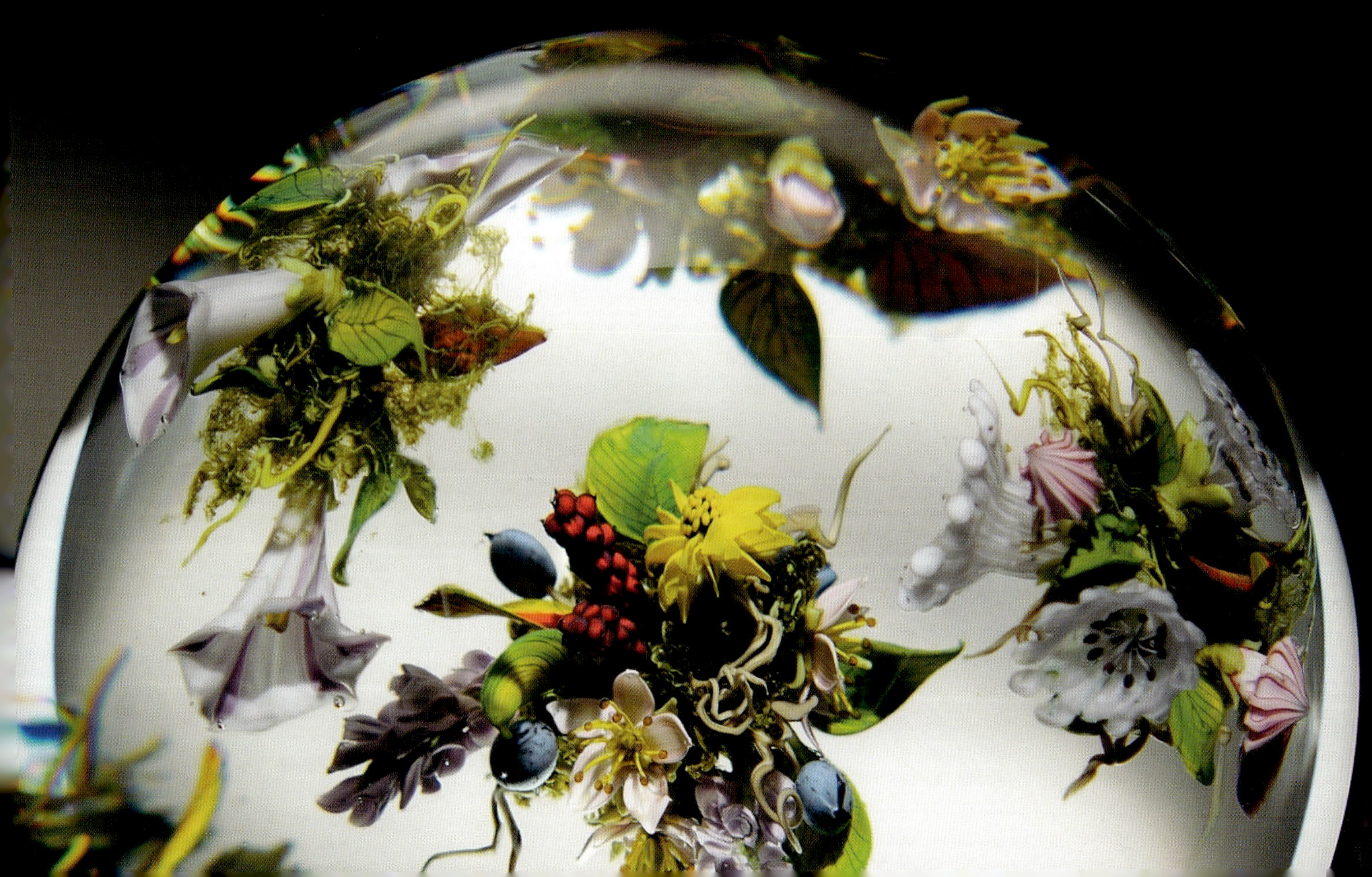

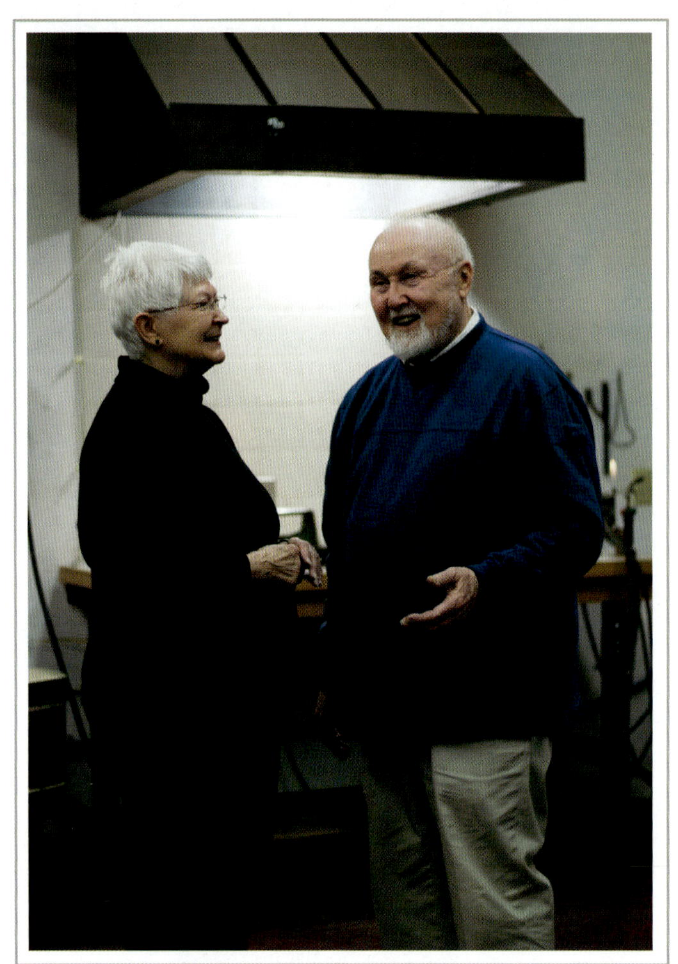

This book is dedicated to my wife, Patricia, whose support and advice over our fifty-six-year marriage has been my inspiration.

Introduction 11

Part 1: The Beginning 21

CHAPTER 1: Get Serious 22

CHAPTER 2: Develop a Work Ethic 28

CHAPTER 3: Embrace Positive Thinking 38

CHAPTER 4: Take Creativity Seriously—Artists Are Professionals 44

CHAPTER 5: Learn from Your Best Teacher—Failure 58

CHAPTER 6: Create a Comfortable Space for Your Art Making 66

Part 2: The Elements of Art 73

CHAPTER 7: How I Define Beauty 74

CHAPTER 8: Craft, Design, and Art 96

CHAPTER 9: Blend the Past with the Present 104

CHAPTER 10: Detail and Delicacy 112

CHAPTER 11: Know Thyself 120

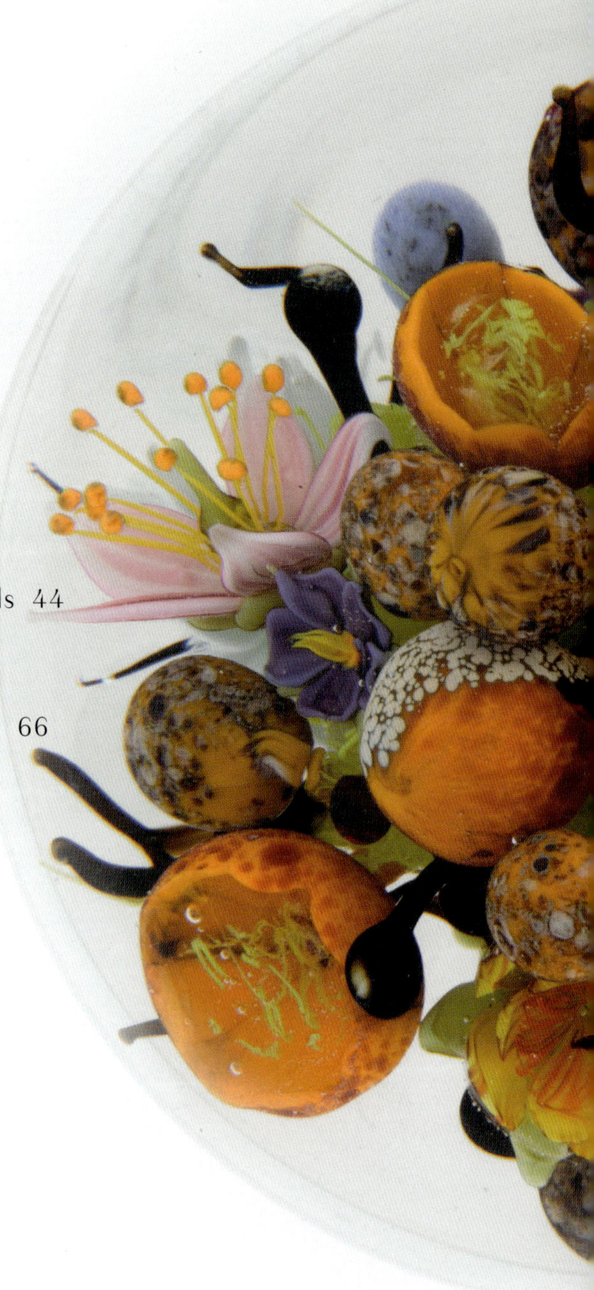

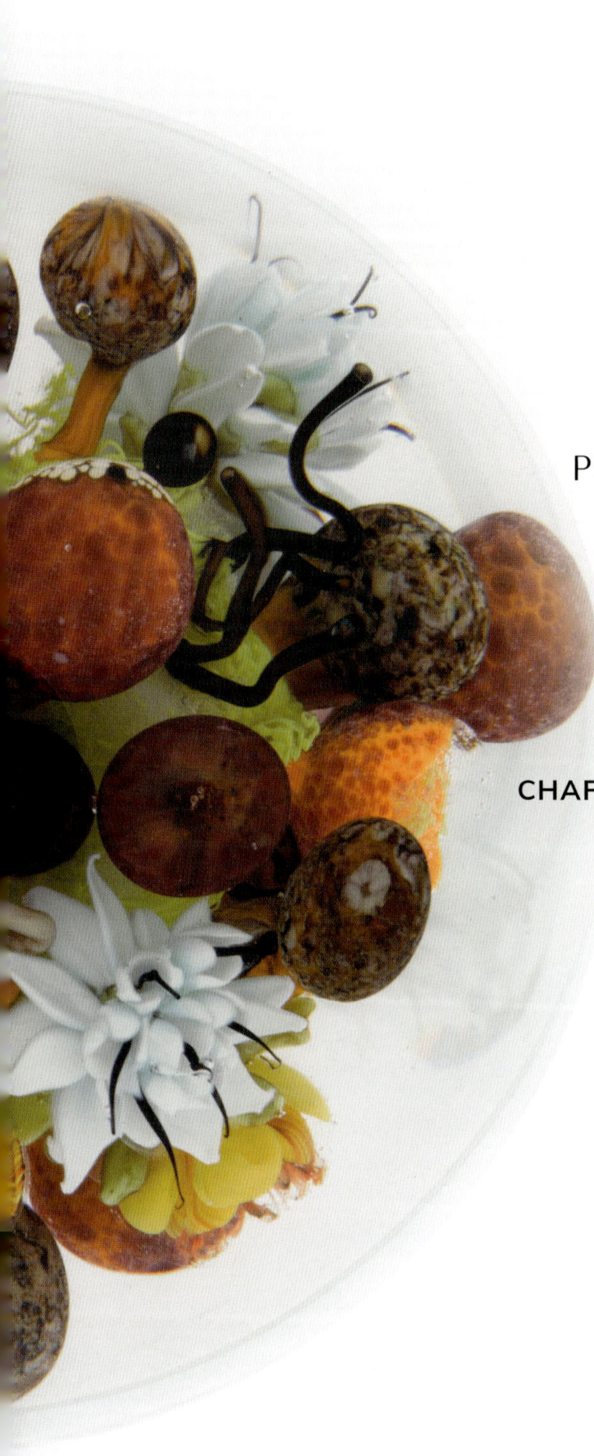

Part 3: Growing with Artistic Maturity 127

CHAPTER 12: It's Not Going to Get Easier 128

CHAPTER 13: Originality 134

CHAPTER 14: Become Obsessed 142

CHAPTER 15: Take Advantage of Anxiety 148

CHAPTER 16: Nurture Spirituality as a Mystical Ingredient 154

CHAPTER 17: Gratitude with Attitude 160

Epilogue 166

Acknowledgments 170

Public Collections 172

Public Exhibitions 173

About the Author 176

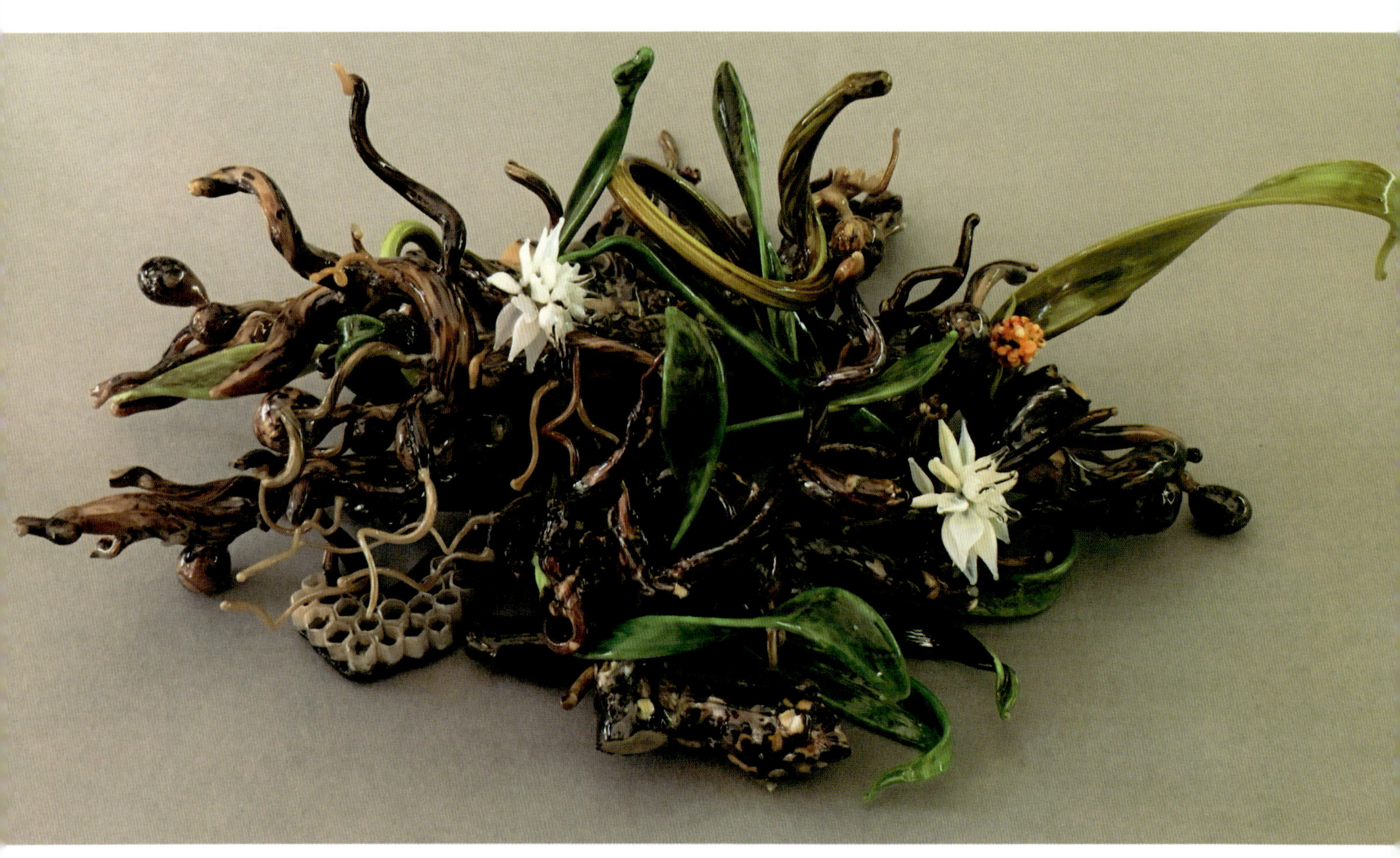

Floral Clump from Walt Whitman's Garden Series
My artistic energy has focused on interpreting nature in glass. The process I use is called flameworking. I use a gas oxygen torch to melt colored glass into flowers, petals, and other botanical components that are later encapsulated in molten clear glass.

INTRODUCTION

Early in my career, my goal was to move from the production of scientific glass to the artistic side of glass.

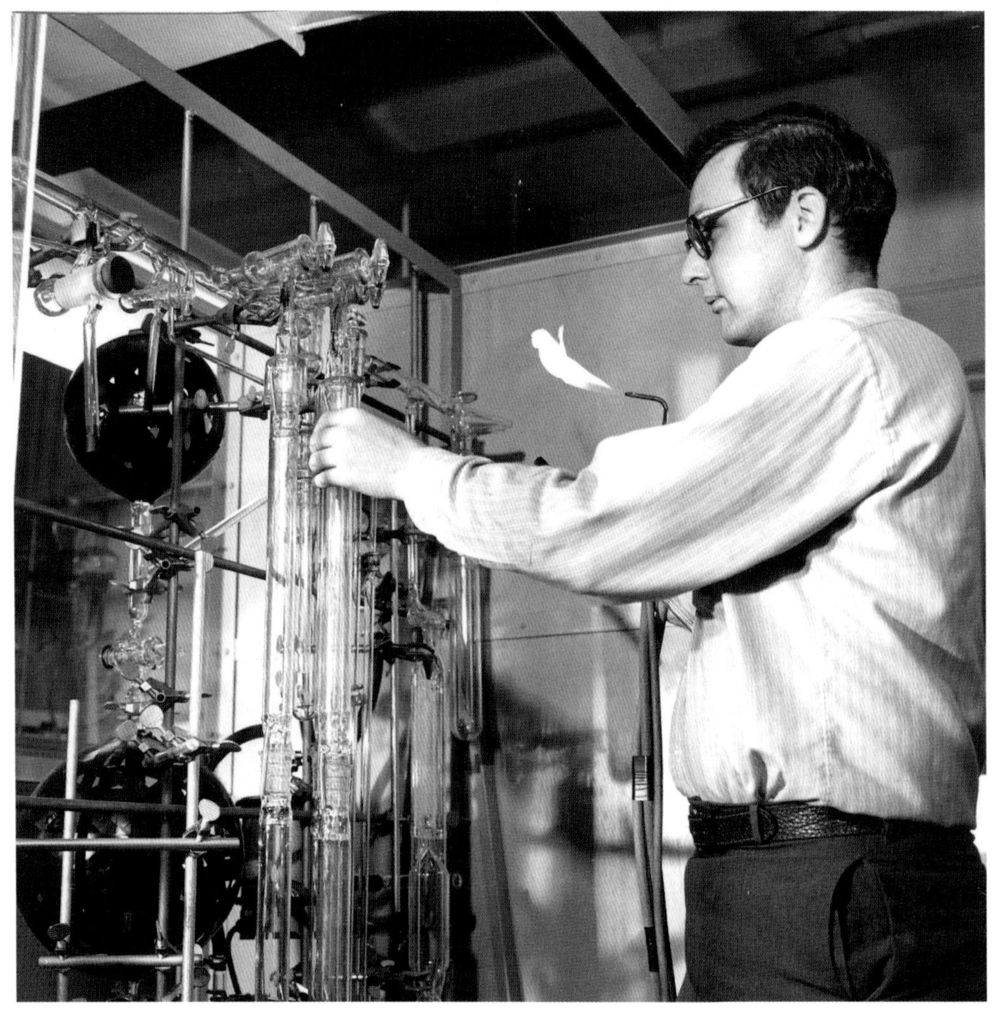

Paul assembling glass high-vacuum system

In 1970, I was working in industry as a master scientific glass craftsperson. Pictured above, I am building a vacuum system, which was used for research in an organic chemistry laboratory.

Over my glass art career, I've gone from a struggling artist/craftsperson to an established artist whose artwork is now represented in more than seventy-five museums around the world. I'm self-taught in the ways of art making, and the recipient of national and international awards.

Early in my career, my goal was to move from the production of scientific glass to the artistic side of glass. When I started my creative journey, I had no idea what path to take other than crafting inexpensive giftware.

After over nine years of working with scientific glass, I upped my game by pursuing more-interesting work on the creative side, building on past glass traditions while, at the same time, striving to craft my floral designs based on a personal response to native flowers. Because I knew of no preexisting road map, I relied on self-directed learning, designing a plan complemented by discussions with artists, art collectors, gallery owners, critics, and anyone I met who was enthusiastic about art.

This collection of essays—fashioned as individual chapters—is a window into a fifty-plus-year career as a studio artist, and the challenges I have met and continue to meet.

What's offered in this book is an outline of a journey that nurtures personal and professional growth. My experiences allowed me not only to advance to new levels of art making but also to build scaffolding on my foundation—a process that continues to this day.

This is not a book focused on my glassworking process. Rather, it's a guide for nurturing personal creativity and the formation of your own plan to reach your full potential, whether you are a creator yourself or someone who simply enjoys the inside story and the endless challenges of art making.

This book opens with advice on how to identify your true interests. In the case of an artist, you will be encouraged to survey art magazines, museums, and galleries, even if it means expense and inconvenience. If you are a writer or musician, focus on what touches your soul, and seek out any and all information in your area of interest. Familiarize yourself with the masters and work toward matching their passion. If you are a collector, become familiar with the history of your particular interests and the evolution of new works of significance. Identify several respected galleries to guide your selection.

In the process, you will find that your interests will expand to cover an area far wider than you had initially supposed—in fact, they may expand into areas you had not known existed, and that is the benefit of self-directed learning.

Your journey will become a lifestyle and a path to educating yourself about the creative world in general and the requirements that will aid you as you work toward a personal voice.

I have difficulty reading due to dyslexia, so I

educated myself by listening to audio books over forty years. This eventually led me to my love of classics. This need to be educated expanded not only my own world, but also my artistic maturity. Among the books that had the most impact was James Joyce's *Ulysses*, which introduced to me a realization that a masterful writer could take an ordinary subject or scenario and reveal the extraordinary depth of human emotion compressed into what, at first glance, appeared to be a mundane day in the life.

I realized that my work could have that same depth of feeling articulated visually in glass, and I labor to create that illusion.

I am writing this book to share what I could have benefited from early in my career. I have written many books and articles on nurturing artistic maturity, pursuing excellence, and taking art to the next level. But this book is intended for a broader audience interested in the nuances of beauty, whether it is being made, sold, or collected.

I hope to lay out a practical foundation to apply your heart and soul toward the upper echelons of a career as an artist or as a collector. This book offers insight into the ingredients that lead to significant work—obsession, spirituality, learning from failure, embracing positive thinking, labor, and the nuances of art, craft, and design, among other topics.

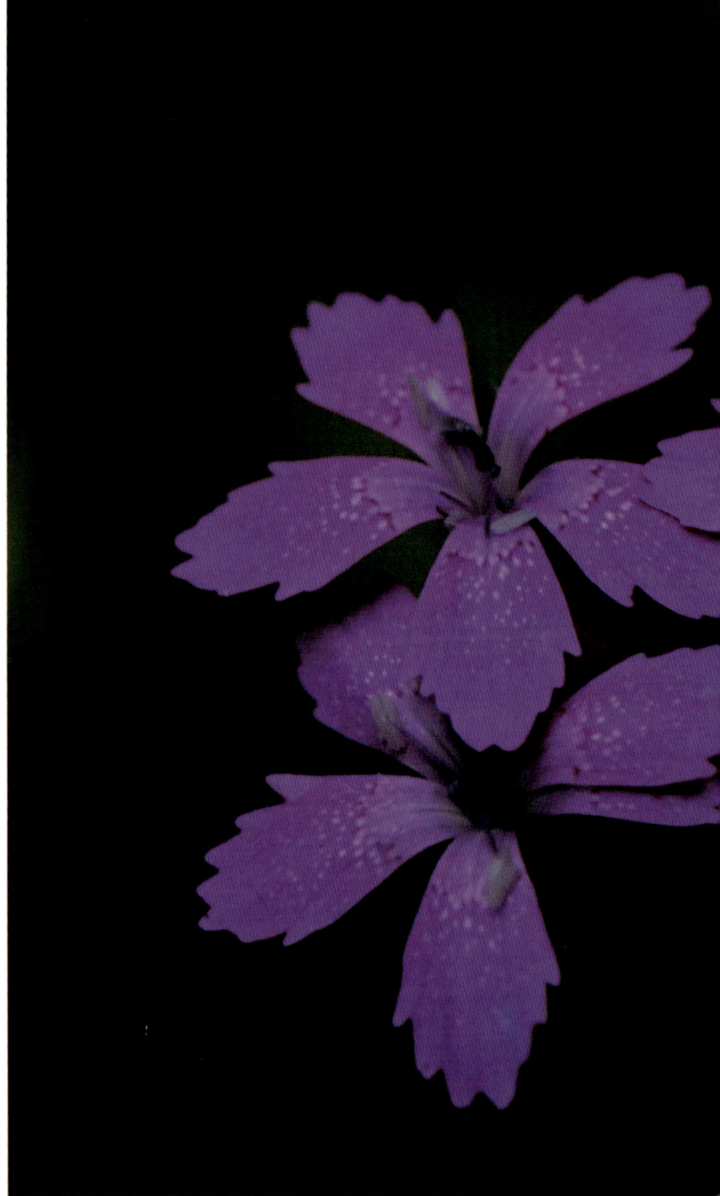

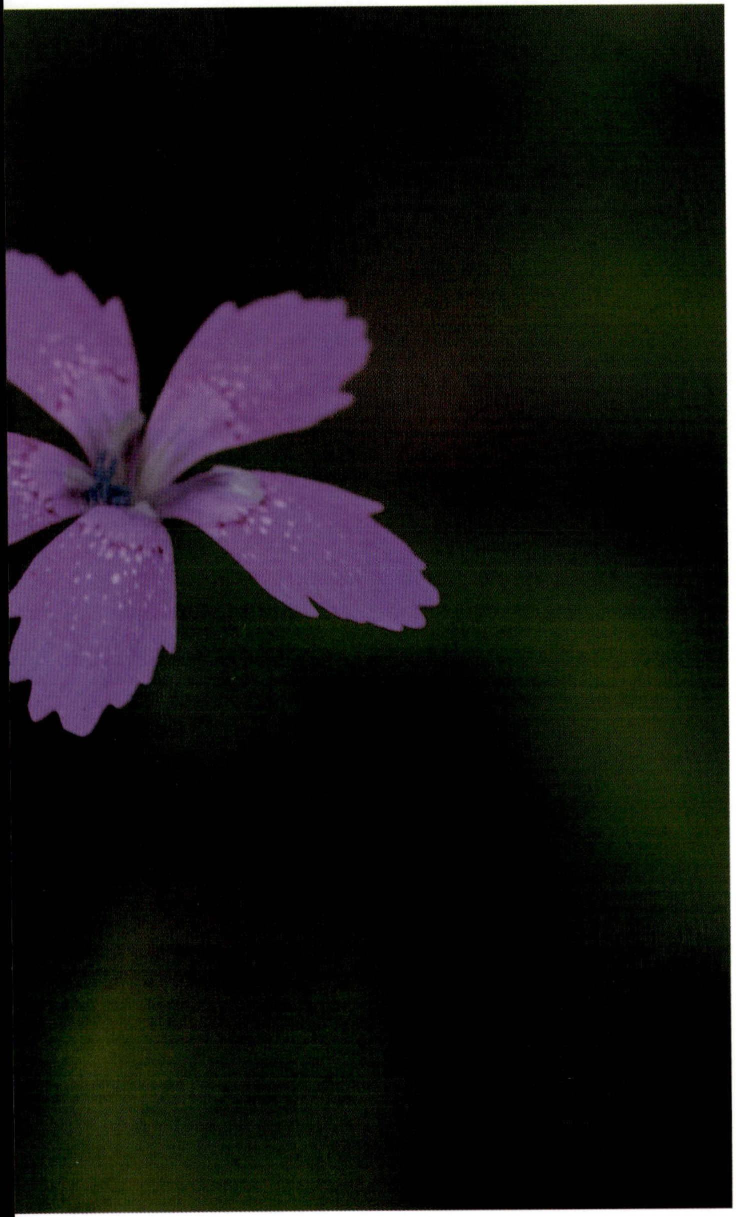

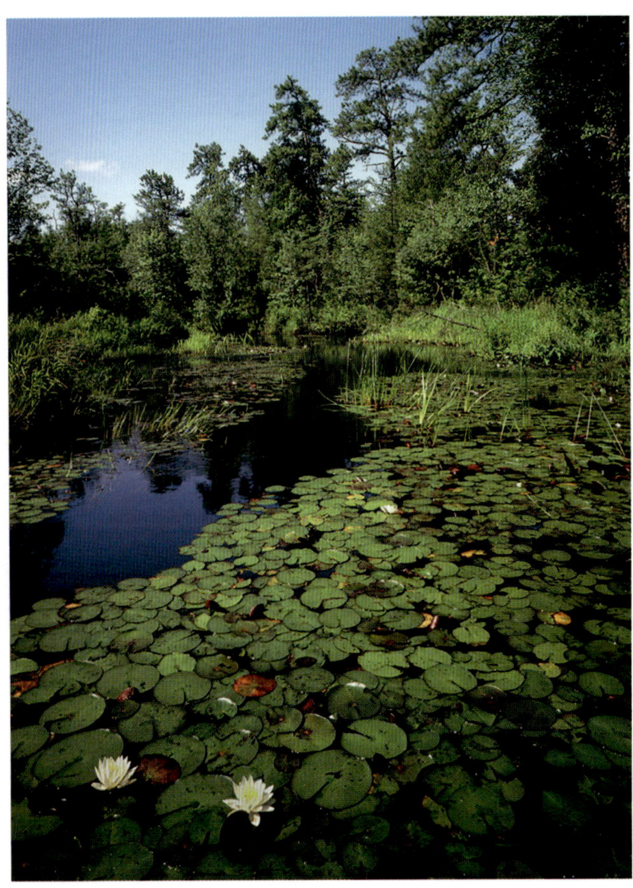

New Jersey pine barrens

Throughout my adolescent years, I enjoyed exploring the woods and swamps near my home and being fascinated with the native flowers. Those memories became the underpinning of a fifty-plus-year career that inspired melting hot glass into a botanical body of work that evolved from craft to my art.

Think back to your childhood fascinations. They may offer clues in identifying your authentic interests.

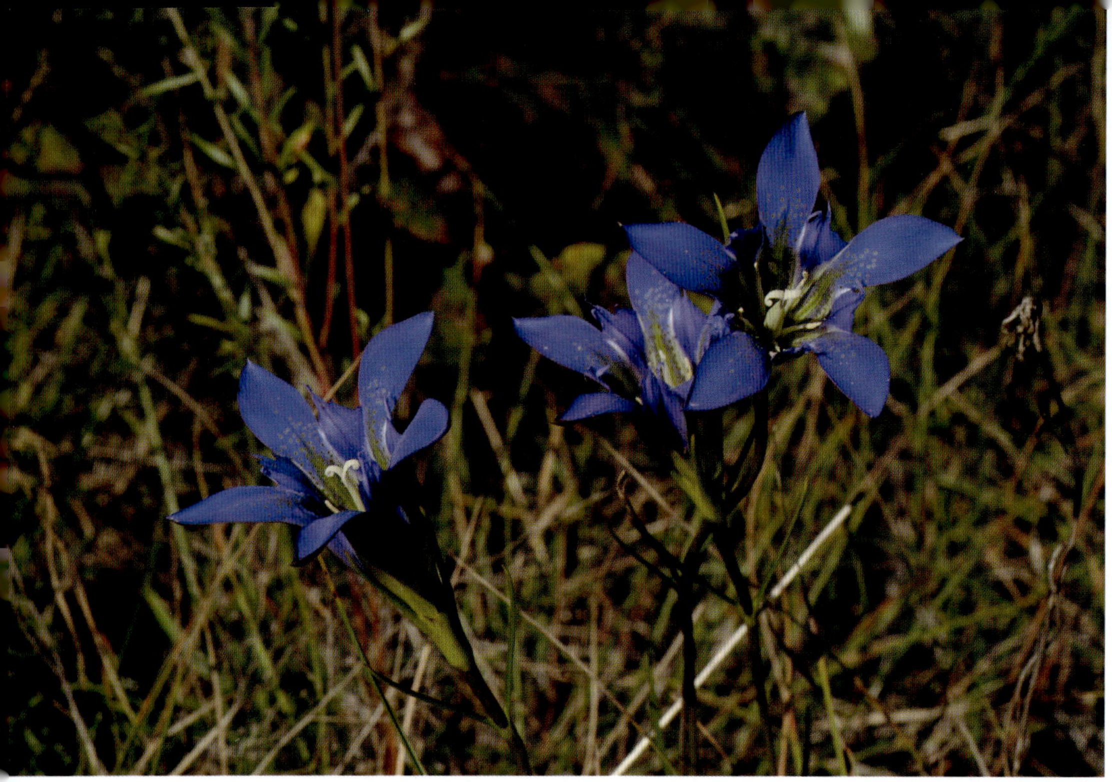

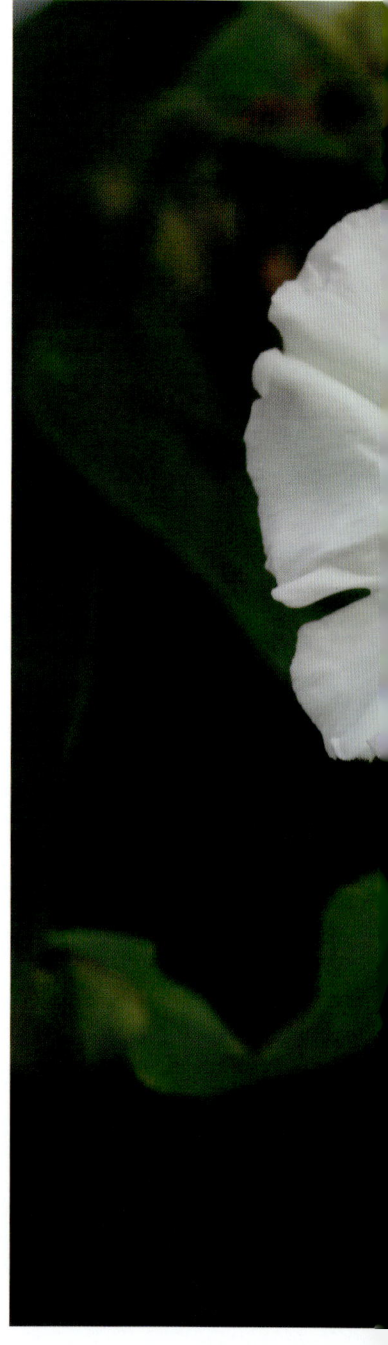

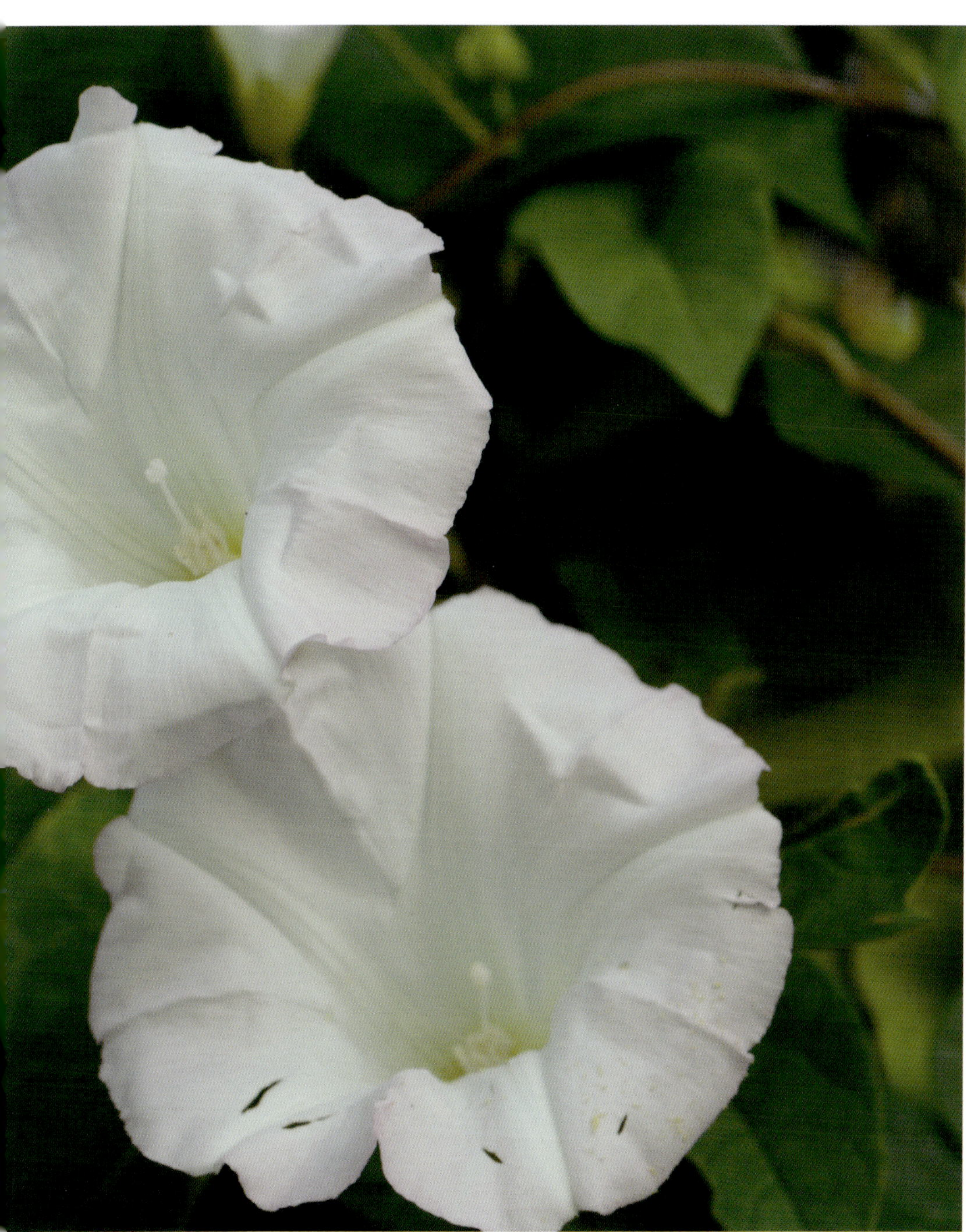

Morning glories
I'm inspired and touched by the nuances of Walt Whitman's response to native flowers: "A morning-glory at my window satisfies me more than the metaphysics of books."

Ultimately, I am not a wizard waving a wand to advance you to the next level, but rather a teacher who will help you better define your own goals. I have grown from my hard-won battles, and this advice is anchored in the reality of a full adult life working in my studio.

Your appreciation of art and beauty is your own path, and it is my sincerest wish that this book will offer insight that could direct you along your journey.

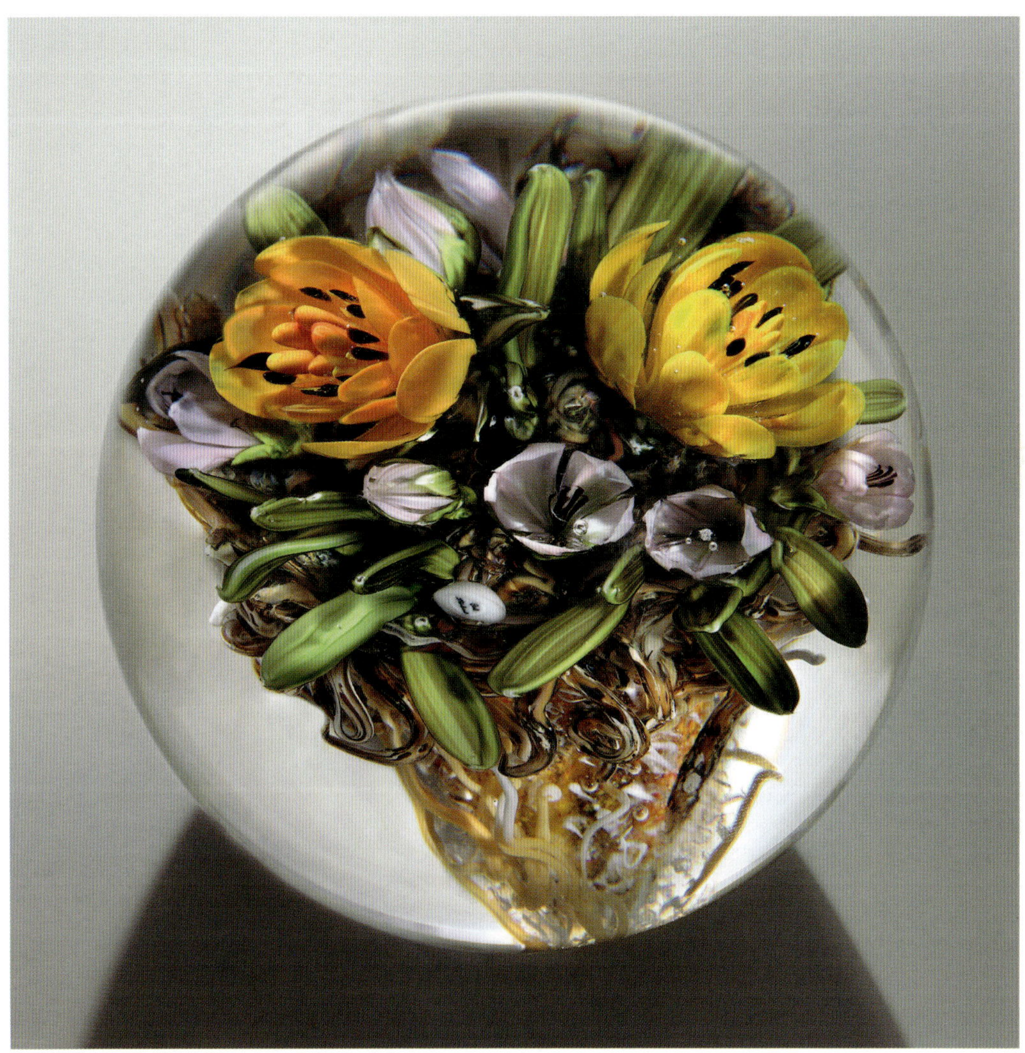

From Walt Whitman's Medicinal Herb Garden, 2021, 4 in.

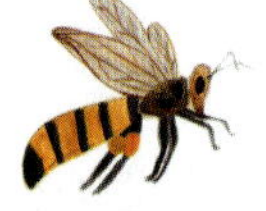

PART I

THE BEGINNING

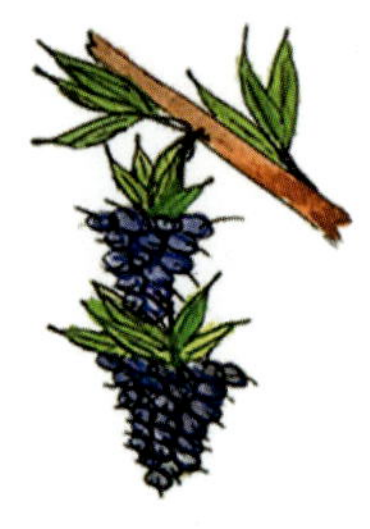

CHAPTER 1: GET SERIOUS

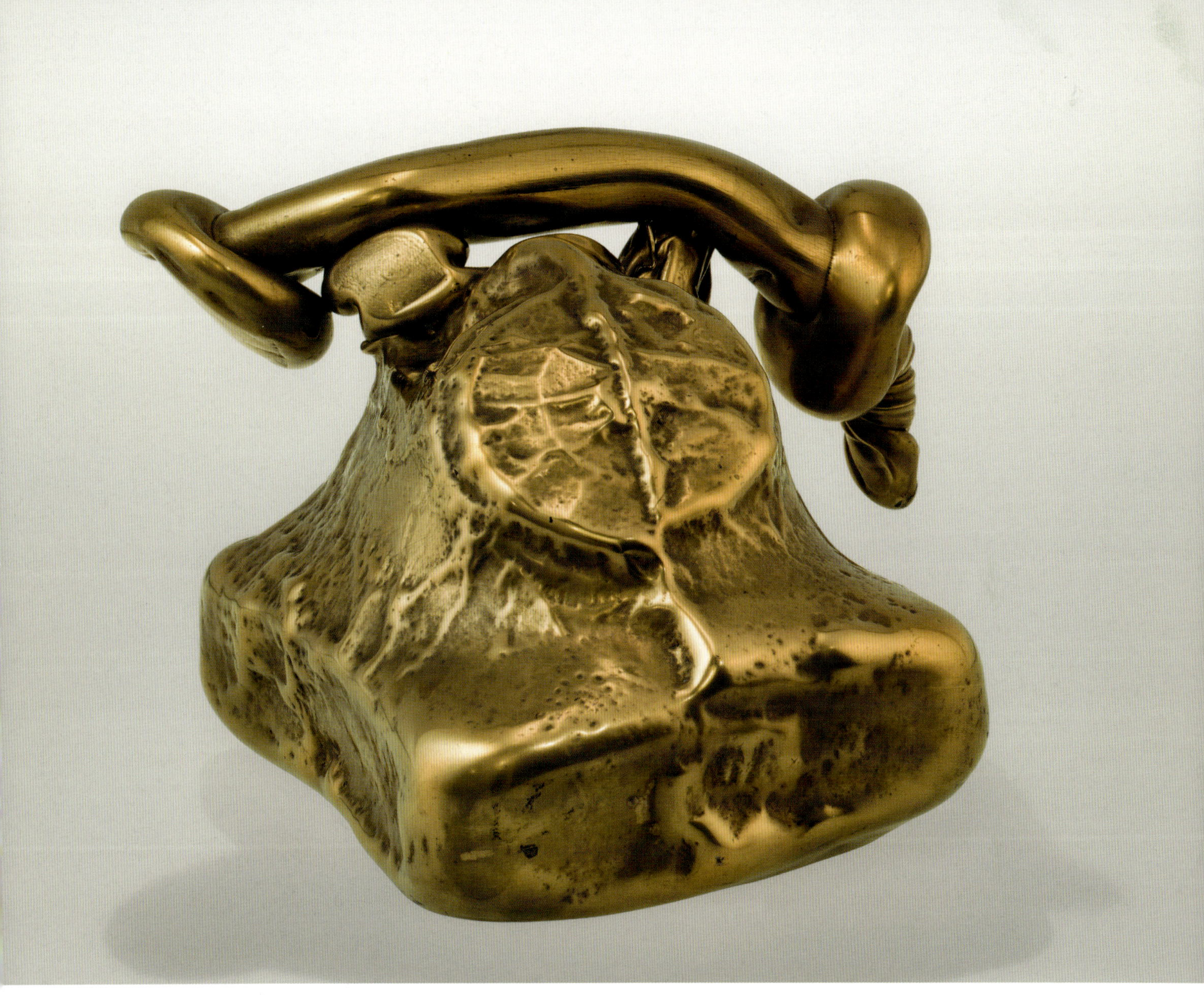

Being introduced to Erwin Eisch's glass art at the Philadelphia Art Alliance in the mid-'60s strengthened my resolve to be on the creative side working in glass. I was excited by his exhibited glass sculpture and the fresh approach he took to blowing glass. It was a novel result representing the future of how glass could become object art.

Prior to this glass exposure, my idea of art glass was glass knickknacks crafted on a torch.

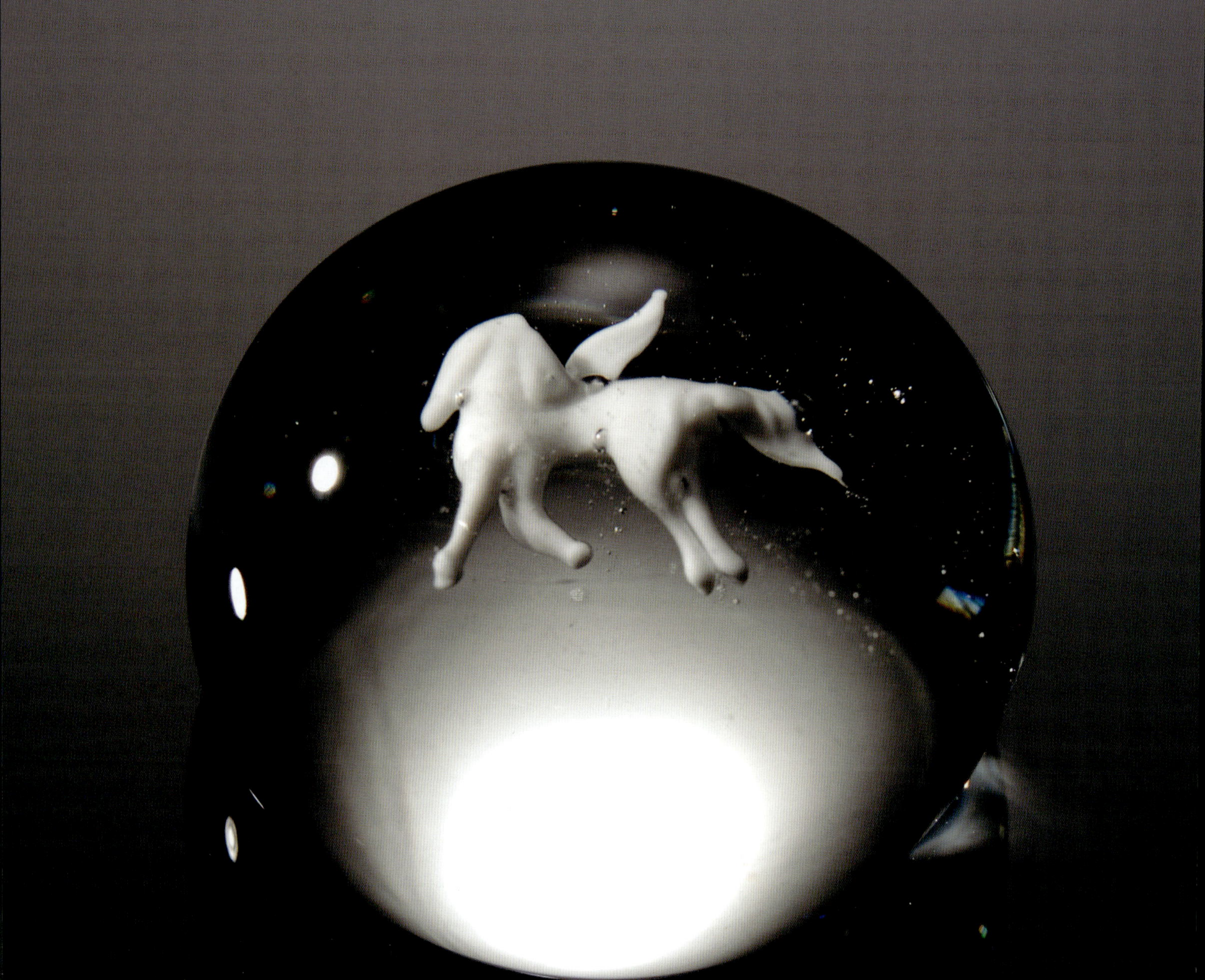

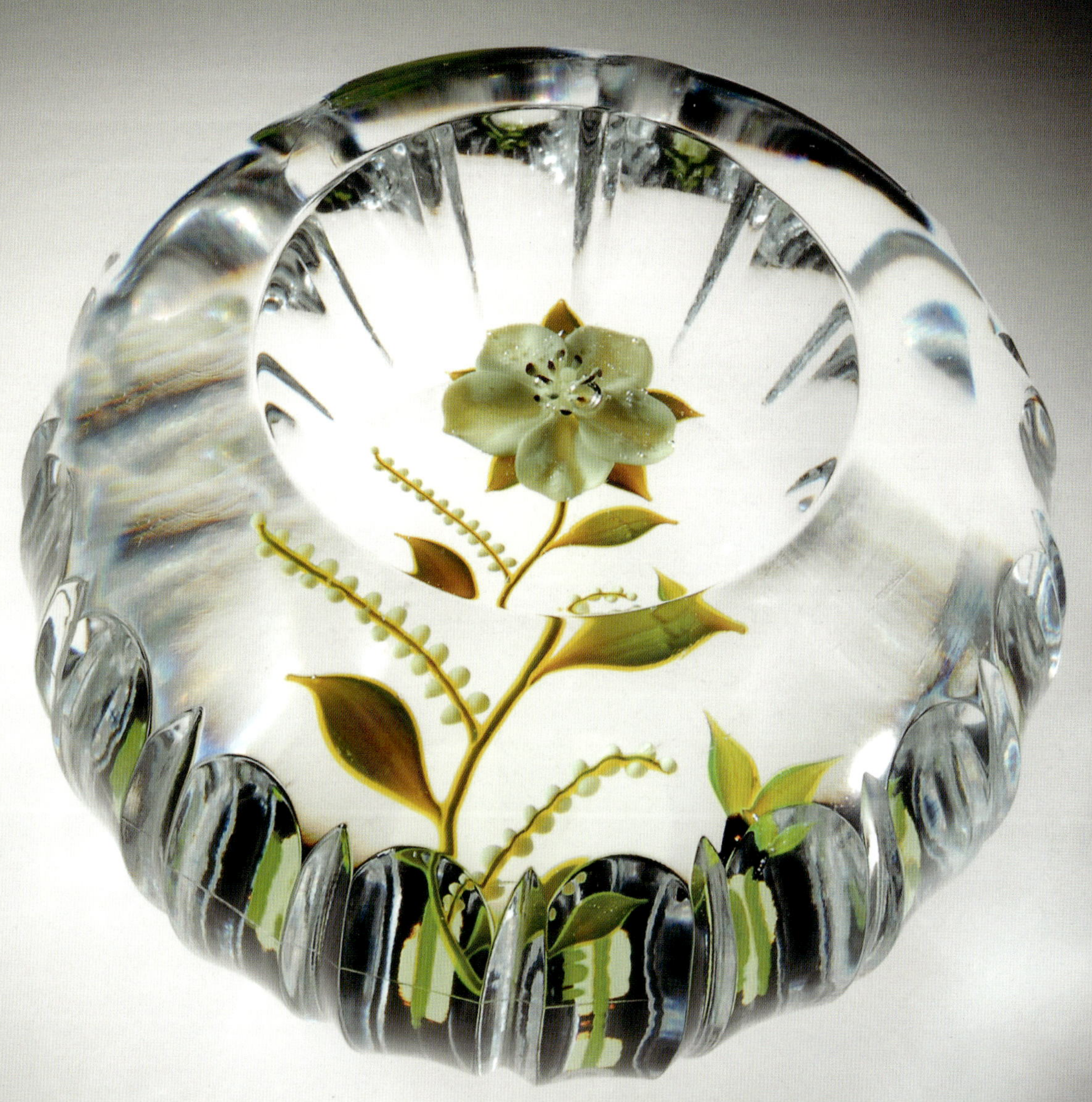

Yellow Meadow Wreath Fancy-Cut Paperweight, 1973, 1¾ × 2⅝ in.

To any person who wants a career on the creative side: Take advantage of the support your family and friends offer by sharing your goals, art-making dreams, and first efforts. You will grow and flourish with positive conversations while learning.

Other than seeking out and being exposed to a wide array of creative endeavors, there are no road maps leading toward a career as an artist. When I was starting out in the late '60s (while holding down a full-time job), my wife, Pat, and I, with the kids in tow on weekends, sought out examples of contemporary art and craft in area galleries. We visited the Philadelphia Museum of Art frequently—as a young family, money was tight, so we took advantage of visiting Sunday mornings, when admission was free.

I was sympathetic to crafted objects and frequently visited a summer weekend craft show in the historic district of Philadelphia.

During these excursions, I would enjoy and learn from the conversations about the work being displayed. These experiences reinforced my dream of one day being an independent object maker full time.

Pegasus was one of my first paperweights. My first efforts in 1969 were animals, but once I crafted a flower to encase in clear glass, my enthusiasm for this supposedly lost art became an important creative outlet. Showing my wife, Pat, and friends my progression motivated me to study flowers, with the idea of new designs that would build on the past. *Pegasus* was one of my first paperweights. When I started to interpret flowers in glass, I abandoned the animals and connected to my childhood interest in flowering plants. The yellow *Meadow Wreath* was one of my first flowers. I added the faceted cutting as a decorative flourish but slowly realized I was detracting from the seriousness of the flower, and I moved away from fancy cutting.

A journey of a thousand miles
begins with a single step.

—Lao Tzu

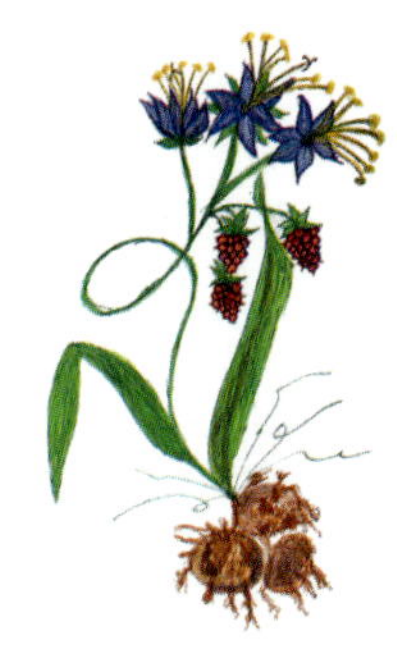

CHAPTER 2: DEVELOP A WORK ETHIC

Inspiration is for amateurs.
The rest of us just show up and get to work.

—Chuck Close

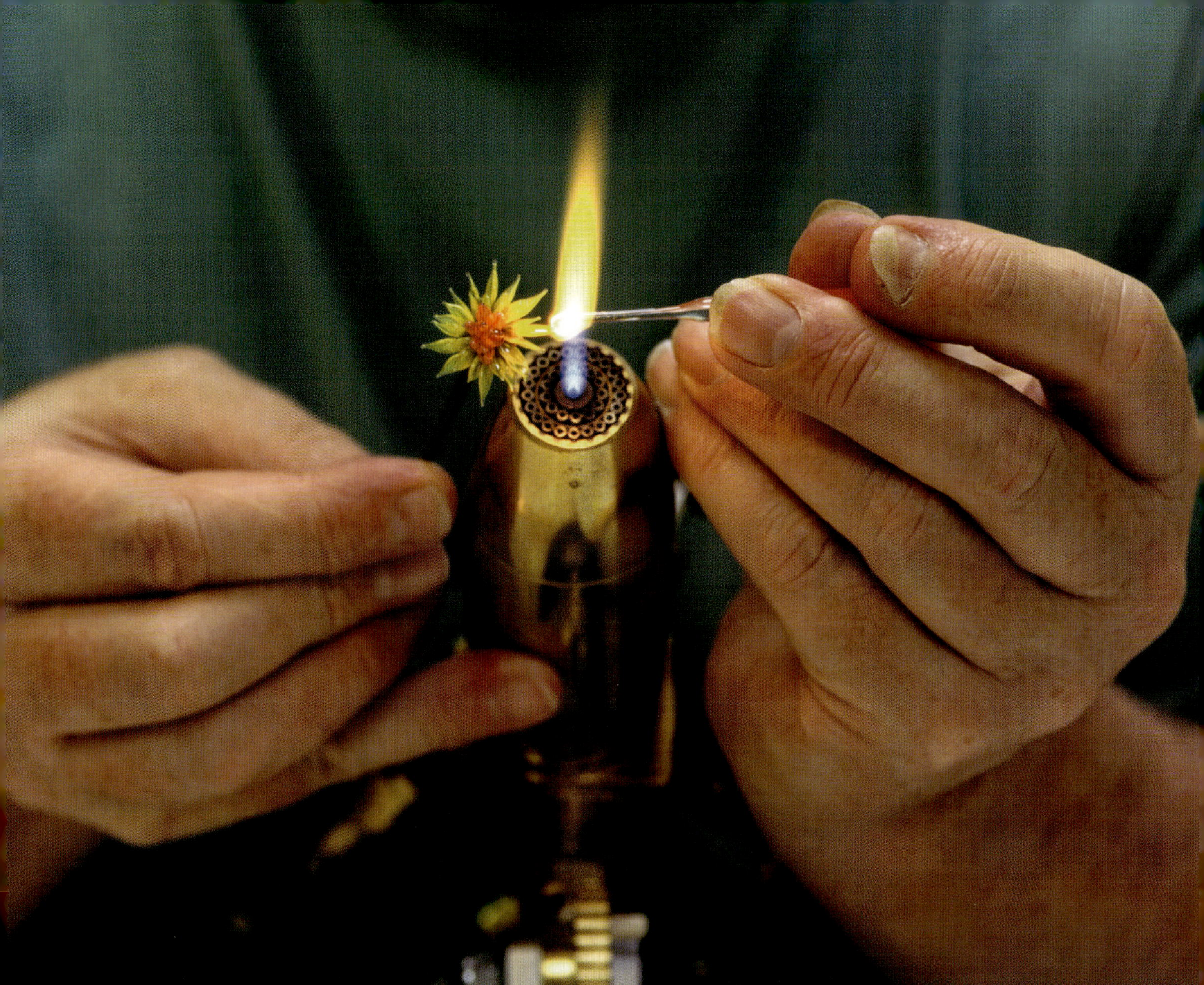

Crafting a flower blossom by melting colored glass in a gas/oxygen flame

By being attentive to the details of a floral design, the process has taught me ways to be creative. Over the years, my routine has guided my techniques to create small-scale components that allow me to mimic the delicacy of nature. It's all about being dedicated to a vision.

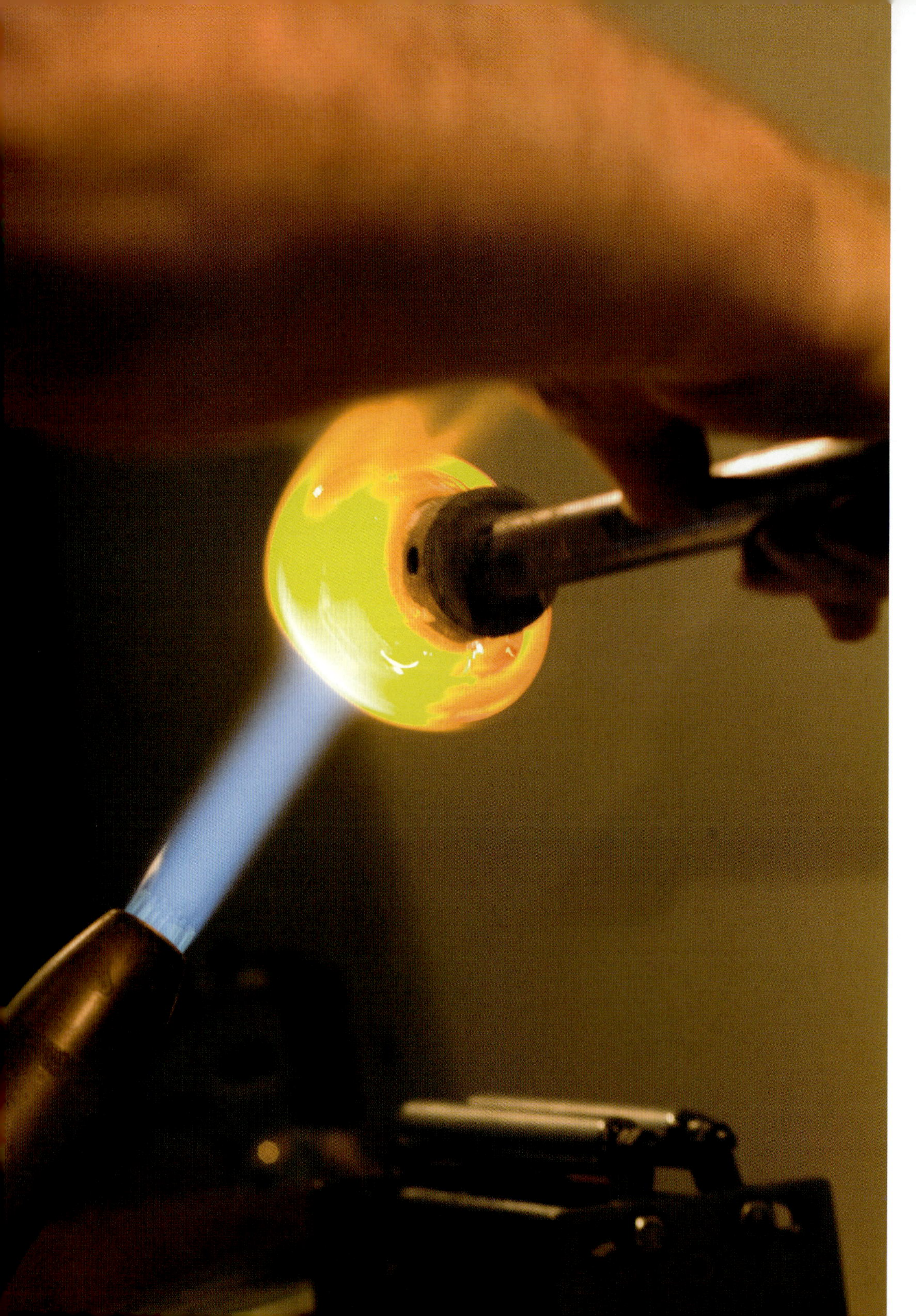

Heating the glass
The material used in great work has a memory, and through skill that memory will be advanced into the present. My challenge over the years has been to build on the past traditions through originality.

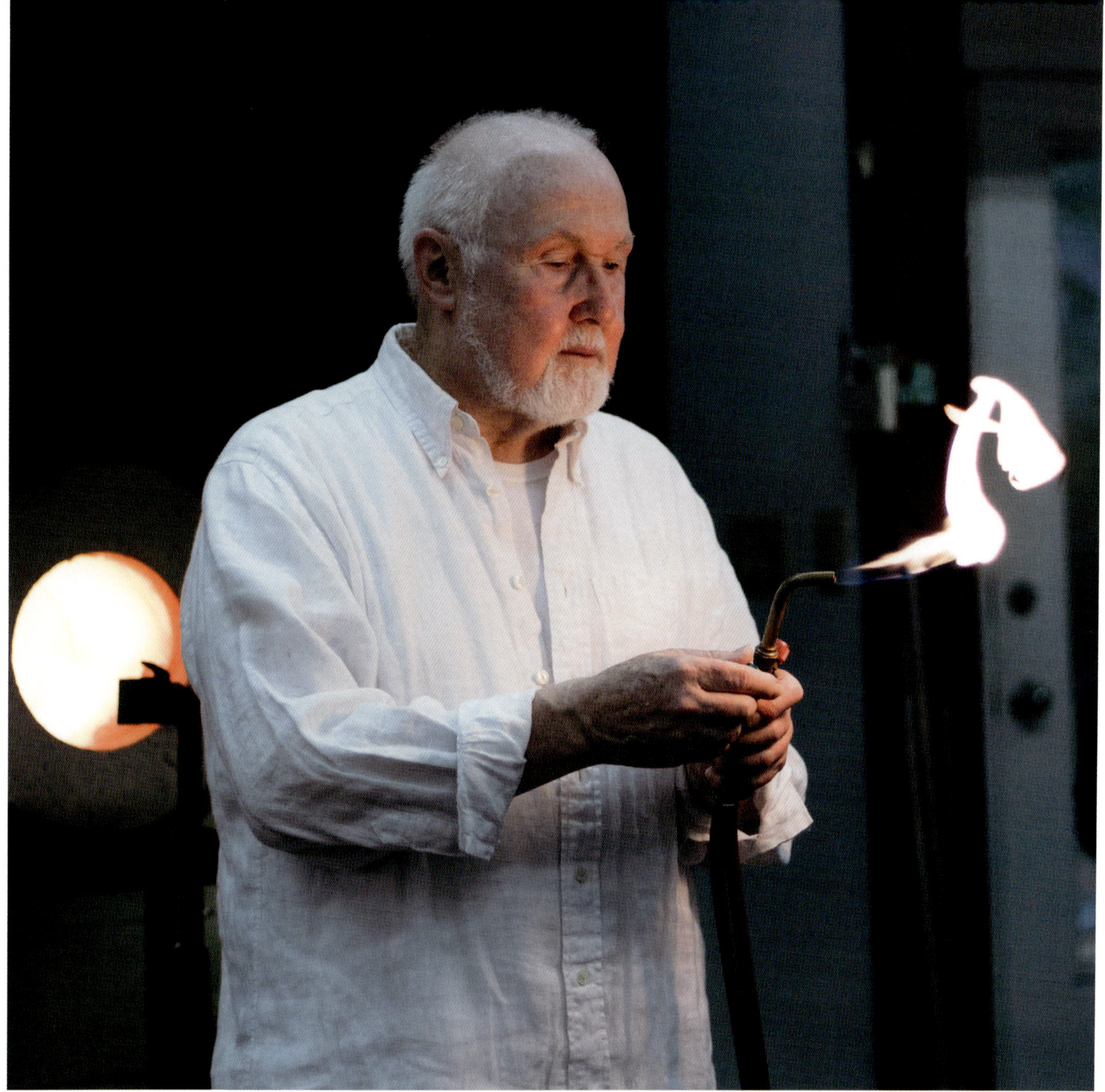

I'm standing in front of the "glory hole"—the word we use to describe the heating chamber. This is the beginning of the process that will encapsulate the glass. Creativity, in part, is about being comfortable with your process. To me, igniting the glory hole is a ritual symbolizing the beginning of a creative adventure.

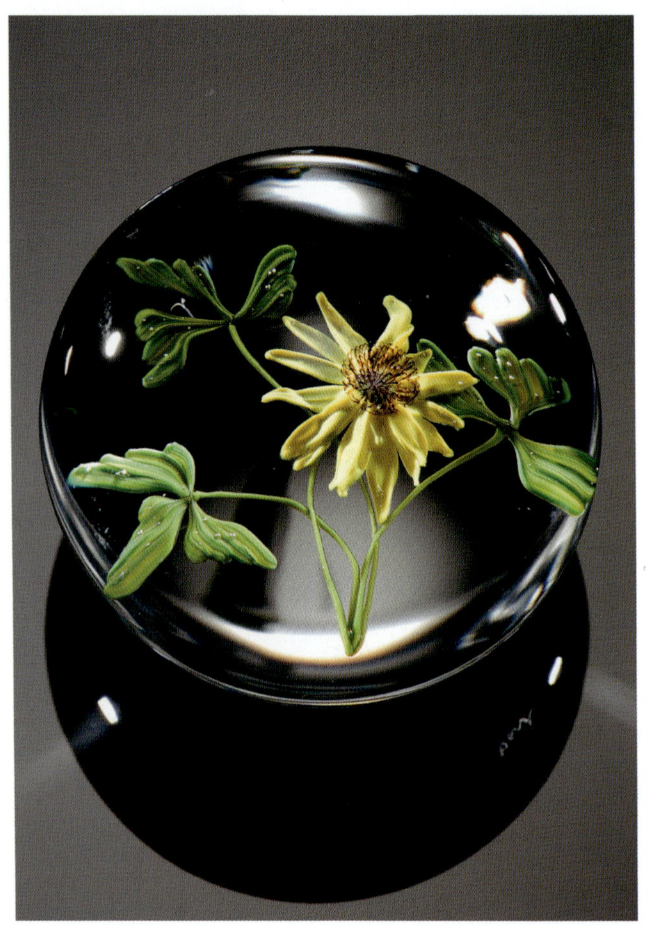

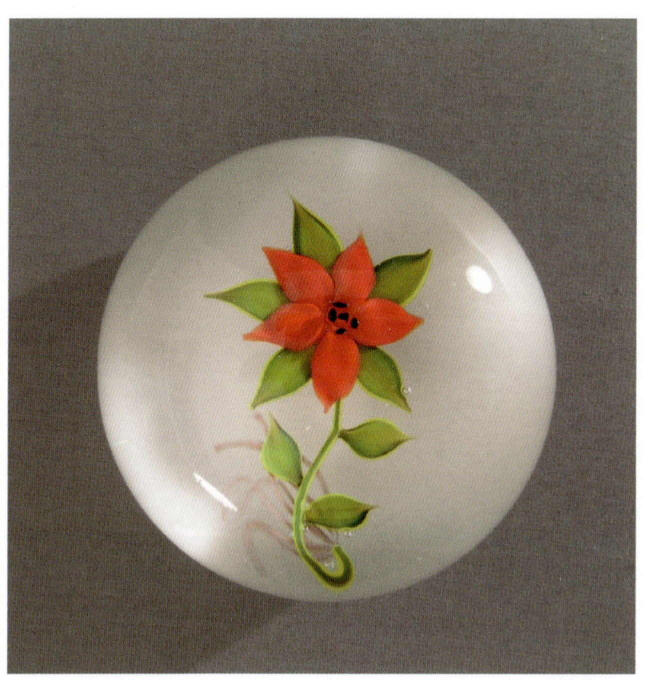

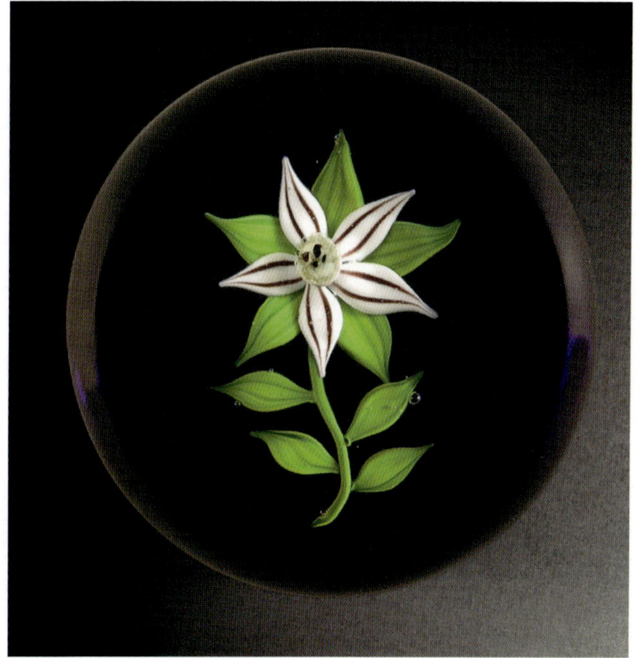

Early works

These early examples represent more risk and tension than my current work represents. When I was starting out, I had limited knowledge, and often the results were spontaneous and out of my control. It wasn't until four years of obsessively hard work mastering my craft that I was able to take the glass to a new level. Throughout my career it's about solving one technical problem after another.

(***Middle***: *Composite Flower Study Paperweight*; mid-1970s; 2⅛ × 2⅞ in.)

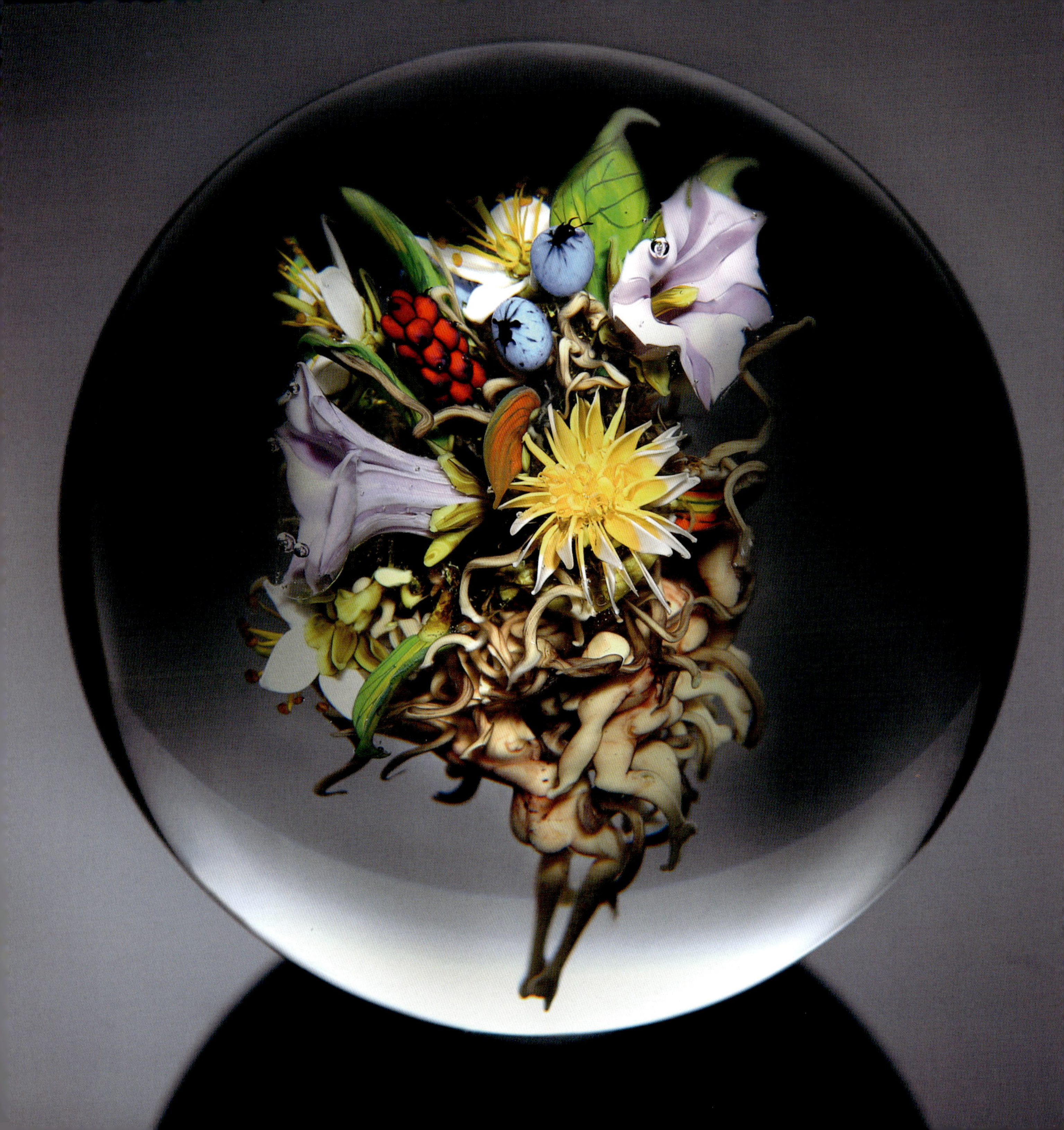

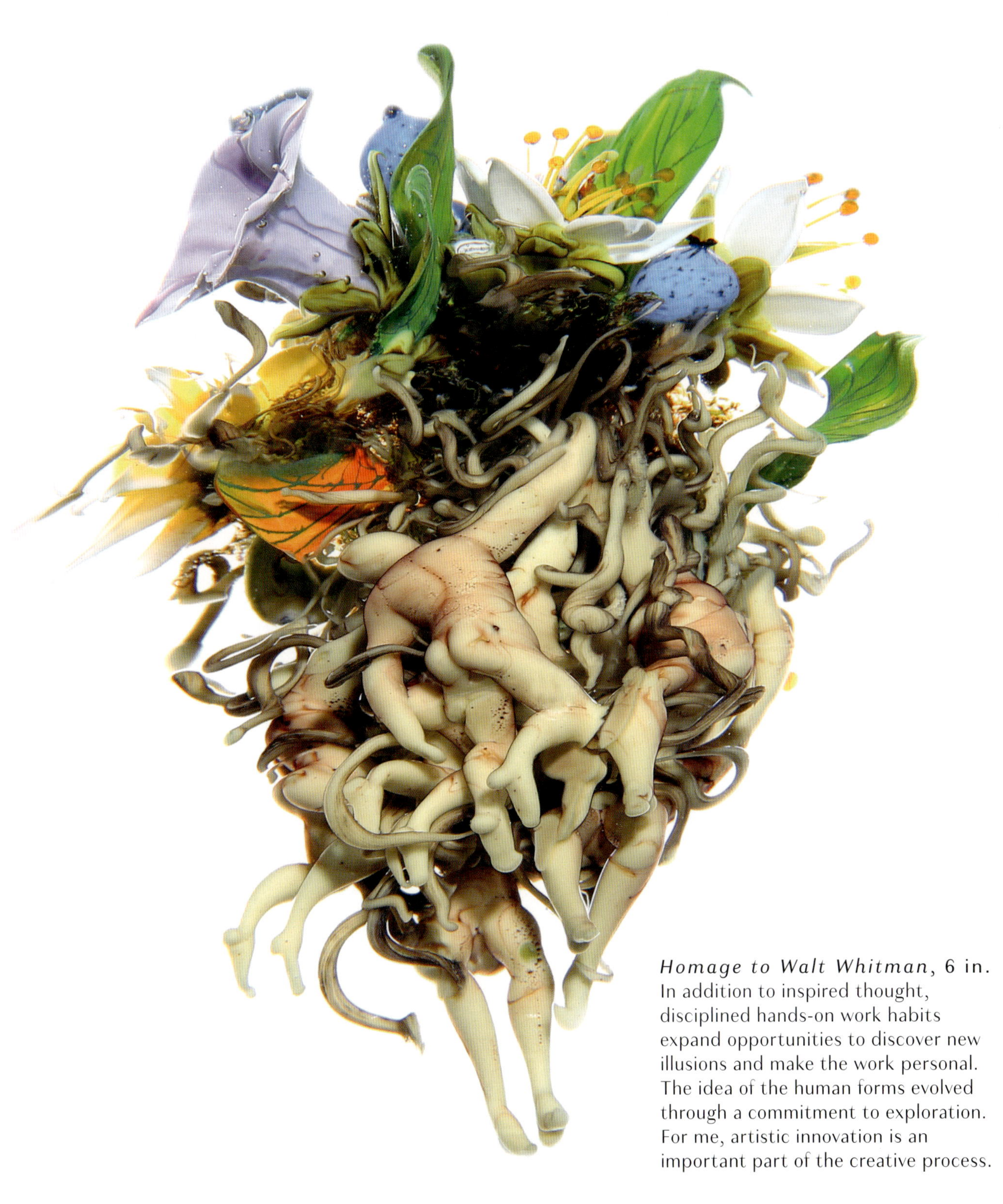

Homage to Walt Whitman, 6 in.
In addition to inspired thought, disciplined hands-on work habits expand opportunities to discover new illusions and make the work personal. The idea of the human forms evolved through a commitment to exploration. For me, artistic innovation is an important part of the creative process.

A regular schedule nurtures success on a number of levels. First, routine saves you the effort of making choices: what time you will work, where you will work, and the order of your tasks. Second, predictability in your work habits provides you with a sense of security, knowing that you are committed to your goals and giving it your best shot. This means a great deal to an artist: routine is the template that allows you to organize.

In addition, a routine facilitates accomplishment, and regular accomplishment is comforting and strengthens one's resolve. Work every day with or without feelings of being inspired. Your best work will show up whether you are inspired or not. The main point is that if you wait for inspiration, your creative output could be minimal at best.

Early in my career, I established a routine of 7:30 a.m. to lunch (around noon), calling it a day around 3:00 p.m., then heading to the gym. This routine fostered family harmony, because my wife and children knew my schedule and we were in sync, both in terms of family time and the kids' natural question of "Where's Dad?"

A morning-glory at my window satisfies me more than the metaphysics of books.

—Walt Whitman, *Song of Myself*

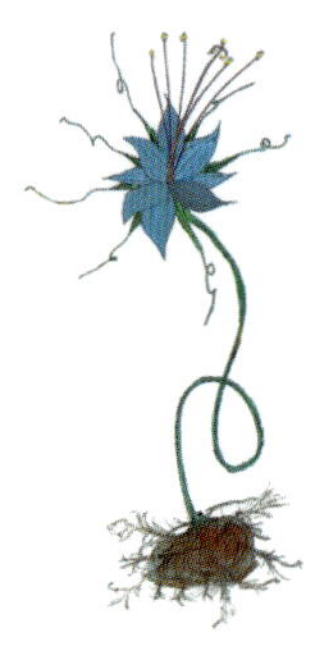

CHAPTER 3: EMBRACE POSITIVE THINKING

The key to realizing a dream is to focus not on success but significance, and then even the small steps and little victories along your path will take on greater meaning.

—Oprah Winfrey

***Earth Cluster with Roots, Flowers and Fruit*, 2020, 4 in.**
Over time, my work has evolved into complex, small-scale sculpture. With a commitment toward excellence, strengthened by positive thinking, the process has shown me how to be creative.

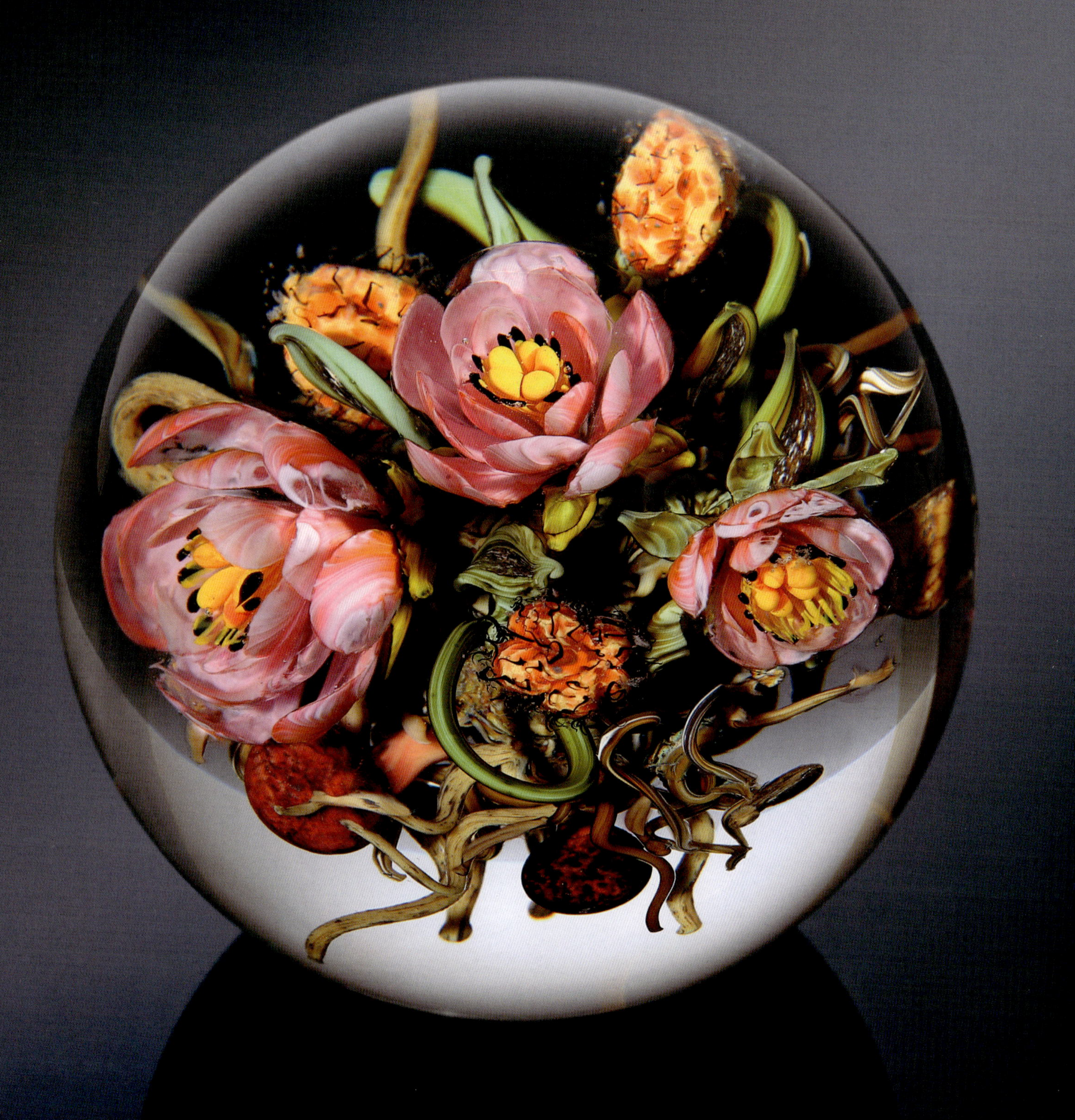

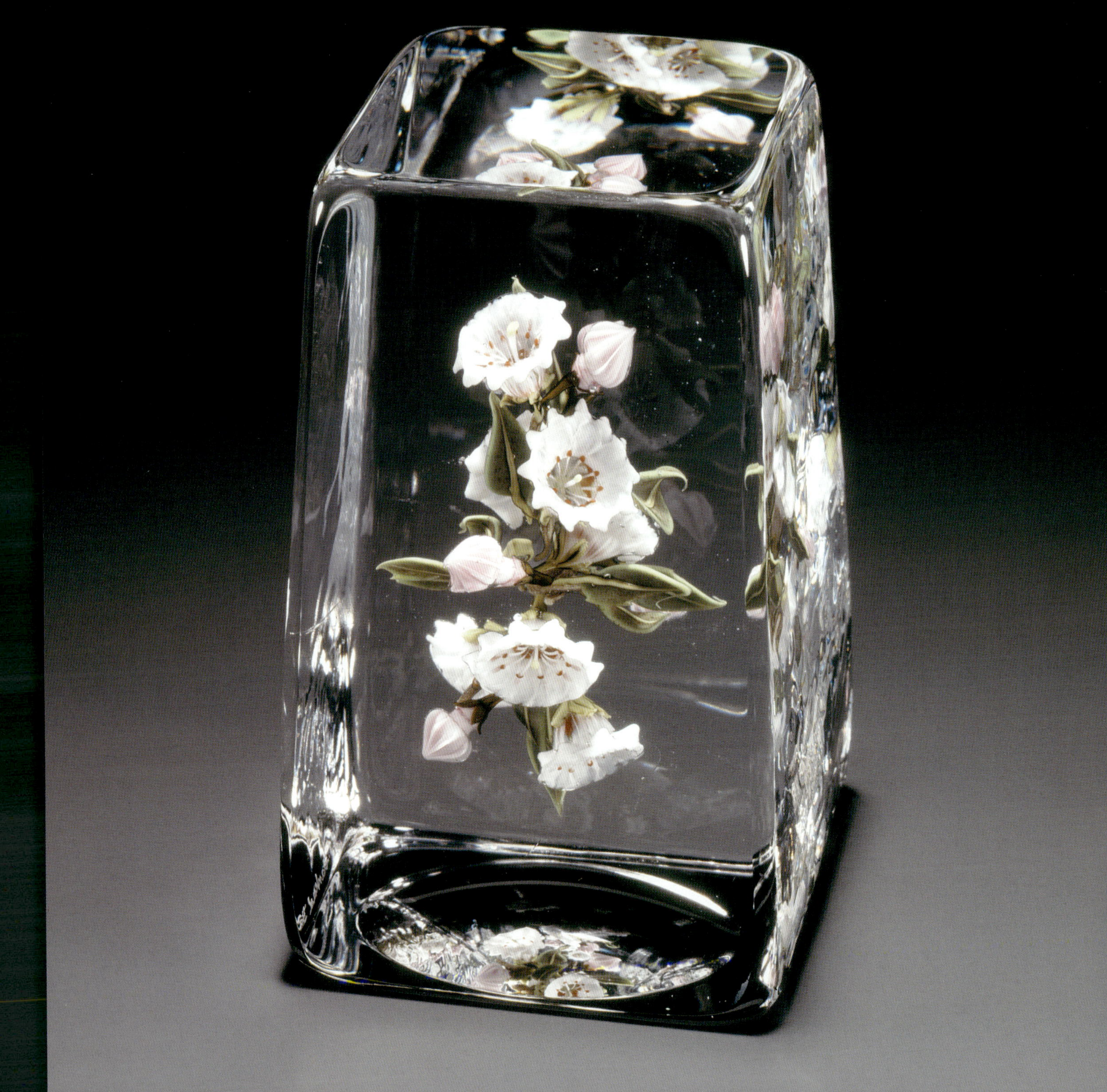

***Mountain Laurel Botanical*, 1994, 5 in.**

In the mid-'80s, while teaching at the Penland School of Craft in North Carolina, I was surrounded by a forest of mountain laurel shrubs in bloom. I arranged a bouquet of field flowers featuring the laurel blossoms in a vase near my work area and was challenged to begin experimenting on capturing the beauty of the mountain laurel in bloom. This was an exercise in positive thinking because, after over five years of on-and-off experimenting, leading to a thirty-day focus to capture the delicacy and intricacy of the blossoms, I nailed it.

As you become more familiar with the philosophy of positive thinking, you'll learn how to take advantage of timeless attitudes that are celebrated by countless numbers of successful people in all areas of life. Once you've identified the area of your creative interest, you'll begin to feel a stronger level of confidence and enthusiasm. Your commitment will lead you closer to making your goal a reality, and your need to be creative will evidence the beginning of your journey in earnest.

After three or four months of working in my utility room, I was getting stir crazy being at home all day, so after work I would go to the local bar to nurse a beer for a change of scenery. On occasion I would talk to a real estate salesman around my age whom I became friends with. I mentioned to my new friend Roy that my little glass-art-making business wasn't doing well. He listened to my story of woe and suggested I read positive-thinking books, which I did. As I read and reread these books, my attitude started to change. My goal was to create exceptional floral glass paperweights and be successful enough to support my family. Over time, instead of thinking I probably would fail, I became more confident about my ability to craft significant objects that people would admire.

I began implementing a disciplined work habit that kept me in my small studio five and a half days a week. I joined a local gym to have a place to go after work, and I started to play 4-wall handball and lift weights. By substituting the gym for the bar, I not only had a place to go at the end of my workday in my small studio, but I was improving my sense of worth at the same time. I soon realized that physical fitness complimented my work stamina in the studio is a necessity.

By embracing classics in positive thinking, most notably The Power of Positive Thinking by Norman Vincent Peale, I was becoming self-motivated. I started to take pride in how my glass art was slowly evolving and attracting the interest of a growing number of paperweight enthusiasts.

Starting out in the early years, with my spiritual life grounded in morning prayers, and with no formal art making education or training but with a sweet naivete, I was focused on the singular objective of making beautiful work by inventing ways to craft native flowers in glass.

With my growing dedication to inventing a botanical language sculpted in glass. I took advantage of my new quasi-business plan of action, that was challenged by building on the significant French paperweight tradition.

There is no guarantee that positive thinking will produce results, but it is a virtual certainty that if you focus on the negative, you will create a self-fulfilling prophecy.

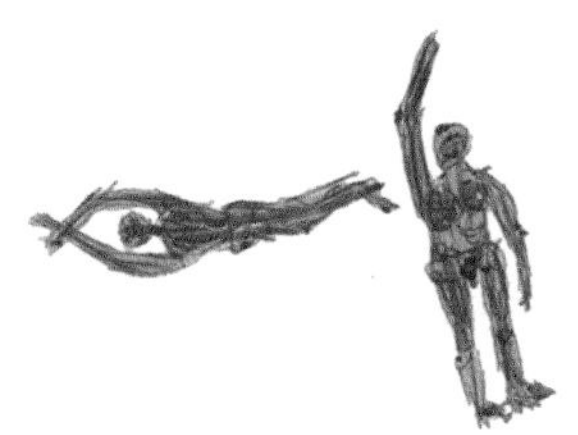

CHAPTER 4: TAKE CREATIVITY SERIOUSLY—ARTISTS ARE PROFESSIONALS

***Golden Orb Floral Triptych*, 2009, 5 3/8 × 7 3/4 × 4 in.**
Inspired by Whitman's poetic celebration of the native flowers from his time period. I hope to pass forward my floral glass sculptures into the future with the same feeling. This work, titled *Golden Orb Floral Triptych* (2009), is arranged clockwise from upper left, with yellow roses, white morning glories, lilacs, and mountain laurel. In the middle is a golden orb floating in timelessness, referencing the metaphysical aspect of the plant kingdom. This labor-intensive effort required weeks of encapsulating the colored-glass floral designs into cubes. Once the arrangement feels visually right, the cubes are cut, polished, and laminated into the panel with a two-part epoxy. The dark background and base are added to complete the piece. The illusion suggests the floral clusters are floating in space.

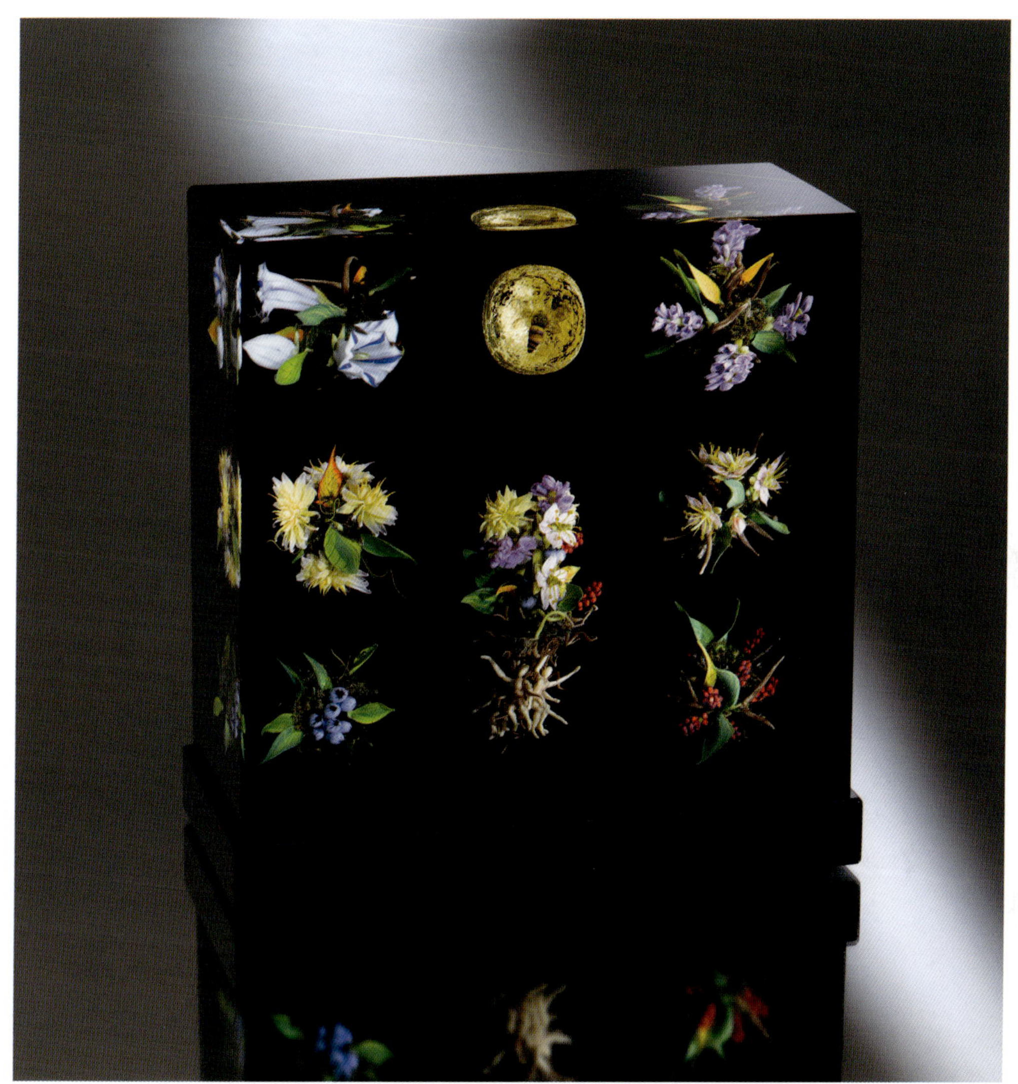

When I was growing up, my parents—who had struggled through the Great Depression—encouraged me to focus on getting a job in a stable company and eventually earn and enjoy a paycheck with two weeks' vacation.

I understood their concern, but I wanted to be on the creative side—at the time, without knowing what the creative side had to offer. I was a dreamer; I loved imagining things, I loved building things, and I felt that creative work could somehow accommodate what was important to me.

I had no role models or resources. My parents, who grew up in the depression and were concerned about me having a good job, never encouraged me to take art courses.

When I enrolled in Salem Community College after high school for a diploma program in scientific glass, I was mesmerized watching the instructor's first demonstration. He fabricated not a piece of scientific glass, but a graceful glass swan. The process, to me, was magical. Little did I know that thirty-five years later, my career would unfold in ways that established a glass art program to complement their world-class scientific glass program—and be honored by having the studio named the Paul J. Stankard Lab and Studio.

Over the next decade, building on what I was taught and working hard to master the scientific glass craft, I became very successful, eventually being responsible for a major corporation's glass shops in three research locations.

However, I could not tamp down the creative urge I felt when I first saw that swan take shape. A decade into my career, I was still eager to try anything I perceived as creative in glass, as naïve as my efforts were.

I quit my job.

The consensus among my friends and family was that I was foolish to give up such an attractive job in industry. But I had a savior: my understanding wife, Pat, understood how unhappy I was commuting each day, and how, conversely, working in my utility room felt emotionally free.

Pat supported my dream of leaving industry, She believed in me more than I believed in myself.

You may not have a supportive partner. But your dreams deserve your full attention and courage. Ultimately, the decision and commitment are yours.

If you have this need to be creative, take it seriously. Make it the most important part of your life's journey. For example: Dedicate time to be creative. Take responsibility for blazing a path for your creative need. Seek out what pulls you in emotionally and challenges you to learn more. What are you looking at? What does it take to do that? How can you incorporate this work into your life?

• As you are starting out, take seriously the fact that your desire to be creative is every bit as worthy as someone else's journey to become a doctor or

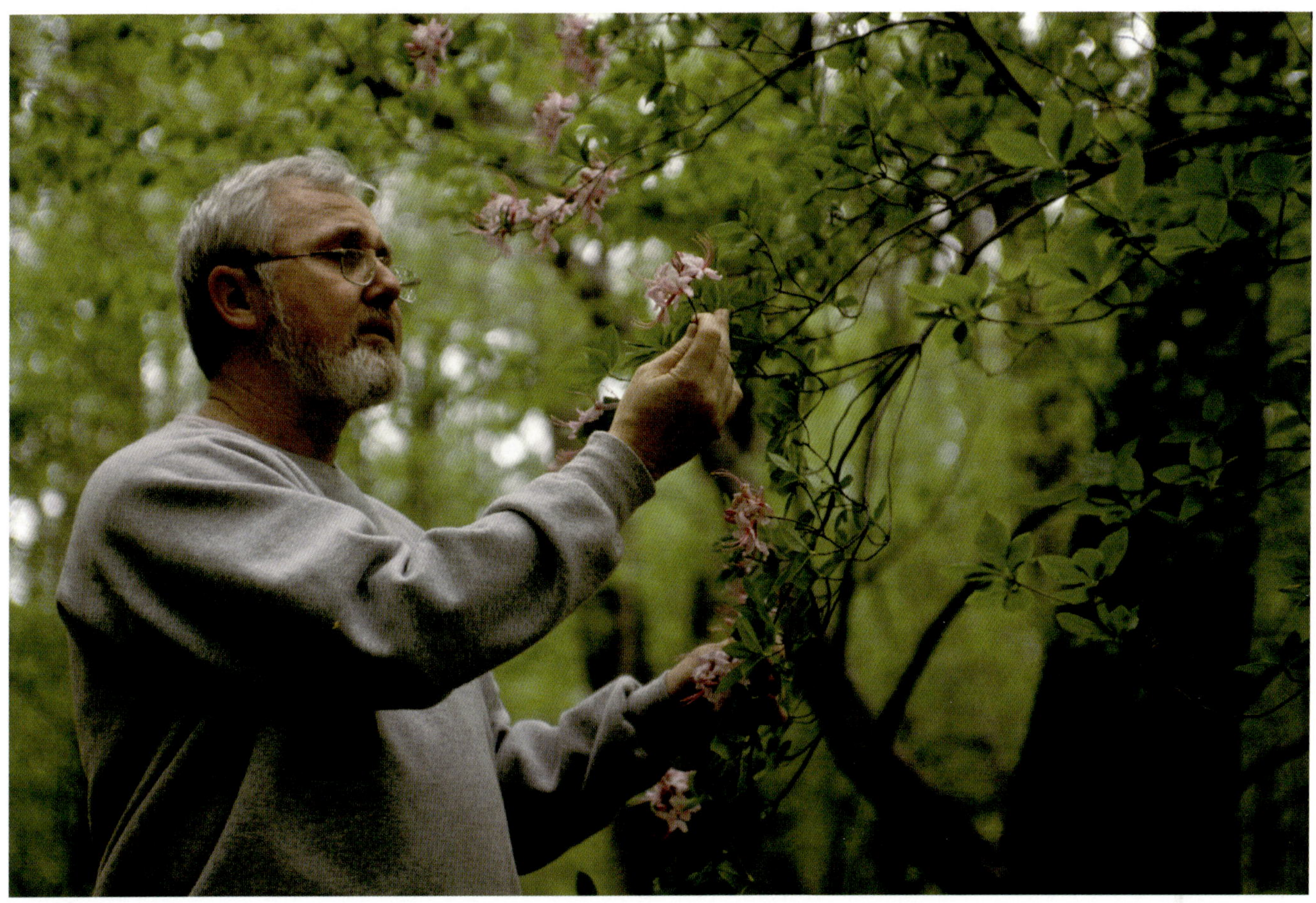

As a maker, I want my work to have its own reason to exist after it leaves my studio. In the studio it's glass; beyond the studio it's a metaphor.

My goal is that my response to nature will have a reality that will attract serious consideration in the future, and document a human response to the beauty around us. I am not a botanist but think of myself as a dreamer who searches for the poetic beauty within botany.

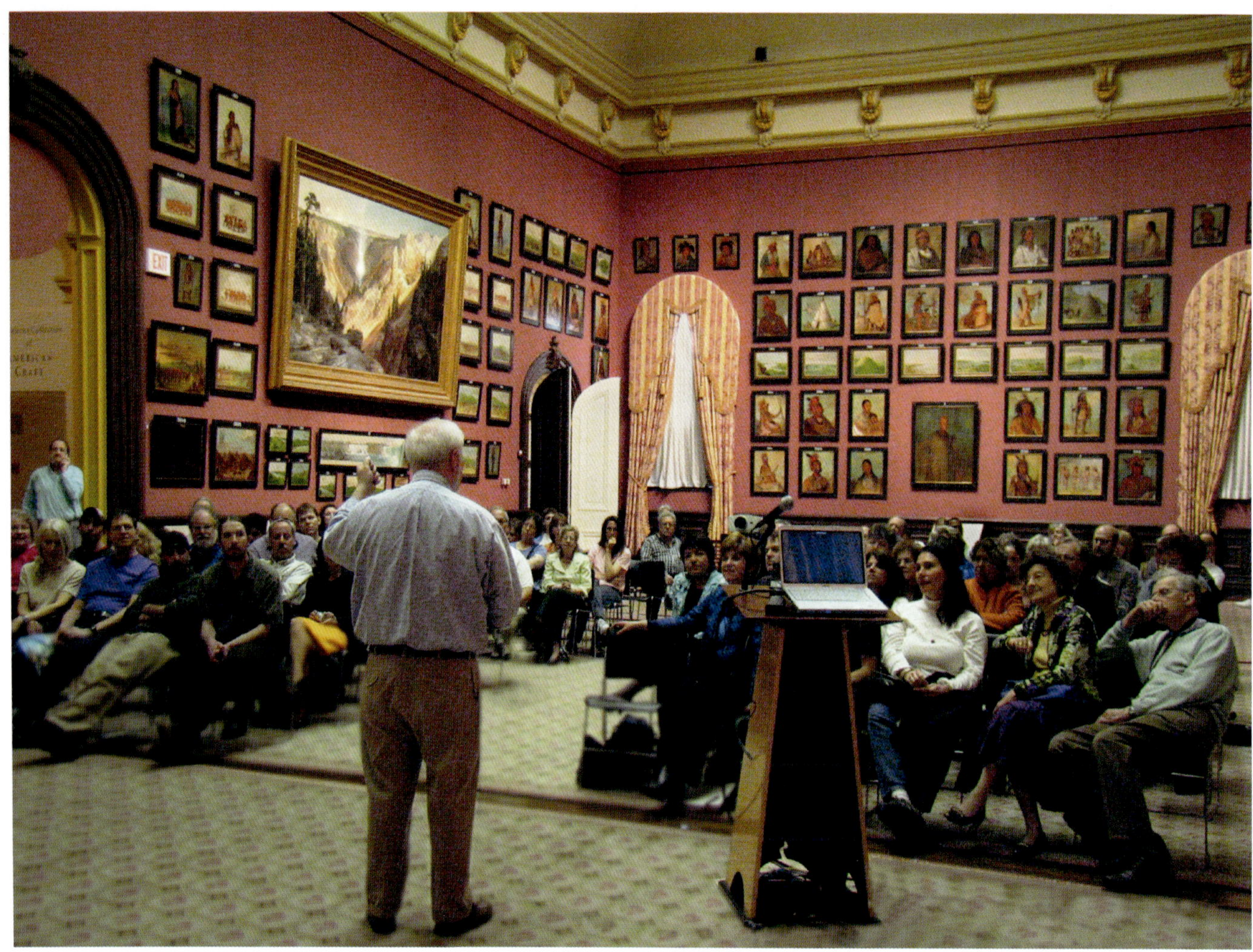

Addressing an audience at the Renwick Gallery at the Smithsonian American Art Museum

In 2006, I was invited to share my world with the general public and members of the Renwick Gallery. This type of opportunity is an honor. People are interested in how artists dedicate their life; in my case, to the art of craft. As you mature as an artist, the community will consider you a professional and will regard you as a resource. You will be invited to speak about your work, lecture to the community and educational groups, and become a valued contributor to the regional culture. As your audience grows and museums begin to acquire your work, or in some cases multiple examples, you will become a part of that institution's family as a contemporary artist.

an accountant. You are just as professional as they are, and over time will have opportunities to interact with other professionals on an equal basis. You are entering a field where, as you mature as an artist, society values your insight and respects your courage that you evidenced when you decided to dedicate your life to art making.

Like any other professional, an artist needs to continually educate themselves in ways that enhance their artistic maturity. Starting in 1972, one of my great joys was listening to audiobooks, which slowly evolved to focusing on the great literature of the Western canon. Audiobooks were instrumental in my self-directed learning, which in turn was critical to my development as an artist.

• Remember, too, that works of art represent your legacy. You have an opportunity through your work to attract an audience long after you are gone.

• You represent your time period; one hopes that your art will reflect your vision into the future to be appreciated.

Your work becomes an artifact of your time. Scholars use the work of artists to understand a time period within the framework of society, whether the work is a functional glass object, such as a decorative goblet, or a fine-art painting or sculpture. Art says volumes.

Commissions are an important part of an artist's livelihood, and this piece, titled *Honeybee Swarm Orb* (2010), 8 inches in diameter, was a major effort that expanded the boundaries of my work. It incorporates flowers, blueberries, a honeycomb, and over twenty honeybees swarming around the center core. This was commissioned by the Robert M. Minkoff Foundation. Robert was an art collector who built a major collection of my work that was documented in a book, *Beauty Beyond Nature: The Glass Art of Paul Stankard*. The traveling exhibit consisted of seventy-four pieces. Robert had acquired my work over two decades and over the course of time, we became dear friends. The friendship revolved around his collecting and supporting contemporary glass community. A project dear to his heart was supporting scholarships and programs such as Salem Community College's glassblowing workshop for twelve at-risk students from Ranch Hope, in Alloway, New Jersey. The program introduced at-risk young men to glassmaking. The point here is that as an artist you meet people who have a philanthropic attitude and use art as a way to enrich the community. This orb celebrates honeybees pollinating plants. In 2020, Robert passed away and the Robert M. Minkoff Foundation donated his collection of 137 Stankard floral glass works of art to the Museum of Glass in Tacoma, Washington.

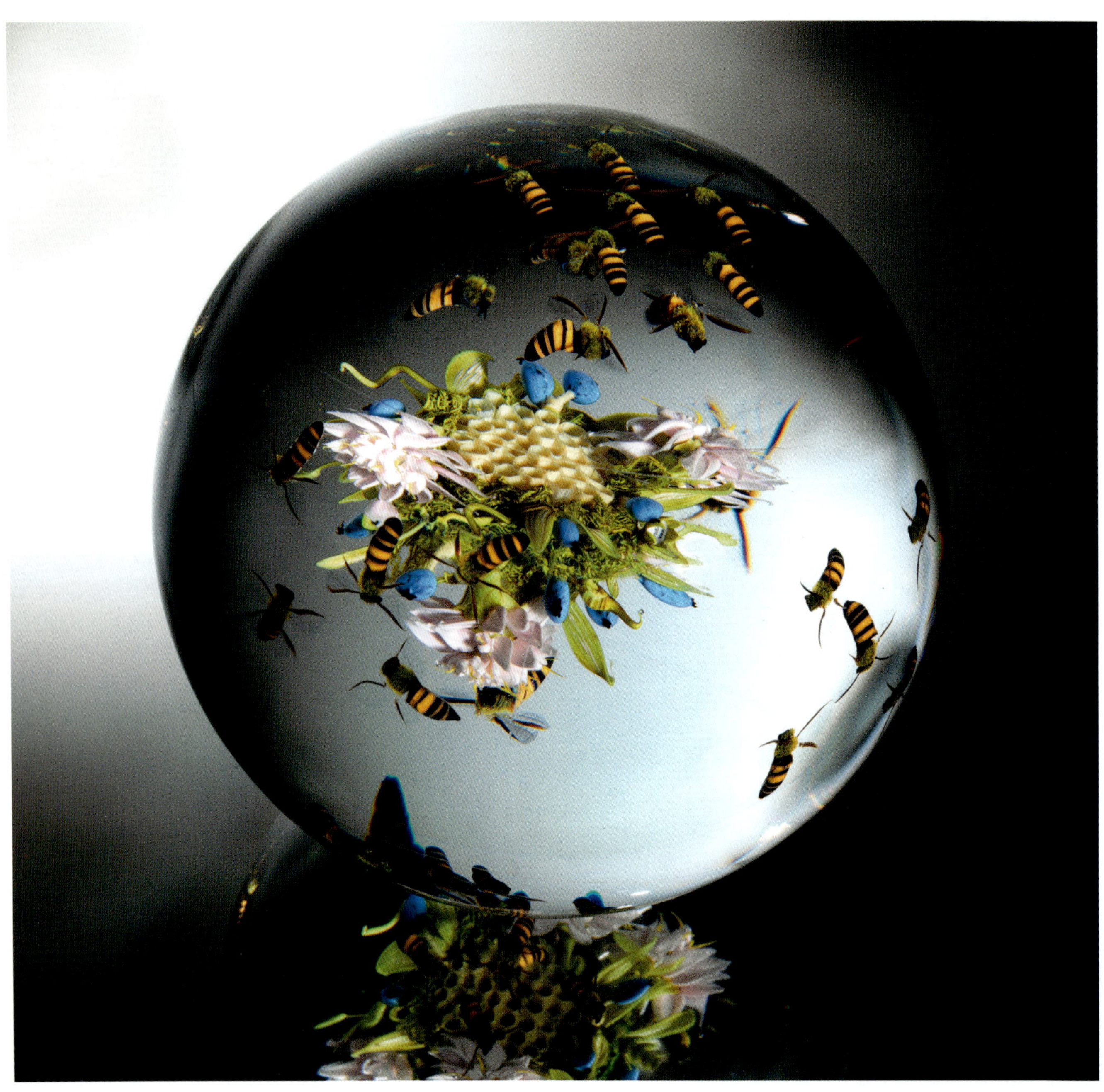

***Honeybee Swarm Orb*, 2010, 8 in.**

Column with Masks, Figures, and Flowers, 2002, 7¼ × 4¼ in.
The idea for the masks was a continuation of the human form. I sculpted small-scale figures to camouflage into the root system, and enjoyed challenging the viewer with the unexpected presence of myth. When I incorporated one figure into the root system, it was often regarded as a curiosity, but when I grouped two or more together, some people suspected that it was a depiction of a suggestive event. I wanted to engage the viewer in a visual dialogue, and the ambiguousness of the human forms clinging to the root system was a wonderful counterpoint to the realistic portrayal of the flowers. I was gratified that people would be engaged with the juxtaposition of the flowers and the figures. While I enjoyed bringing in these references, I wanted to go beyond the figures and reference humanity in other ways. The masks evolved over the next few years, and people became equally curious about them. This time, though, the symbolism was not so benign. Some viewers thought of them as death masks, and that series was often overlooked in the marketplace. But now, this body of work (from about 2000–2006) is experiencing success on the auction block.

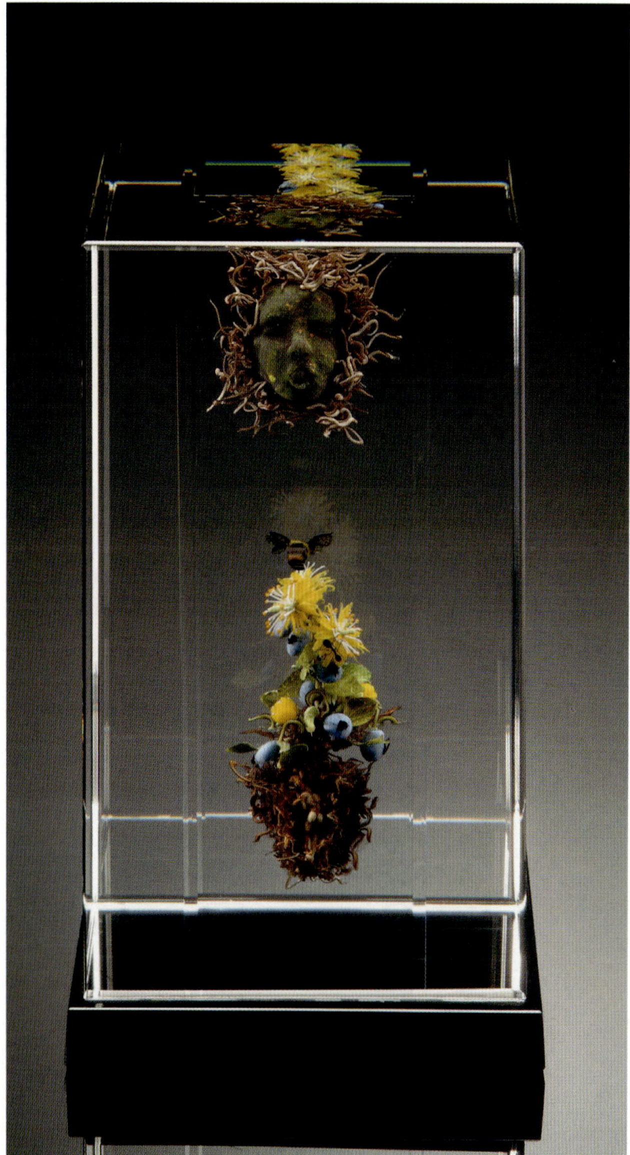

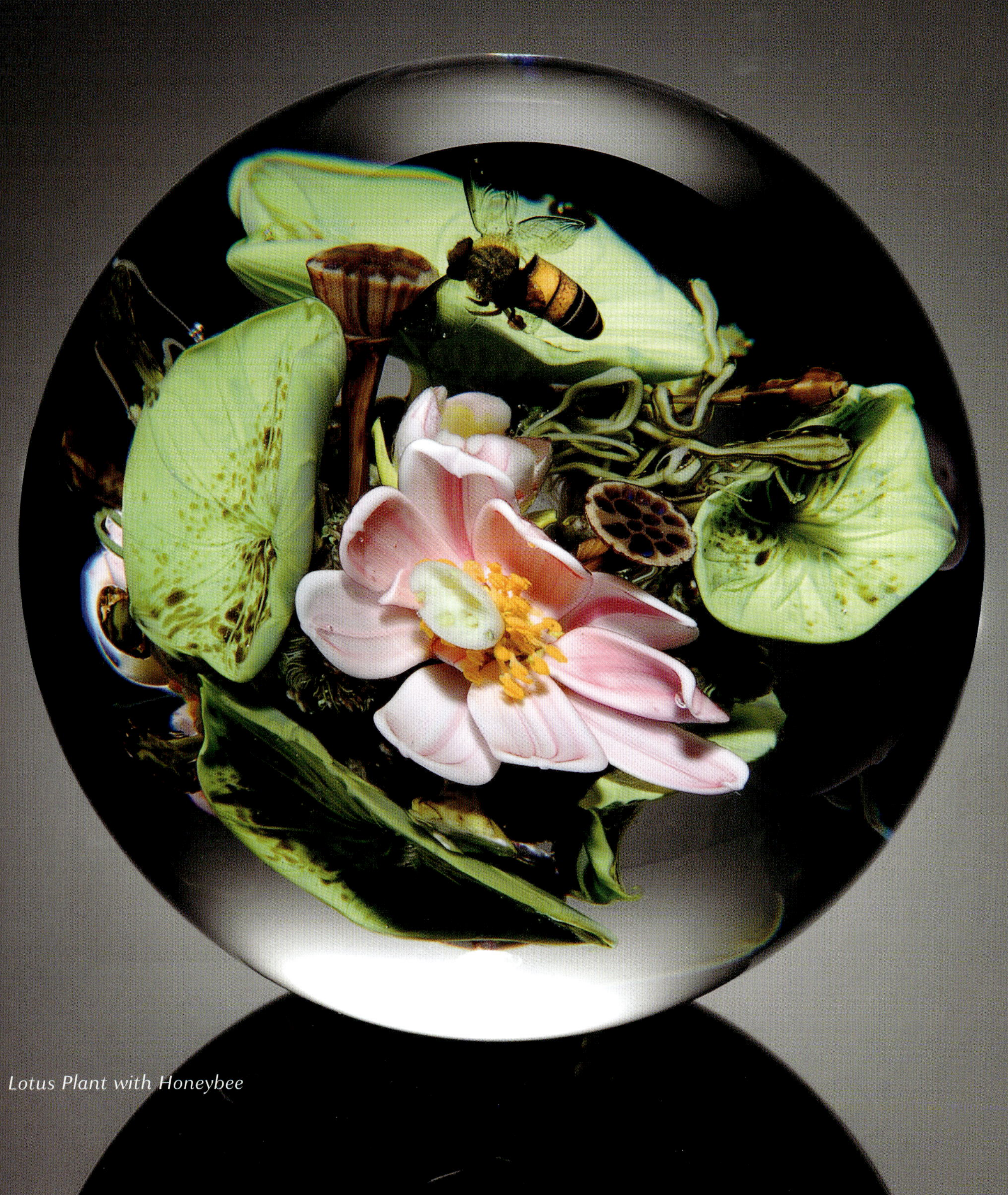

Lotus Plant with Honeybee

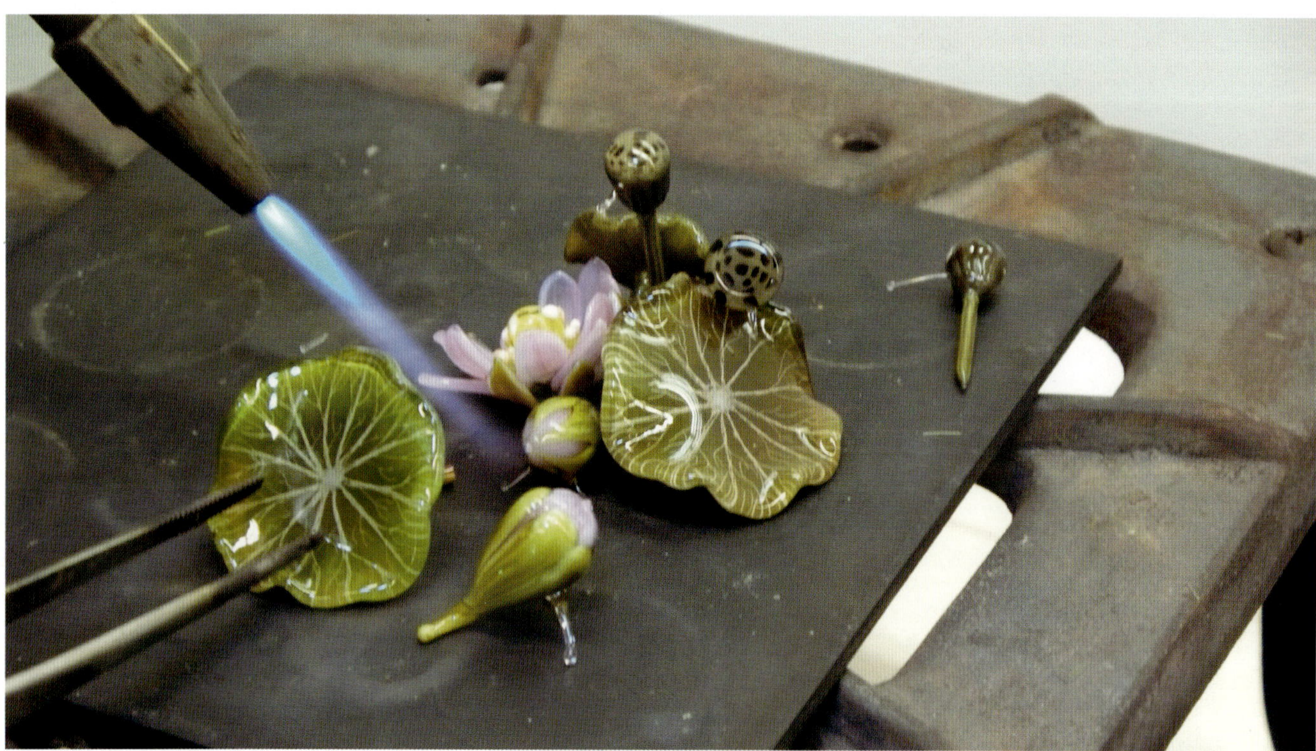

I was interested in portraying water lilies and lotuses and took the day off and drove the forty-five minutes to Longwood Gardens with my two assistants to familiarize myself with the subject. Longwood Gardens, a world-class, 1,000-acre botanical complex of gardens and meadows in Kennett Square, Pennsylvania, near the Delaware border, was inspiring to me because I wanted to learn more about how native flowers were cultivated into ornamental flowers for formal gardens. Over the years it has been a wonderful resource. In addition to the gardens, they have a thorough library.

As referential as my work has become, the core of my imagery is based on truth to nature. I think of my creative point of view as suggesting organic credibility based on stylized designs. People think my flowers are real. There are times some people think that I have somehow invented a way of suspending flowers in molten glass.

To me, artistic success is all about knowing your subject and nuancing the visual information that you're sending into the world.

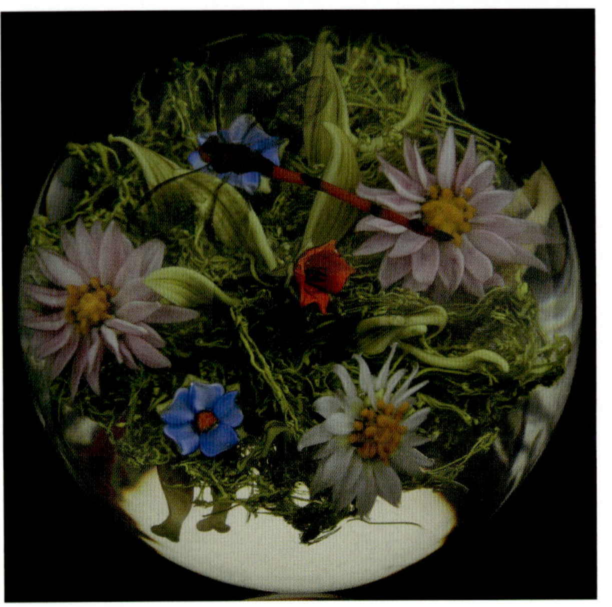

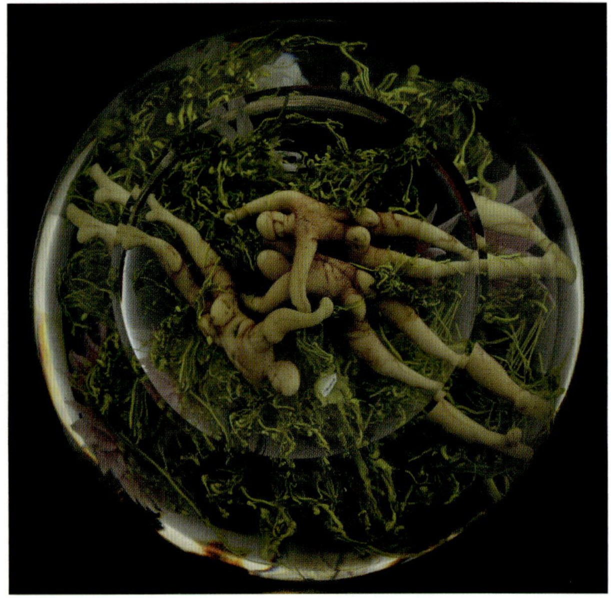

Trips to the Pinelands, a 3-million-acre undeveloped forest in South Jersey, have been an important resource for my professional and spiritual reinvigoration. My referential *Daisy Bouquet with Damselfly and Figures* incorporates intricate detail with complex stamens, veined leaves, and insect. One of my goals is to make the labor invisible. This goes back to one of my ambitions—to make the work believable, by protecting its botanical credibility.

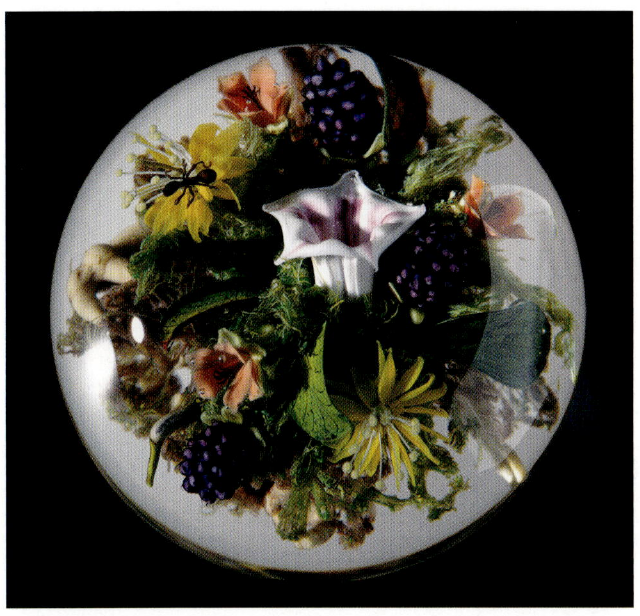

***Blackberry Bouquet Paperweight*, 3¼ in.**
As I was working toward building on the French tradition, I moved away from the stylized floral patterns to focus on the native flowers of North America. My particular interest in this design and others similar was to explore the illusion of negative space.

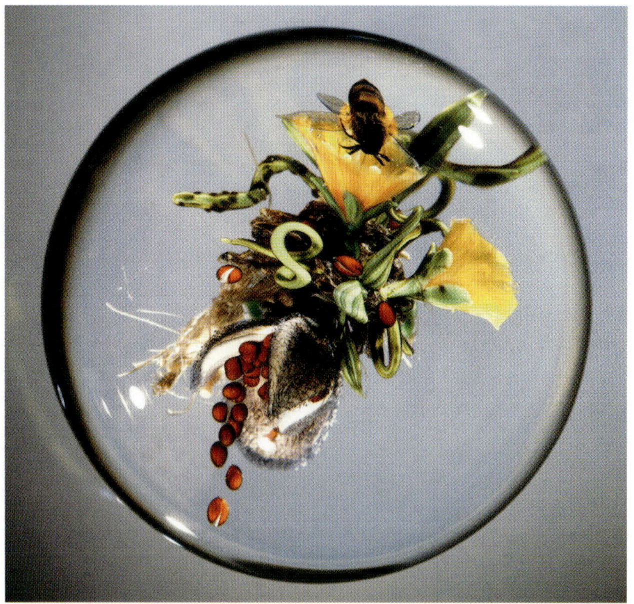

***Flower, Honeybee, Seed Pods Spilling Seeds*, 1997, 3¼ in.**
This design is about fecundity: the honeybee pollinating the blossom, and the seed pod swelled open, spilling seeds. The seeds dropping from the pod were an interesting challenge, suggesting kinetic movement. I think of it as a botanical portrait with the life cycle of the plant portrayed.

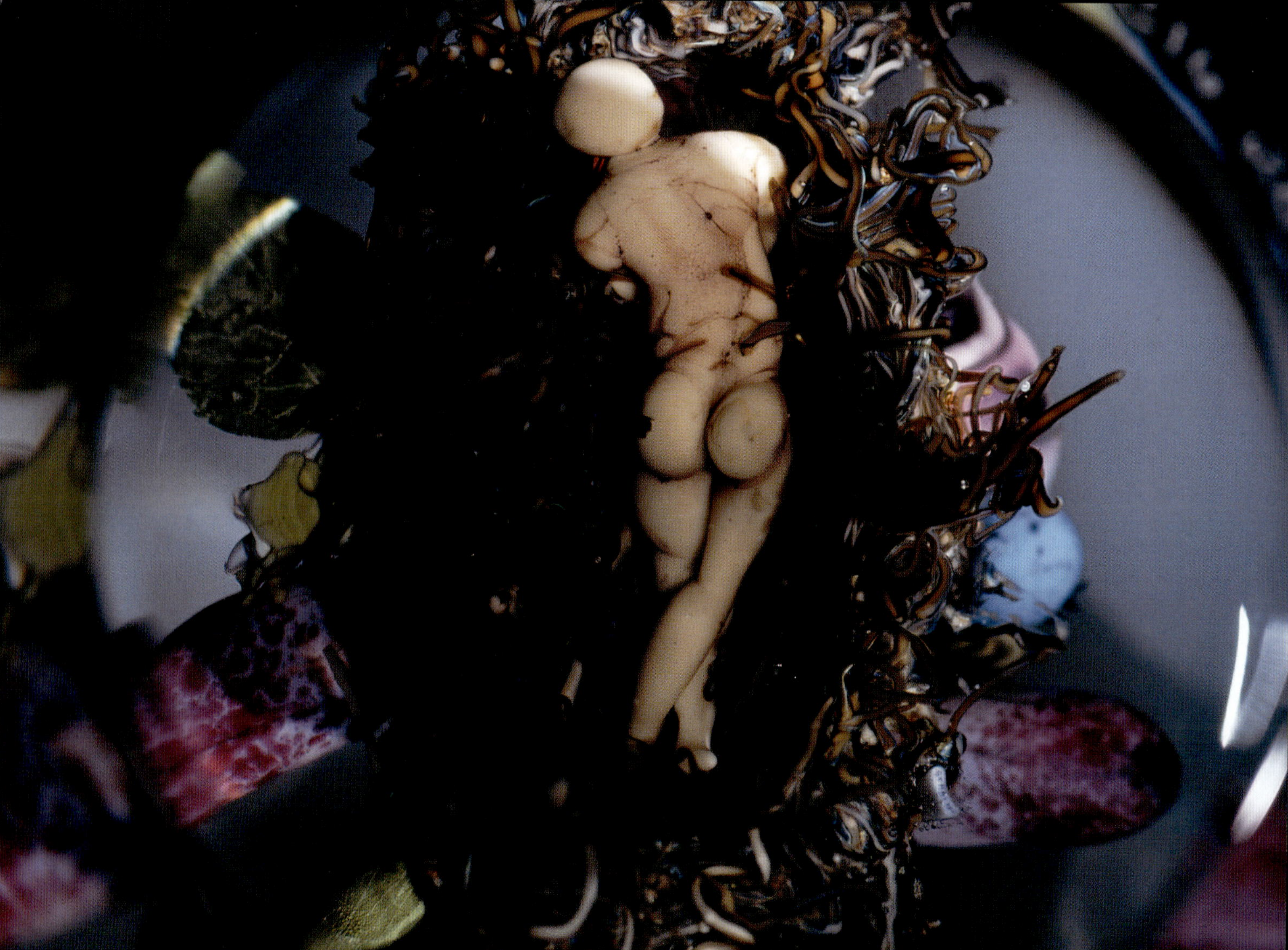

***Figure Nestled in Moss under a Gooseberry Bouquet*, 2001, 3¼ in.**
A single human form suggests (for me, at least) solitude and communing with nature. Interpretation is personal; my response to the design is no more or less valid then another person's take. The viewer's primary focus is the botanical motif. But once you turn it over, it's a totally different experience that is part of the visual story.

Creativity takes courage.

—Henri Matisse

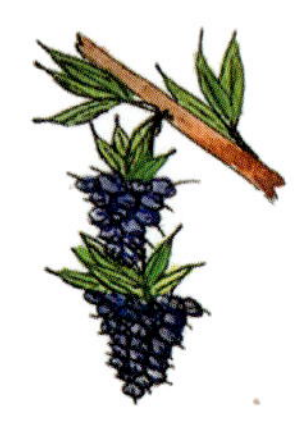

CHAPTER 5: LEARN FROM YOUR BEST TEACHER—FAILURE

Every adversity, every failure, every heartache carries with it the seed of an equal or greater benefit.

—Napoleon Hill

For me, the creative process is a combination of certainty and spontaneity. The risk-taking when inviting spontaneity into my efforts is often a gamble, but when it works, you know that you have advanced your aesthetic in a special way.

Not every gamble pays off. However, in the creative world, failure is a step toward success.

Over the years, I had experimented with casting panels that would incorporate my botanical vocabulary, believing that someday I would build a furnace in my studio and experiment to create floral designs that would multiply my scale—taking my work to a new level and doing things that had never been done before. In my studio I was successful sculpting small-scale work at the torch, utilizing the flameworking process I had mastered.

In 2012, Wheaton Arts and Cultural Center in Millville, New Jersey, invited a group of known artists to create a major piece to commemorate the fiftieth anniversary of the studio glass movement. I enthusiastically accepted the challenge to work in this world-class glassblowing facility. I had help from talented assistants; among them was Beccy Feather, who worked for weeks crafting honeybees with me in preparation for a major effort to cast a 75-pound block with additional Wheaton staff. My dream was to create a major breakthrough piece combining flameworking and casting. This goal involved over a month in preparation. The honeybees would be the theme of the cast-glass panel. The effort, from my perspective, was herculean.

I had the benefit of experienced artist Hank Murta Adams, as well as Skitch Manion and staff, who facilitated this cast block with honeybees floating in and around golden orbs.

It was a major effort dealing with a 2,000-degree, 75-pound block of hot soft glass. It was placed in an annealing oven for a seven-day cycle. This was so far beyond my comfort zone that I eventually lost interest in large-scale work. I realized, shortly after completing this experiment, that my aptitude and passion centered on my small-scale work, which I was dedicated to. The 75-pound block did not turn out well; in fact, it failed with internal cracks. After living with it for a year, and not being emotionally involved with the results, I destroyed it.

However, this was not a failure: I knew, once and for all, that my dream of building a casting furnace in my studio, and my belief that it would open a new body of work, was just that—a dream. Chasing the dream of a large-scale project was not where I belonged. I have tremendous respect for the sculptors who can push the size limits with cast glass or any other material. But that's not me. In retrospect, this endeavor was a huge success, because it gave me permission not to worry about doing large-scale work, but to continue to experience success with my small-scale efforts. I am an artist whose work engages people to experience a dialogue when they pick up one of my intimate objects and hold it in their hand.

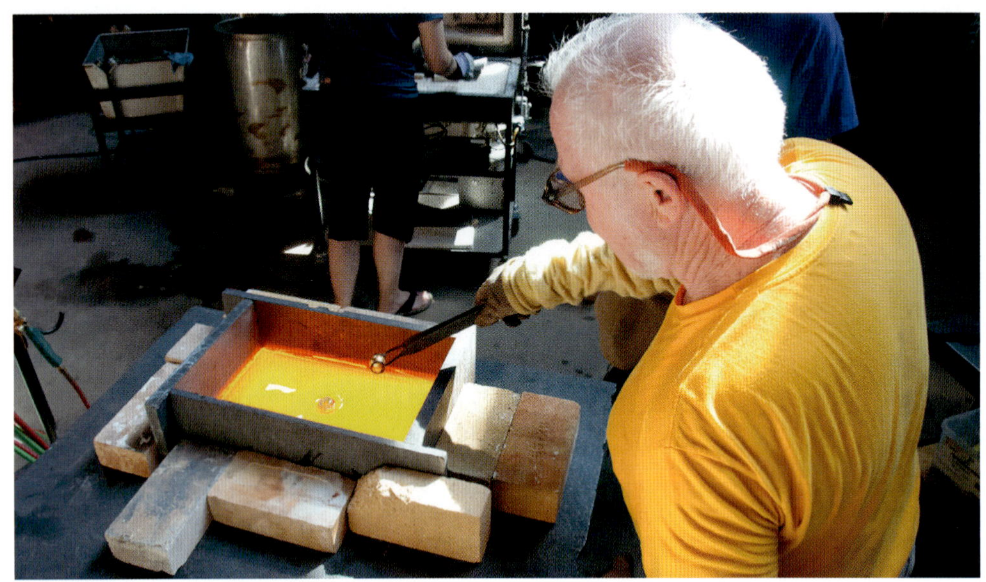

This is an experimental effort that was part of my exploration of how to cast a large floral panel. Here I am adding components onto the molten glass to ready it for the last casting. The work was done at the Wheaton Arts and Cultural Center glass studio.

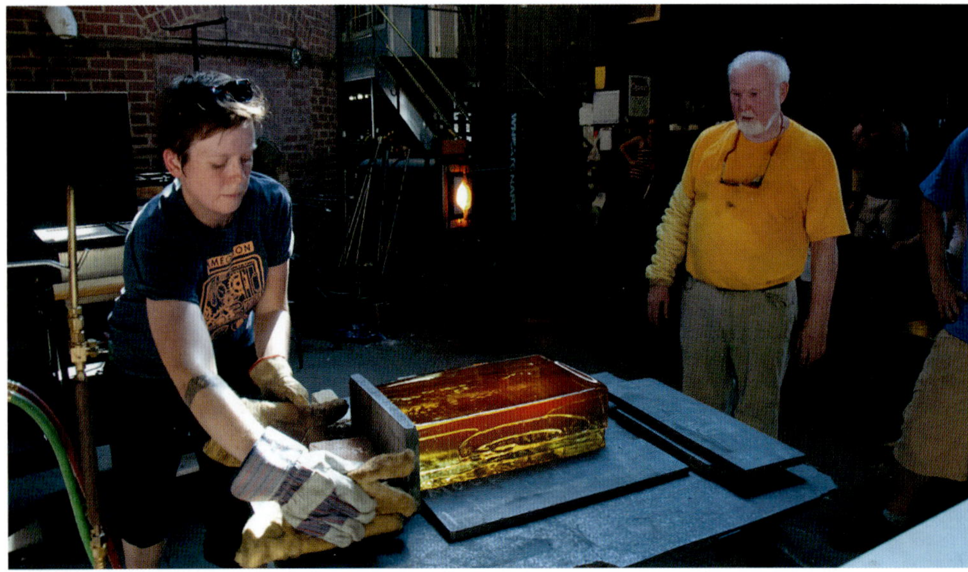

Casting honeybees in a block

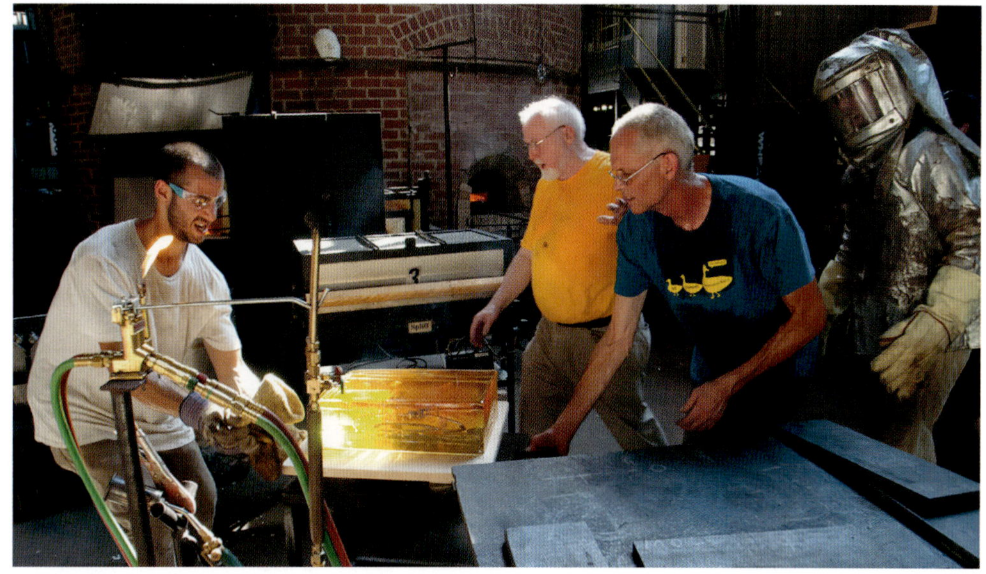

Preparation for placing the hot cast glass in the annealing oven

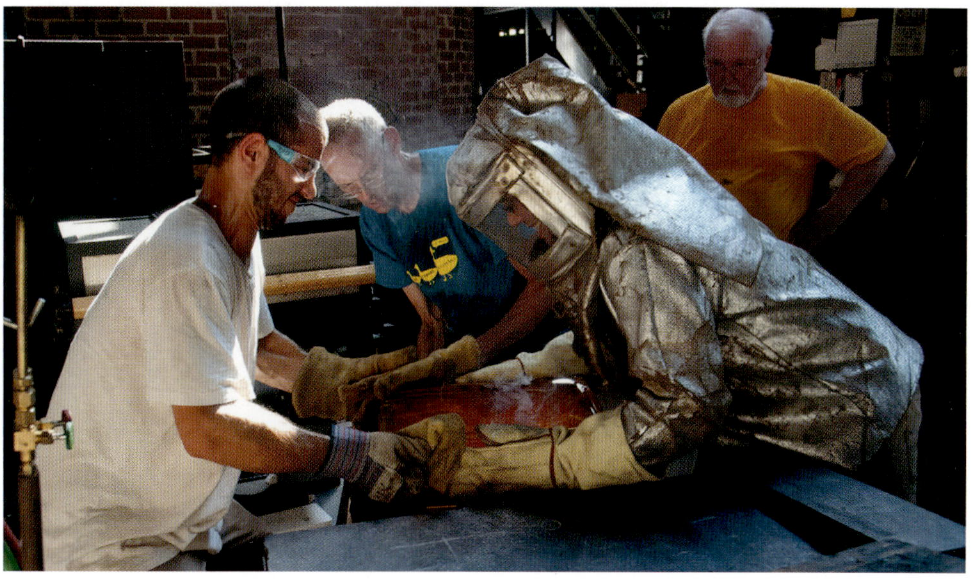

Lifting the glass to place it in the annealing oven

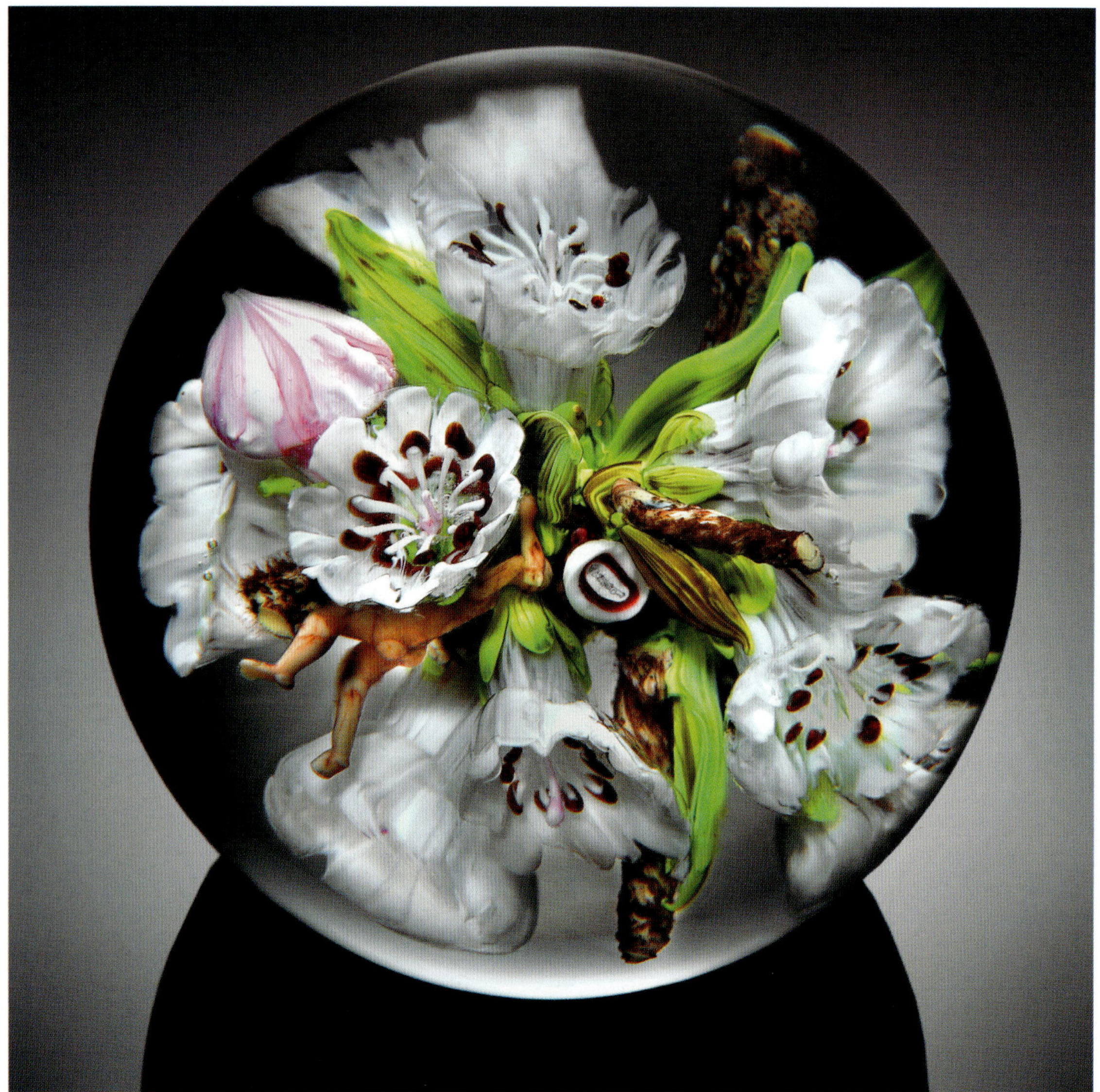

Mountain Laurel Blossom Bouquet with Human Form
This was the result of experimenting and being persistent—over five years of periodic experiments and failures. Sealing the stamens with the red tips into the trumpeted, creased blossoms was a breakthrough for me. I had to use my insights from the many disappointments to literally invent a way to accomplish the illusion.

In other words, I realized how important it is to know who you are.

I am not a scientist, and certainly no Thomas Edison, but I do understand his approach. He regarded his many "failures" as experiments that took him closer to success.

Planning and documenting the experimental techniques going into an artistic effort is critical. You need to chart where you have been in order to plot where you are going.

For example, while I was teaching at Penland in 1986, I became enamored by the mountain laurels in bloom that populated the woodland areas of the campus. While I was familiar with that particular flower, I had not paid close attention to it. But, finding myself teaching in a creative environment surrounded by the beauty of nature, I picked a bouquet of field flowers. The bouquet was dominated by a mountain laurel spray. I used it to decorate my workbench, symbolically celebrating the spirit of creativity at the glass-melting torch.

I came home with the idea of experimenting with the mountain laurel. I failed. Stymied by two weeks of failure, I put a few of the efforts on the shelf and destroyed the worst of them.

Over the next six years, I would periodically try to solve the technical puzzle of representing the flower, which was very complex because the stamens were secured in a cup-shaped blossom; as the flower wilted, the stamens sprung out of the holster to pollinate the plant.

The colors were especially challenging because I was seeking the unique translucence that captured the complexity, beauty, and uniqueness that led many botanists to consider the mountain laurel among the most attractive shrubs in the Northern Hemisphere.

I don't believe in failure. It is not failure if you enjoyed the process.

—Oprah Winfrey

My experimentation with this elusive design was discouraging.

Eventually I came into the studio with this need to take the mountain laurel design to the next level. I made a commitment that I was going to solve the technical and aesthetic challenges.

After ten or fifteen experiments over the course of a month, I was failing again. I felt that my labor and costs not only had failed to produce results but had drained me emotionally.

When I was about ready to give up, one night—right before I went to sleep—an idea floated into my mind. I could position the stamens in the translucent blossom by creasing the floral segments and adding clear glass to interpret the fidelity of the flower.

When I woke up the next morning, the idea was fresh in my mind and I was anxious to get to the studio. I immediately started to work on my idea and became very excited by what I perceived could be a breakthrough.

This was not the first time that my mind, in my relaxed mode, had solved an aesthetic challenge. Earlier, in 1979, I wanted to present my floral designs in a new form. I could not invent the floral paperweight that I had dedicated my talents toward, because others beat me to it in the mid-1800s in France.

I was driven by an obsession to do something fresh with my botanical vocabulary.

Over the course of six months, I set aside Friday and Saturday mornings to experiment with this new series. I "failed" many times and reconciled the efforts to the cullet bucket (a fireproof container for hot-glass waste), with a few going on the shelf.

The "failures," to me, were experimental studies. I had always relied on experimental efforts to refine my work, but this was a much more ambitious and systematized effort leading to a new form.

That mindset I developed in the late '70s changed everything. The studies on the shelf were disappointing in many ways. But they were also encouraging: I was lifting my flowers out of the traditional paperweight form and into a rectangular block, showing a plant suspended in clear glass.

Once I was confident with the result of my innovation, I destroyed most of the failures—with the recognition that they were not really failures, but studies that amounted to rungs on the ladder. They lacked the refinement that I demand from my work, but they were my teachers.

It's only when you risk failure that you discover things. When you play it safe, you're not expressing the utmost of your human experience.

—Lupita Nyong'o

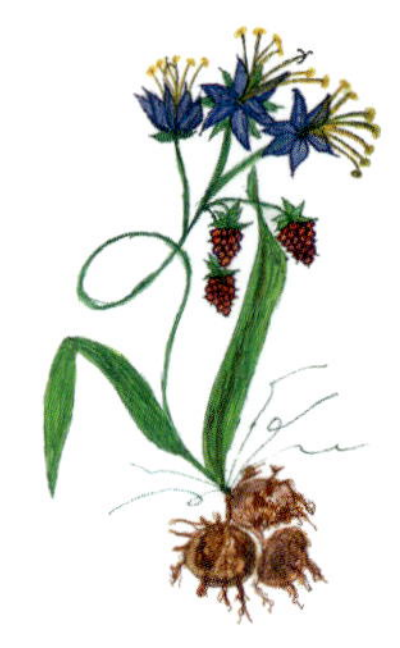

CHAPTER 6: CREATE A COMFORTABLE SPACE FOR YOUR ART MAKING

I always prefer to work in the studio. It isolates people from their environment. They become in a sense . . . symbolic of themselves.

—Richard Avedon

Make your studio as comfortable as your living room—you'll be spending more time in it as you move forward.

For the first three years of my career, I worked in the corner of my utility room. My bench was across from the furnace and water heater. At the time, the environment matched my level of ability and technical knowledge. It was comfortable.

As my work progressed, I connected the utility room to a 600-square-foot addition that was disguised as a two-car garage (I was worried about violating zoning ordinances). It felt spacious, and the additional room allowed me to bring in an assistant and buy new equipment.

All went well, but after twenty-seven years I was feeling the pinch. I wanted to experiment with larger forms. A small house next door was for sale; it was on a dead-end street that connected to my property. I thought it would be a wonderful transition if I could work in a larger studio away from my residence.

It was a difficult decision. On one hand, I was fifty-six years old and knew that a larger studio could facilitate new work that would advance my dreams. However, it was a risky, complicated, and expensive proposition. It required me to go to the municipal zoning board and retain an attorney to represent me for a commercial variance in a residential neighborhood.

I was apprehensive about this step—if I were turned down, I would likely have to move or rent a commercial space. (This turned out to be a rewarding experience, though: the zoning board was aware of my career and complimented me as they approved my application.)

It was a major financial commitment. I added 1,800 square feet to a two-bedroom cottage.

I didn't build anything that would attract attention. In fact, I wanted to blend in. I was investing in my career. I was creating a comfortable sanctuary for my art making dreams.

The new facility affected my career in expected and unexpected ways.

Having additional space allowed me to do more-ambitious work and take advantage of part-time assistants. One unexpected benefit was that having a large space accessible to the public—not connected to my house—provided Pat and me more privacy when museums scheduled studio visits for their members.

Over the last twenty years, my most valued time has been arriving at the studio between four and

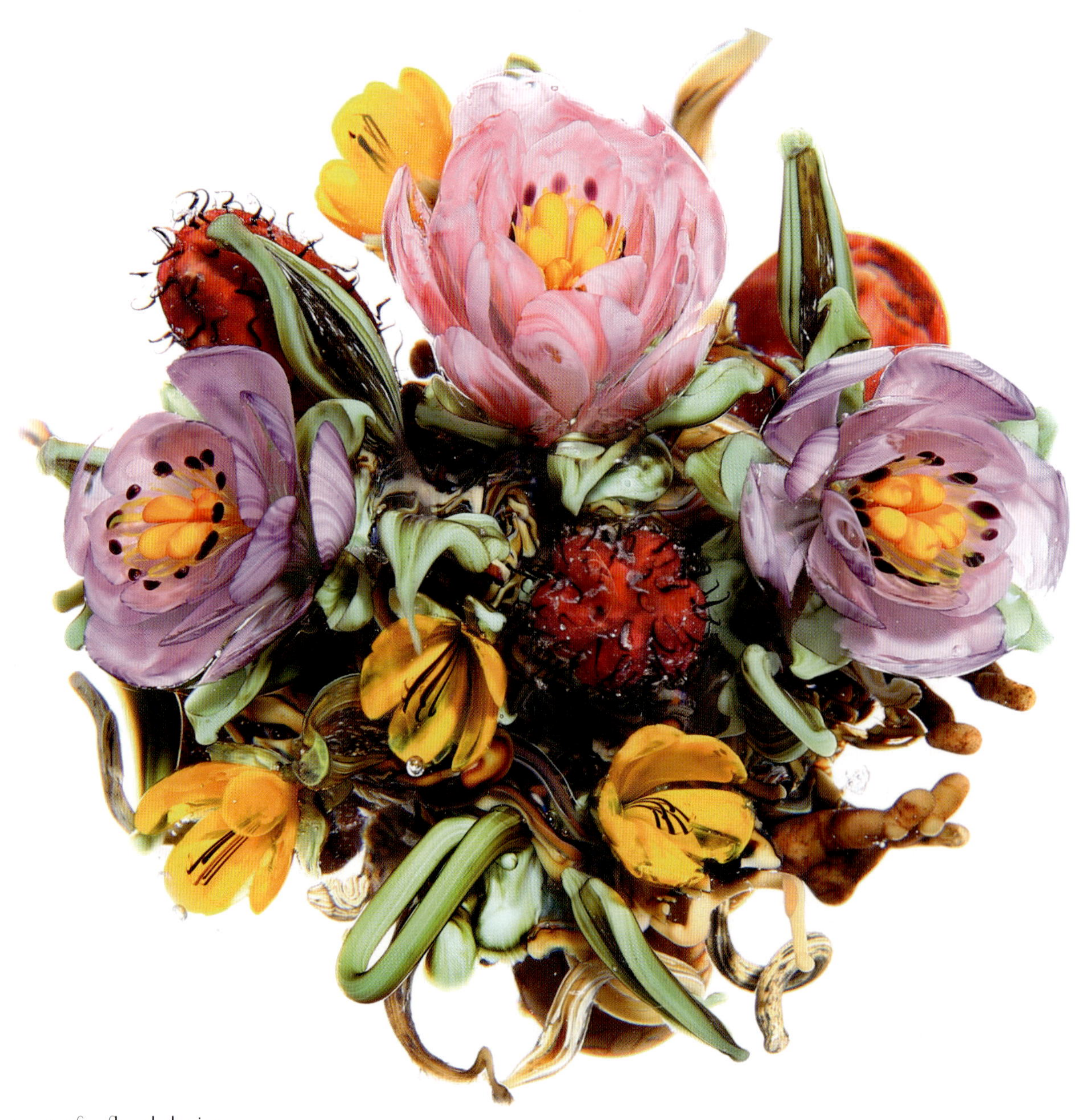

Close-up of a floral design

five in the morning. Prior to opening the studio door, I stargaze, fascinated by the scale of the universe. I feel humbled by the magnitude of the experience and spiritually enlivened by the majesty of God's design.

My studio is a blend of the practical and the spiritual, as are the ingredients of art. You blend the physical and metaphysical in ways that allow you to share your feelings.

Think about your space as your spiritual sanctuary and as a sacred place crucial to your work. The adornments you choose should challenge you, not distract you. My space is not decorated with niceties. The cultural clutter references opportunities to be explored and refined.

Don't neglect the relationship between your workspace and the quality, range, and evolution of your art making. It's not about creating an extravagant environment. It's about investing in a quiet space that doesn't distract you from your work, a space that is special to you.

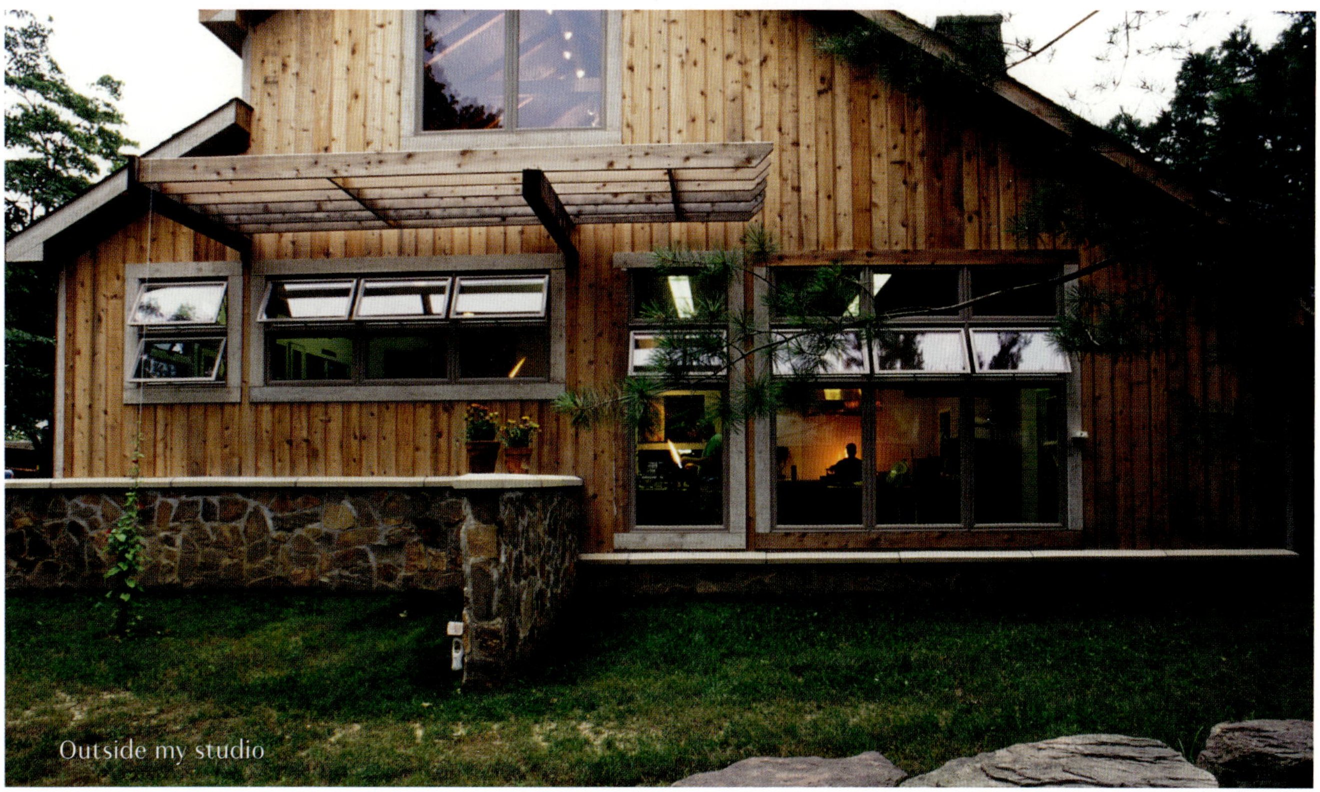
Outside my studio

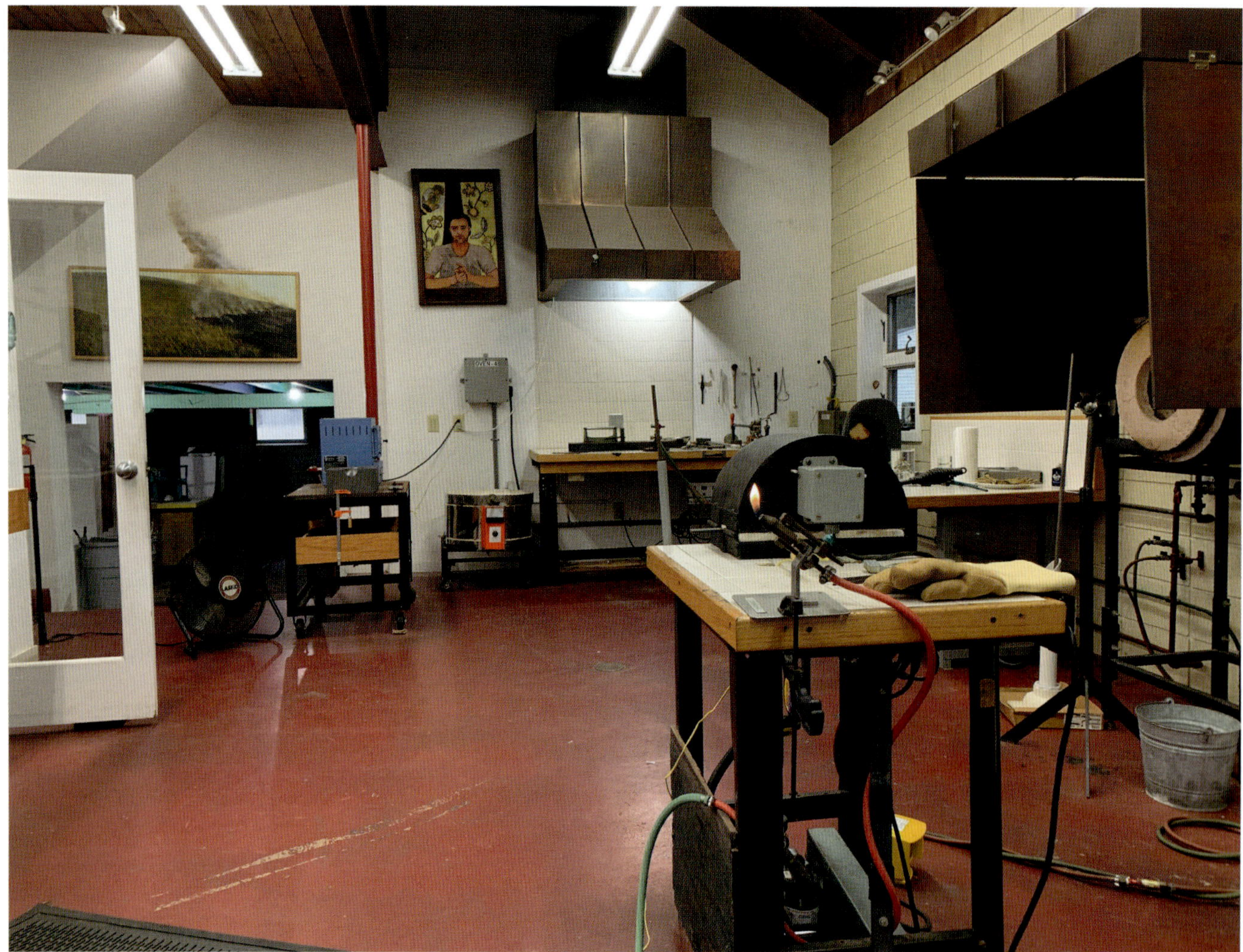

Inside my studio

This area is dedicated to encapsulating the colored glass flowers into the molten glass. After working for twenty-seven years in a 600-square-foot garage, the 3,000-square-foot studio had a very positive influence on my work. For one thing, I had room to bring in added equipment, allowing me to pursue more ambitious projects. Also, I could provide a comfortable work space for my assistants.

To have a sacred place is an absolute necessity for anybody today. You must have a room or a certain hour of the day or so, where you do not know who your friends are, you don't know what you owe anybody or what they owe you. This is a place where you can simply experience and bring forth what you are and what you might be.

—*Joseph Campbell*

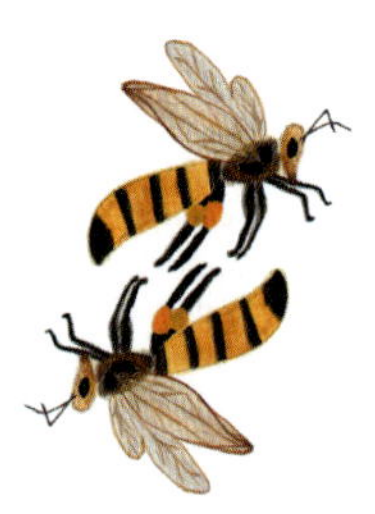

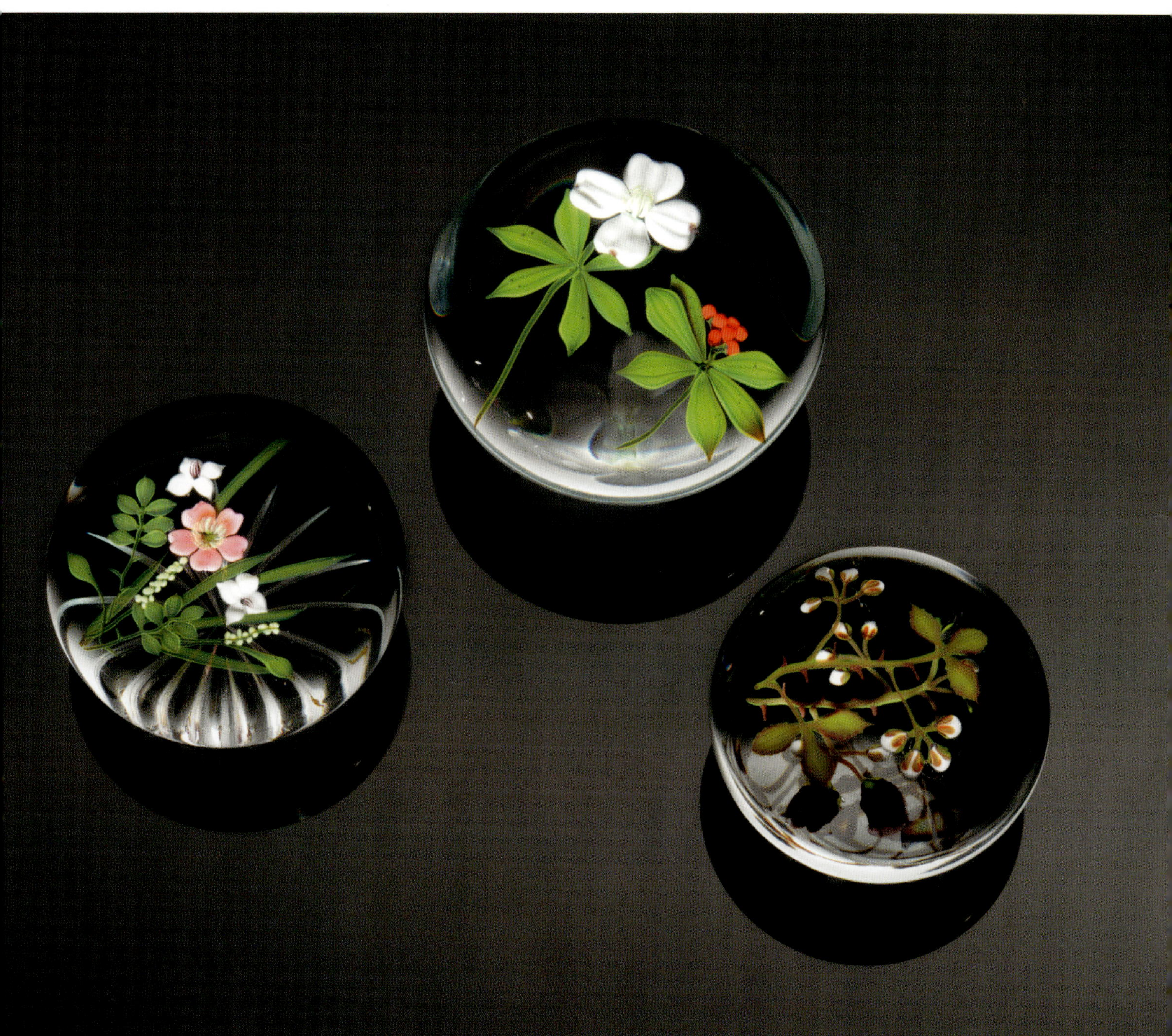

Aesthetics is a branch of philosophy that investigates the nature of art and the metaphysical properties of beauty. As an object maker, I apply my emotions with technical skills to create works of art that people can relate to and derive pleasure from. The more personal my interpretations of nature are, the more accessible my art will be to an audience across all cultures.

I believe that beauty and spirituality are entwined in a fascinating balance between skilled craft and imagination.

I'm not a student of philosophy; however, I constantly think about the nature of beauty in the context of my art. While writing this chapter, I revisited a book titled *Philosophies of Art and Beauty: Selected Readings in Aesthetics from Plato to Heidegger*. I found its works by Plato, St. Augustine, and Immanuel Kant the most attractive and relatable.

It's beyond the scope of this book to offer a dissertation on aesthetics, but even a cursory examination of some main points lends an interesting perspective on beauty.

For example, Plato evaluated beauty in a higher realm and expected viewers of works of art to bring an informed opinion about beauty that would enhance their experience.

St. Augustine was less interested in logical deductions related to beauty than Plato. Augustine was more motivated by the spiritual realm—particularly by crediting human appreciation of aesthetics as a gift from God. St. Augustine wrote that God is responsible for elevating our senses to beauty, and that beauty is inextricably linked with virtue, truth, and thoughtfulness. In short, all these elements of beauty celebrate the godly realm.

Kant's philosophical territory is both vast and complex, and when he talks about the inherent beauty of an art object regardless of function, I easily relate to Kant's attitude. For example, when I craft small-scale sculpture as homage to the plant kingdom, I am not concerned with botanical accuracy; it's about a personal response to how the poetry of nature touches my soul. The challenge is to translate my emotional experience to the glass and thus share my interpretation and feelings with the viewer.

Beyond the material's memory, spontaneity plays a special role in my pursuit of expression. The spontaneity associated with risk-taking can teach creative people different ways to present ideas.

It's not about getting it right—it's about allowing magic to happen.

My artistic maturity has evolved with my relationship with object making. The process has showed me inventive ways to balance beauty with truth to the material, skilled craftsmanship, and personal expression. I've been fascinated by what I perceive to be a magical result under the heading of spontaneity.

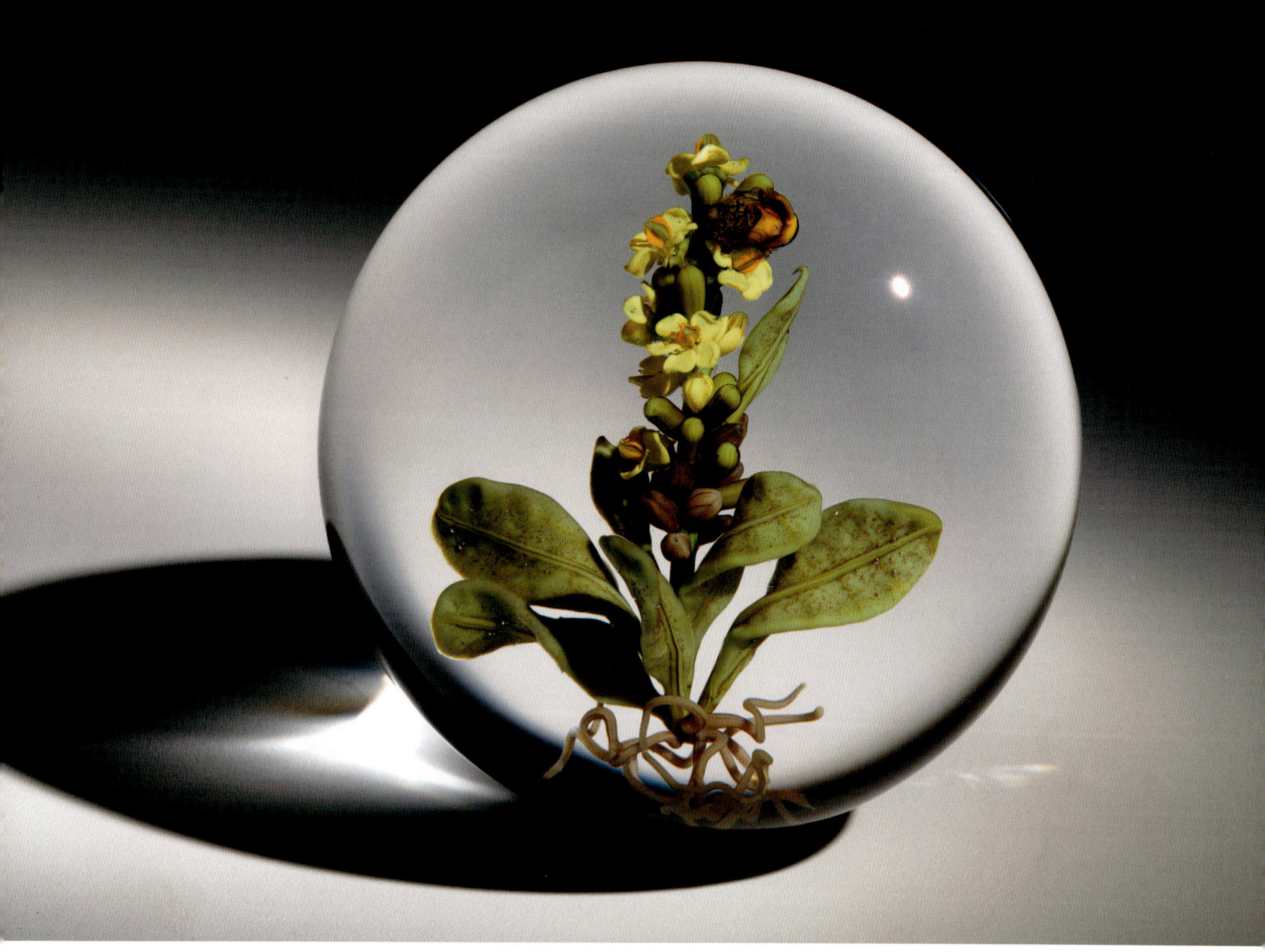

Common Mullein

This common mullein, from the paperweight series, shows a level of detail and truth to nature that distinguishes it from its antique French forerunners. At this stage of my career, I was focused on botanical accuracy. I saw the specimen that inspired this during one of my woodland walks. I knew this plant as a child, but it wasn't until the early '80s that I was inspired to research this flowering plant and share this common mullein with a wider audience. I learned during my research that early pioneers used the broad leaves for insulation of their clothes and boots from the cold and also diapers for their babies.

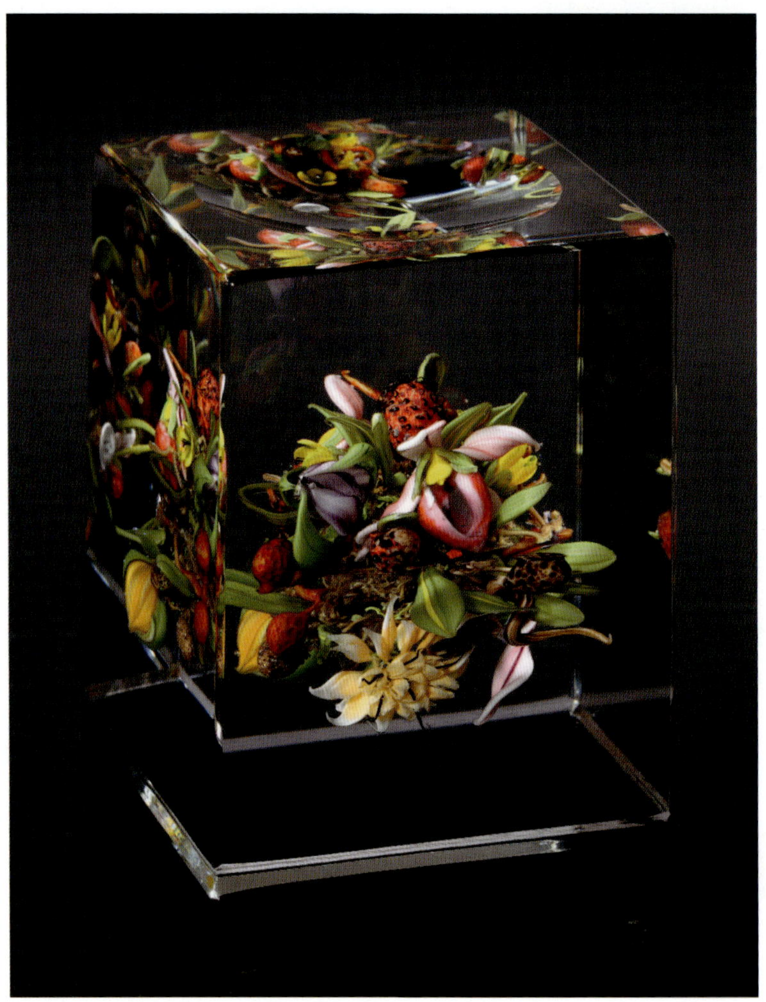

Paphiopedilum Orchids with Field Flowers and Figures, 2020, 4.5 × 3 in.

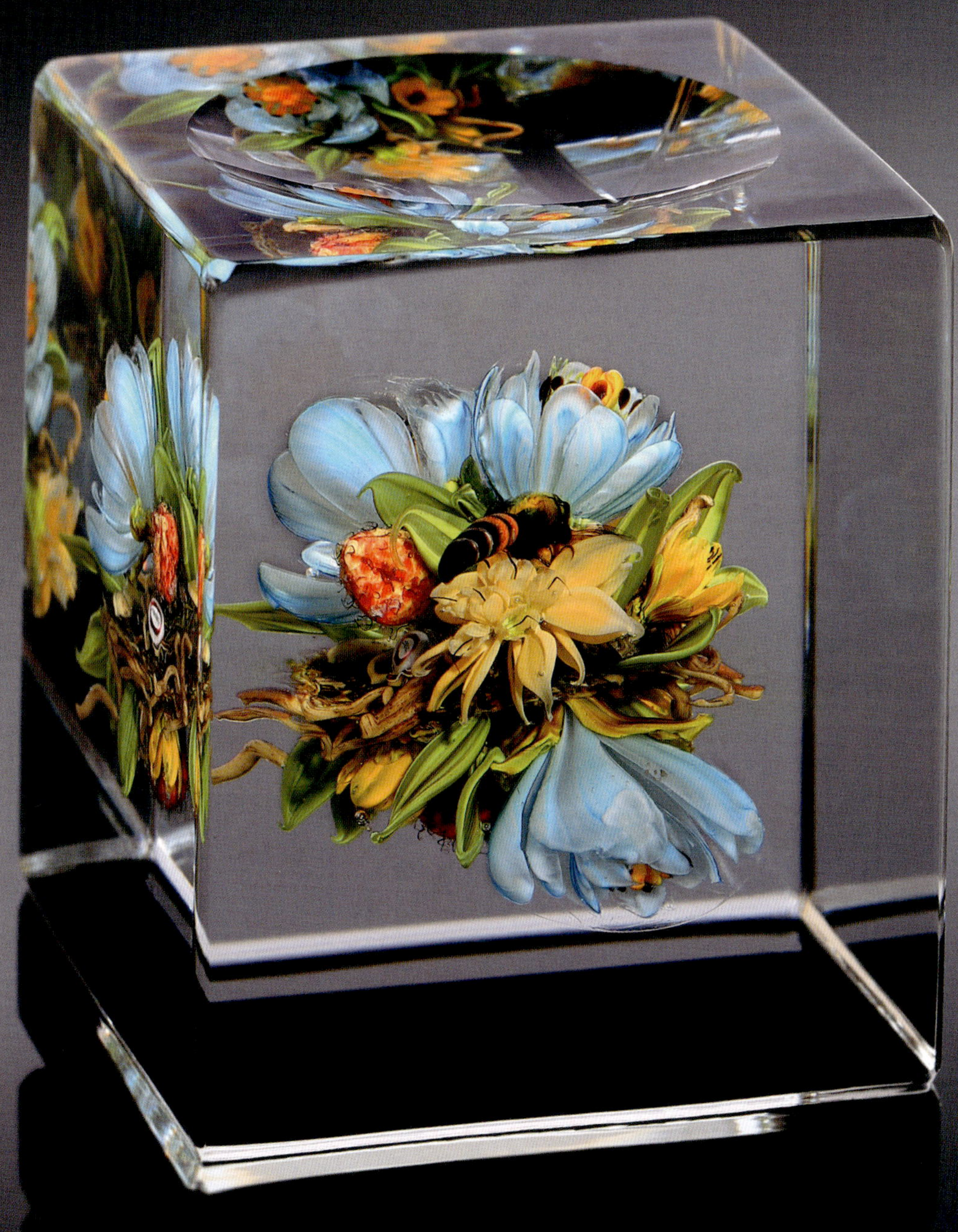

Emily Dickinson's Garden Bouquet, 2020, 4 × 3 in.

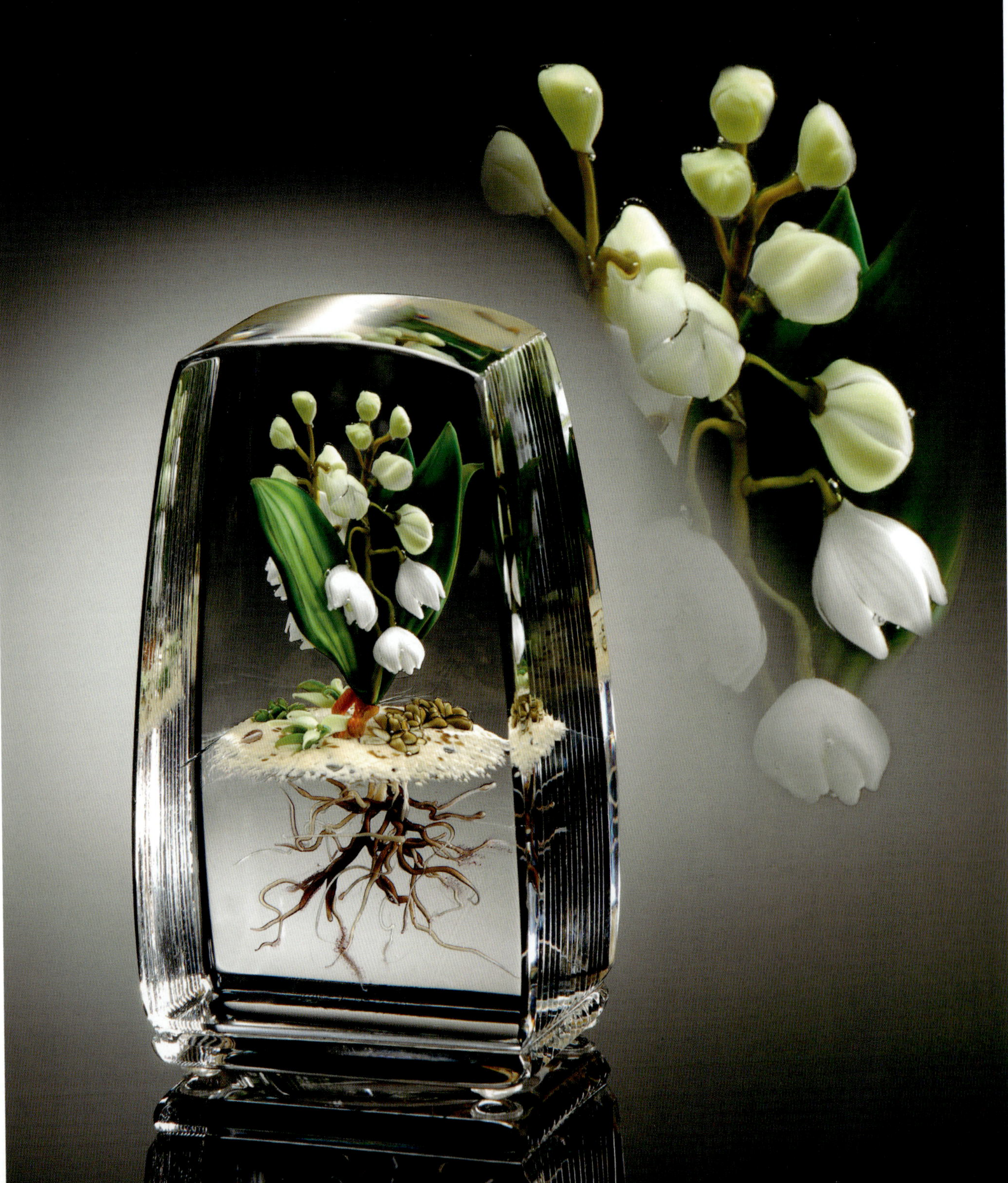

Lily of the Valley

This botanical is a tribute to one of my mother's favorite ornamental plants. The botanical format was a way to explore, in a symbolic way, the mysteries under the earth as a counterpoint to above. This format, which I titled the Botanical series, was a breakthrough in scale and complexity in the early '80s. It allowed me to bring more visual information into my body of work. This series was one more step toward a fresh approach while building on the French tradition of the mid-nineteenth century.

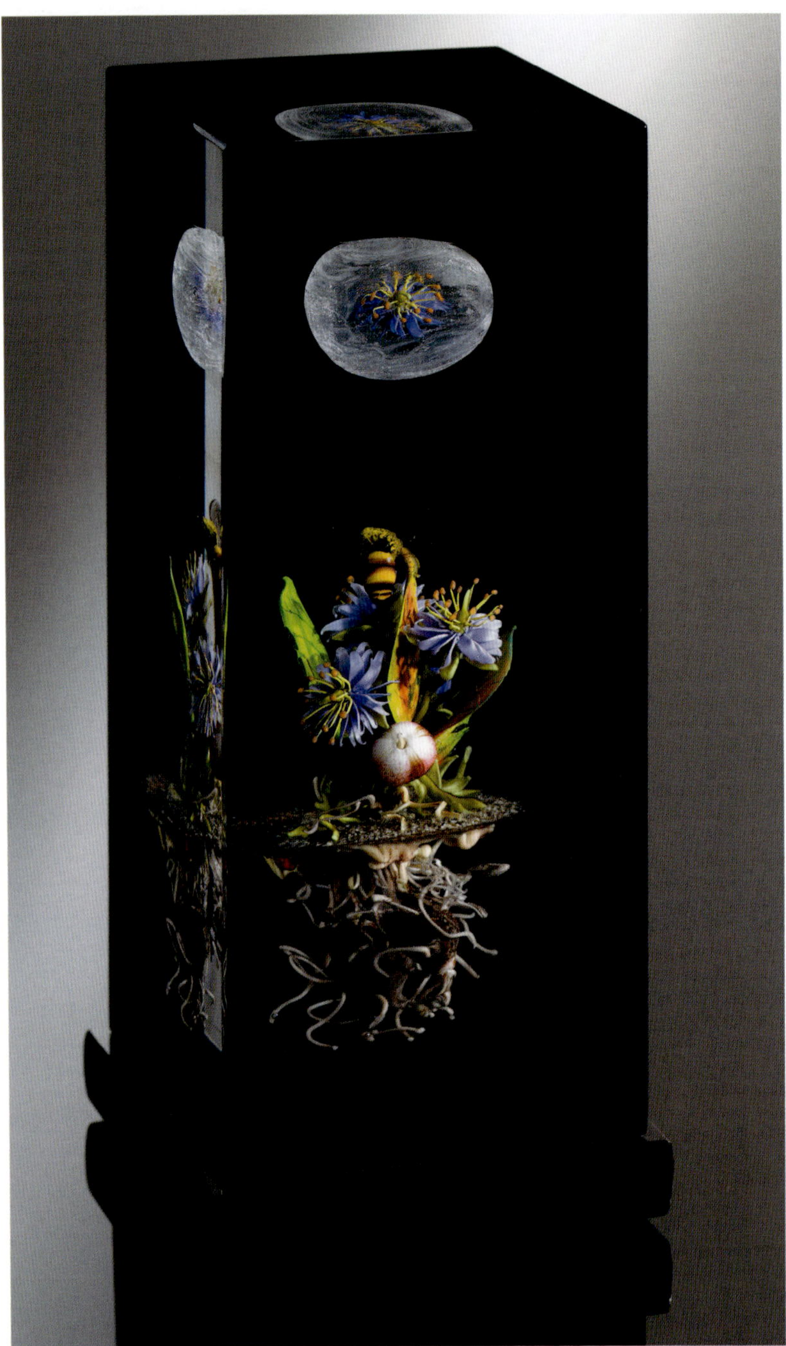

Cloistered Botanical with Floating Orb

"Cloistered" references a sheet of dark glass laminated to the form that offered an illusion of the plant floating in space. The floating orb suggests a surreal portrayal of a spiritual offering. There is a certain drama associated with the dark environment that is pleasing to the viewers yet allows them to be curious and respond in their own personal way.

Opposite:

Bouquet of Flowers, Fruits, and Insects

This close-up of an orb displays a cluster. To me, there is something magical about the timeless quality of this interpretation of nature. I love the idea that I am suspending my creation in a timeless form.

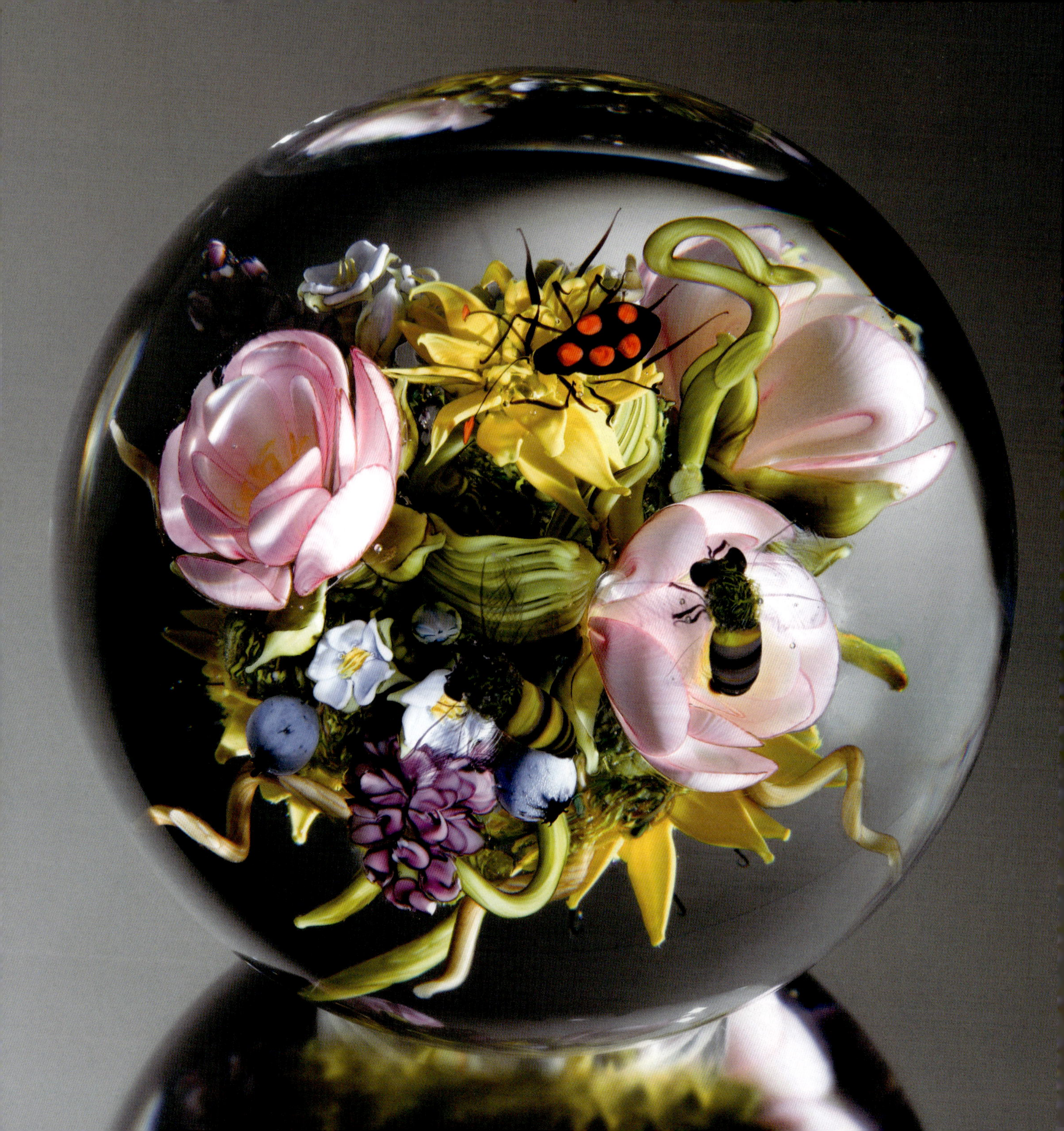

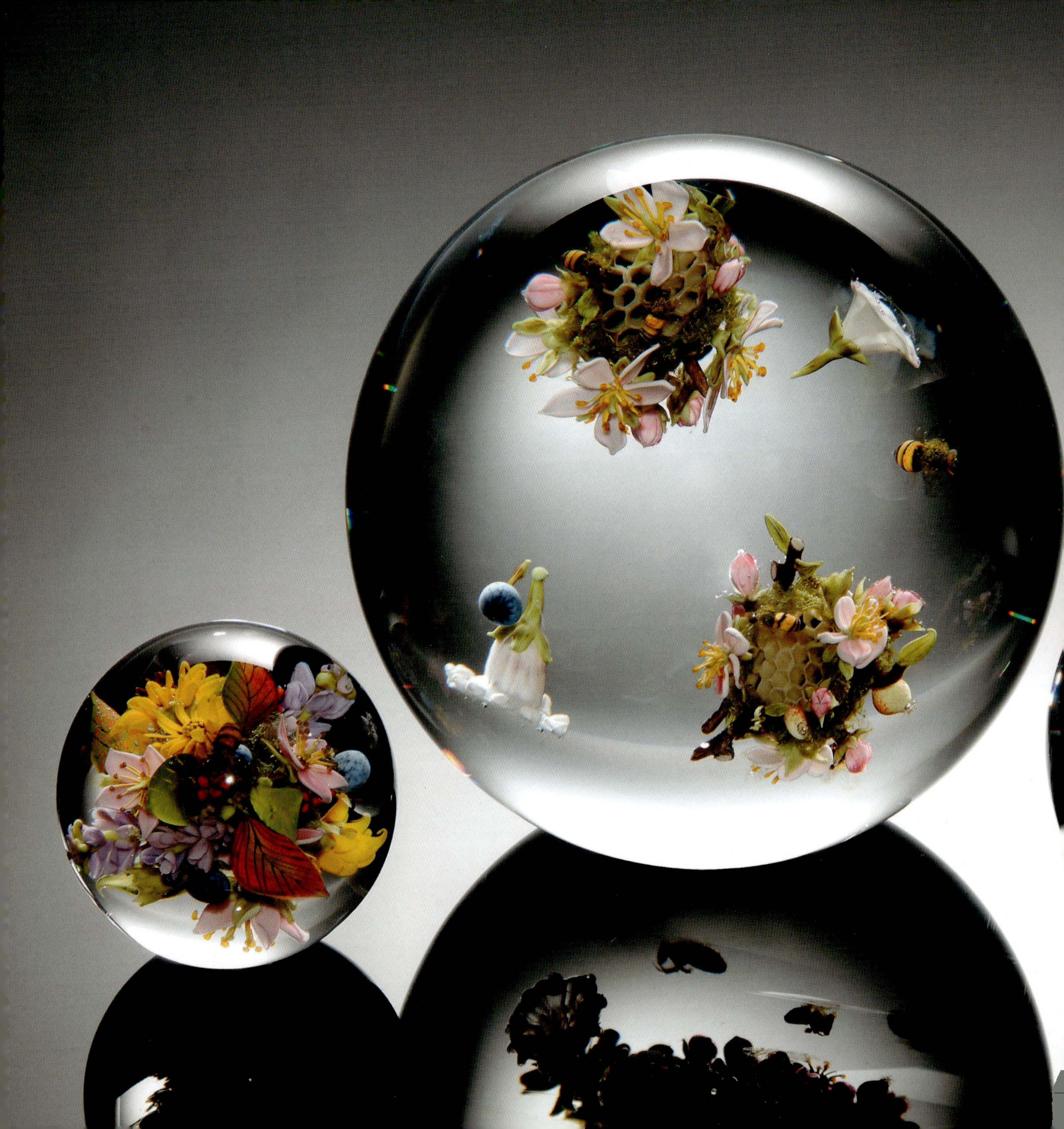

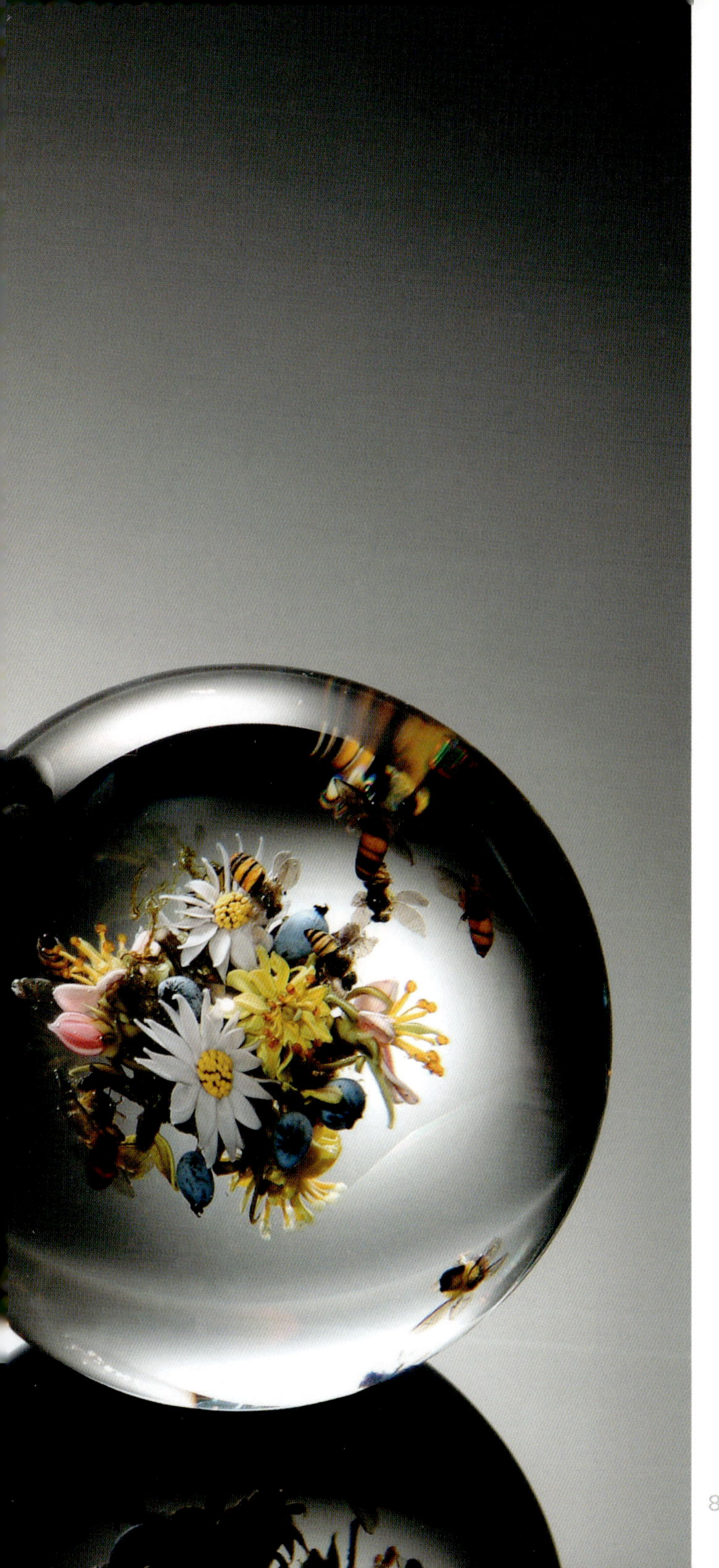

Grouping of Three Orbs

This series first evolved in the first few years of the 2000s. What initially appealed to me about the orb format was the uniformity of the magnification of a 360-degree sphere. The paperweights were magnified only from the top view, and the botanical series had no magnifying-lens quality to the form. The orbs were also larger in scale than the paperweights. The fact that the orbs had no top or bottom left it to the viewer to choose not only how to display them but what could be discovered thanks to the format. These three pieces represent a range from 4 to 6 to 8 inches. To this day, I continue to be fascinated with the optical illusions associated with the clear, nondistorted view offered by the uniformity of the shape.

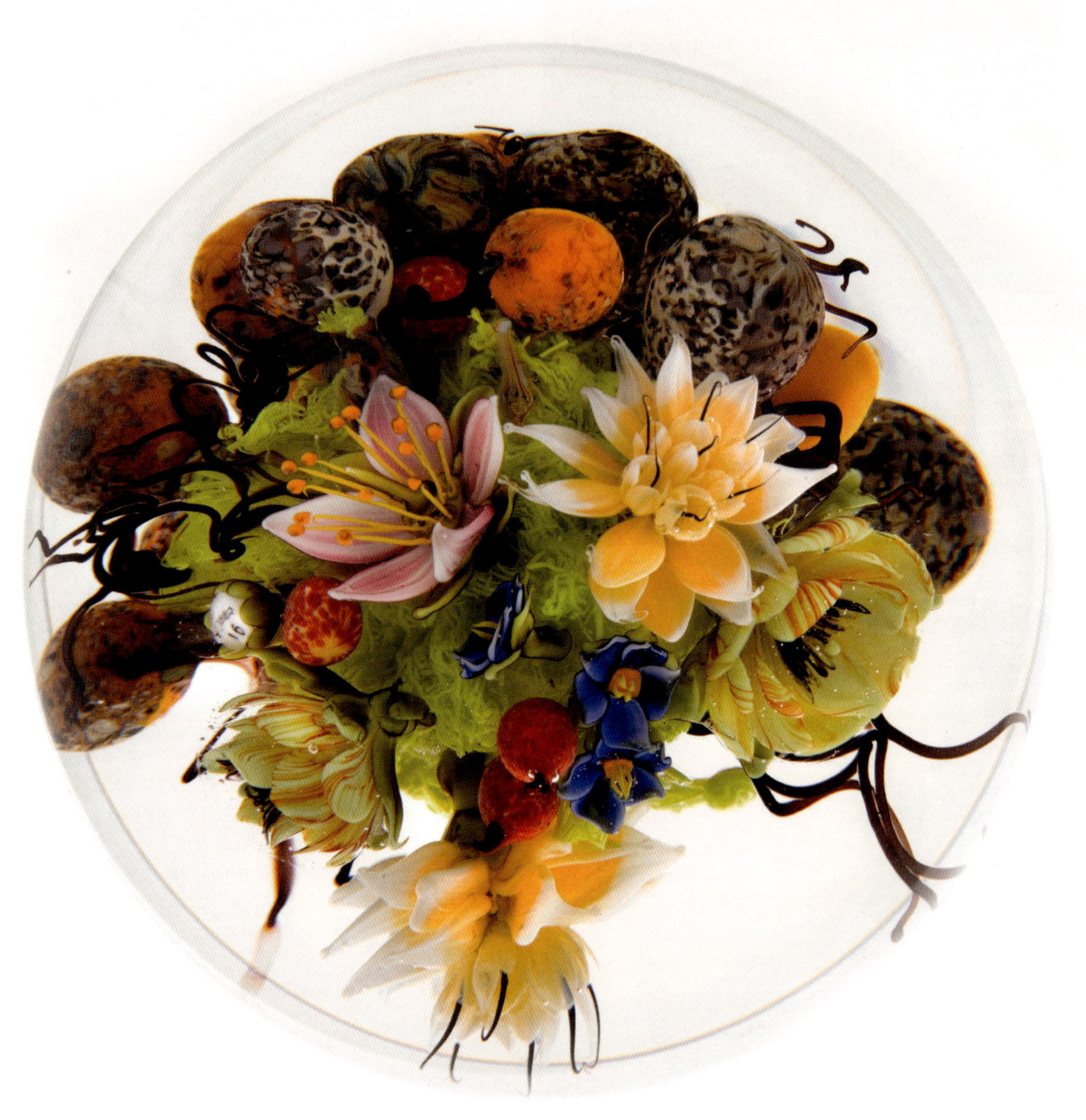

***Flowers in Bulbous Form*, top side**

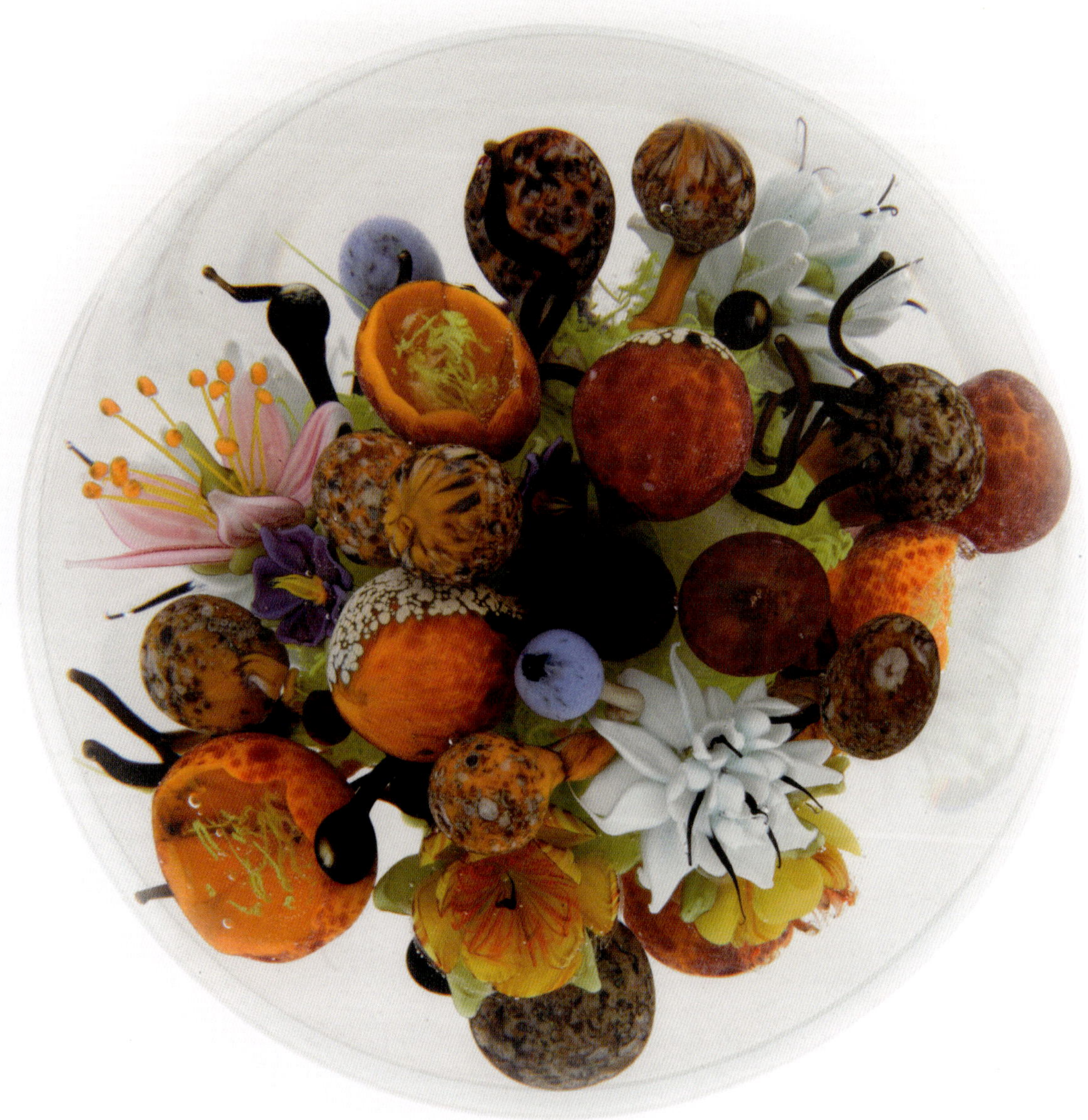

***Flowers in Bulbous Form*, underside**

While I reference a top and bottom, in some cases there is no indication of the most attractive orientation for this object. It's really up to the viewer. This piece, shown in two different perspectives, is a result of my interest in bulbous forms. For me, bulbs offer a fascinating food and healing source associated with a flowering plant.

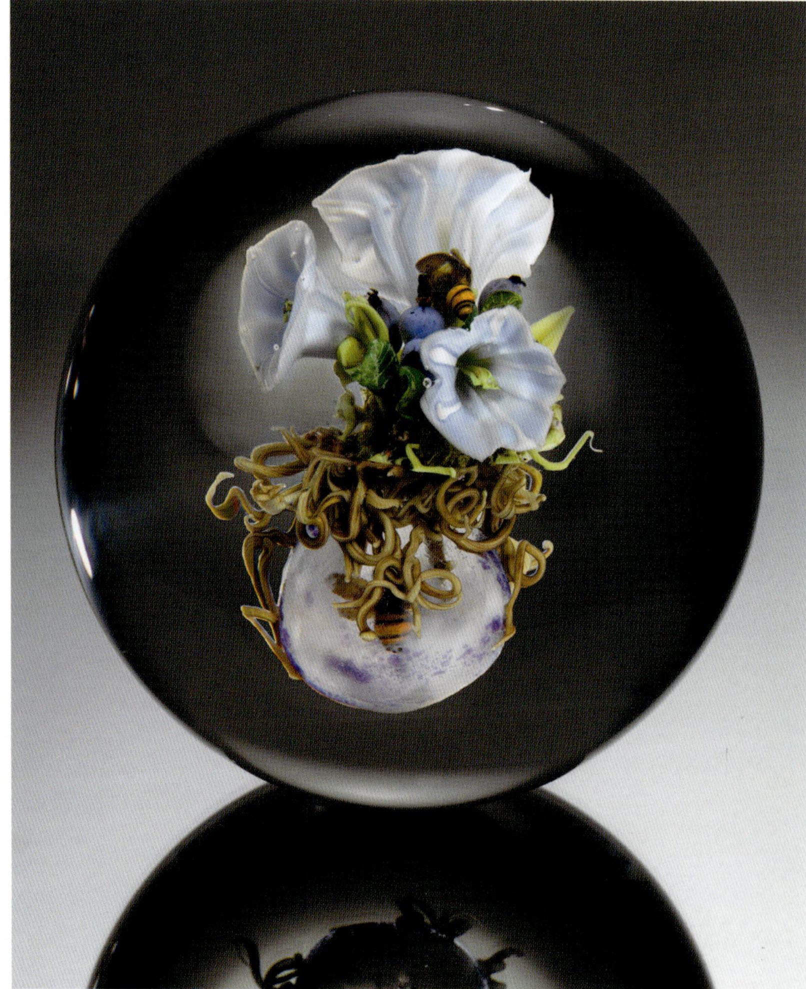

Morning Glory in Bulbous Form with Bee

This 6-inch orb incorporates morning glories and an ambitious root system clinging to a bulb that encases a bee. I love interpreting. It is satisfying to bring my menu of illusions into designs that present the plants in an intelligent but unusual setting. I think of much of my work as botanical anomalies, believing that if you searched the plant kingdom you most likely would eventually come across a similar specimen, just as unique. The unusual interpretation of the plant does not take away from the organic credibility.

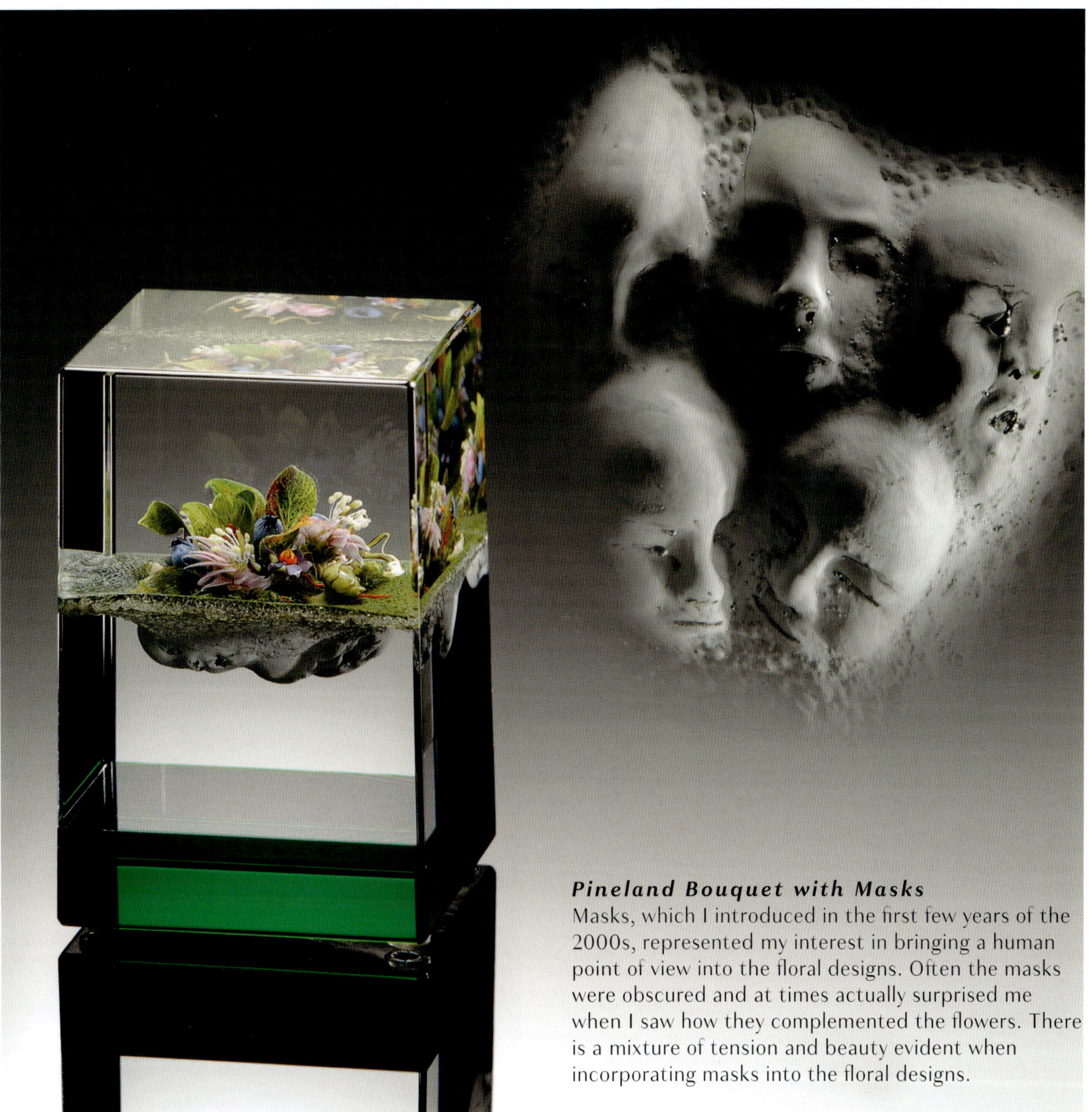

Pineland Bouquet with Masks
Masks, which I introduced in the first few years of the 2000s, represented my interest in bringing a human point of view into the floral designs. Often the masks were obscured and at times actually surprised me when I saw how they complemented the flowers. There is a mixture of tension and beauty evident when incorporating masks into the floral designs.

Assemblage

This work has evolved by incorporating dark-glass backgrounds. When I say that this is one of the later works in my evolution, it is not to negate what has been done before. This assemblage is yet another variation of the theme. As I spent time with the panels, they revealed more opportunities to be innovative. This particular work took advantage of floral designs that have evolved over the years with subtle variations. In a way, this summarizes my commitment to flameworking colored-glass flowers and bringing myth (as represented by the golden orb and the human forms) into the presentation.

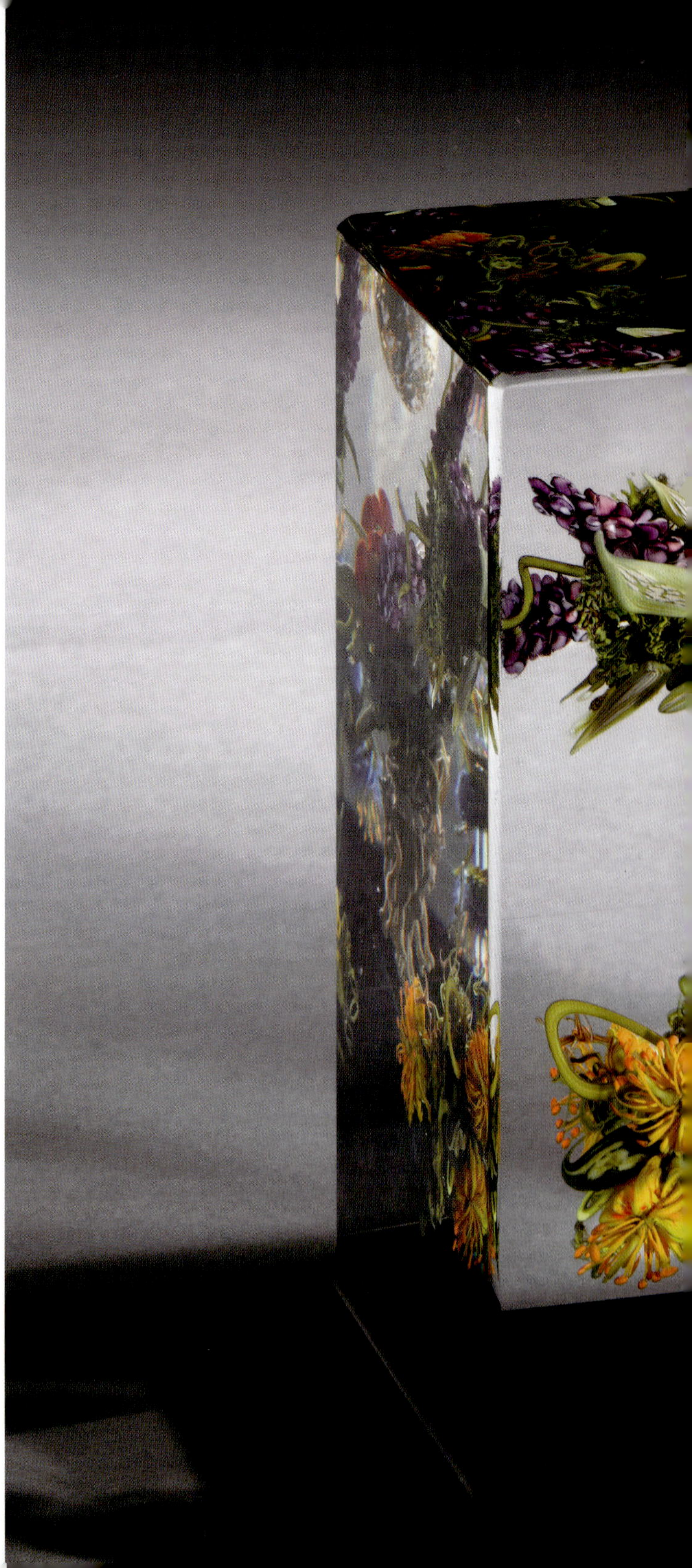

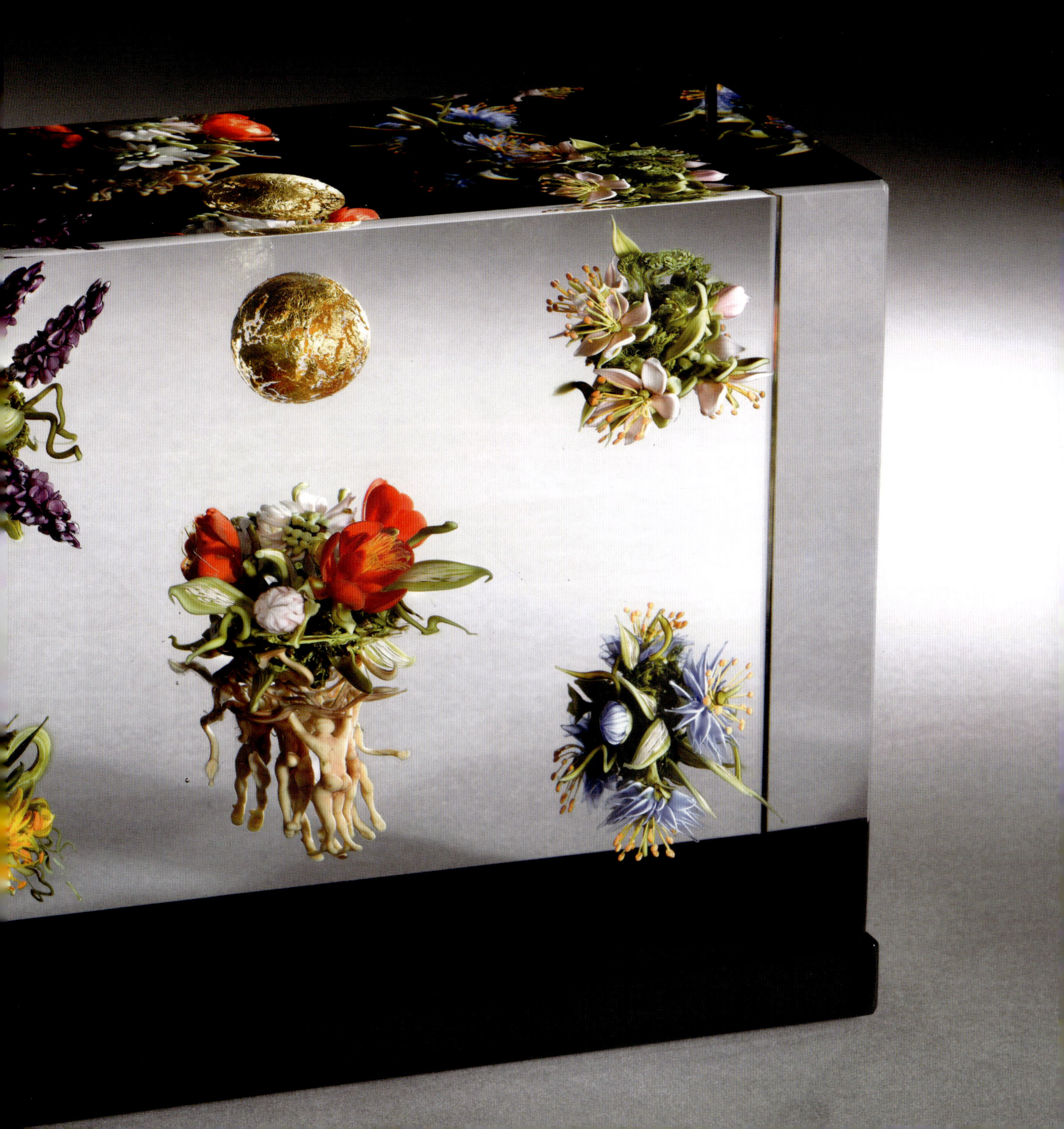

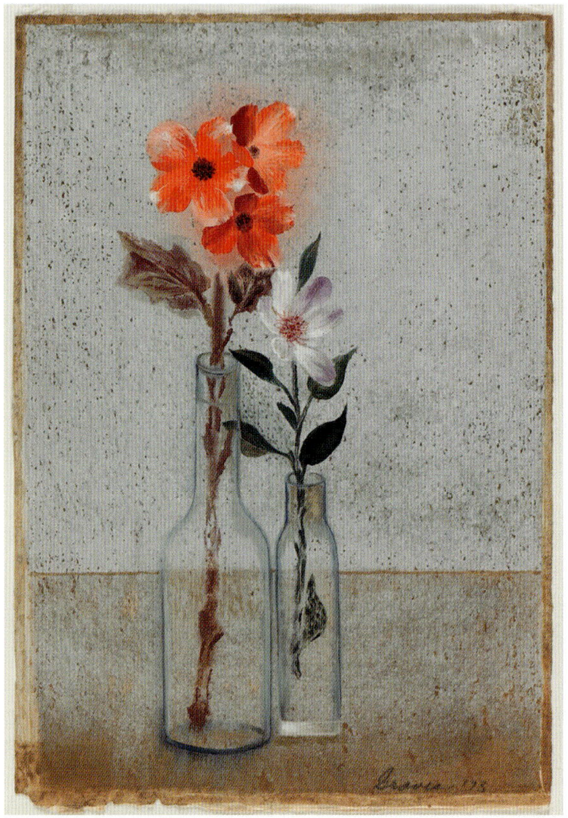

Morris Graves Painting
Winter Bouquet #12
Seattle Art Museum; 2009.52.97; *Winter Bouquet #12*; Morris Grave, born Fox Valley, Oregon, 1910; died Loleta, California, 2001; 1973; Tempera on paper; 13/ ¾ × 9 ½ in.; Gift of the Marshall and Helen Hatch Collection, in honor of the 75th anniversary of the Seattle Art Museum; Photographer: Elizabeth Mann

One of my core beliefs that I promote to students is that in order to do excellent work, you have to know what excellence is. My self-directed learning entailed not only forty years of listening to the classics from audiobooks, but also seeking out great work in museums.

Great work has a peculiar tension that can be mesmerizing. When I first viewed Leonardo da Vinci's *Ginevra de'Benci* at the National Gallery in Washington, DC, I was awestruck by the painting's beauty. The fact that Leonardo da Vinci painted it 541 years ago—yet it feels so modern—is mind-boggling.

The words of St. Augustine move me verbally the way that da Vinci's work does visually. I think Beauty is the ethereal substance of the mind and heart that heightens our senses in praise of God. This is evident when, over the course of my travels, I've been introduced to beautiful art that touches my being and leaves me perplexed.

As a modern example, I've enjoyed, and professionally grown from, many years of experiencing the nuances in the floral paintings of Morris Graves. Why did I meditate on Morris Graves's work when I had no intention of being a painter? His paintings—which glow with nuanced beauty—inspired me to find ways to inject into my own work a higher level of spirituality inspired by my idea of excellence.

I was in New York delivering work to Leo Kaplan Antiques, Ltd., which at the time was one of the leading dealers both in antique French and contemporary paperweights. They were located close to the Whitney Museum on Madison Ave. After spending time at Kaplan's, I enjoyed visiting the Whitney Museum, and at the time there was a retrospective collection of Morris Graves's floral paintings. I was touched by the beauty and ethereal quality of the paintings. I found them to be unusually beautiful. This was the beginning of my study of Graves's career.

In summary, what I have addressed in this chapter is what you might call my philosophy of beauty. As an artist, I believe that a commitment to beauty is part of an overall philosophical dialogue. For an artist, this dialogue is a continuum—once the work leaves the studio, it has its own reason to exist, and the historians and philosophers who study beauty will—if my work is significant—place it into an American aesthetics continuum.

The artist is a primary component of an experience that has profound cultural value.

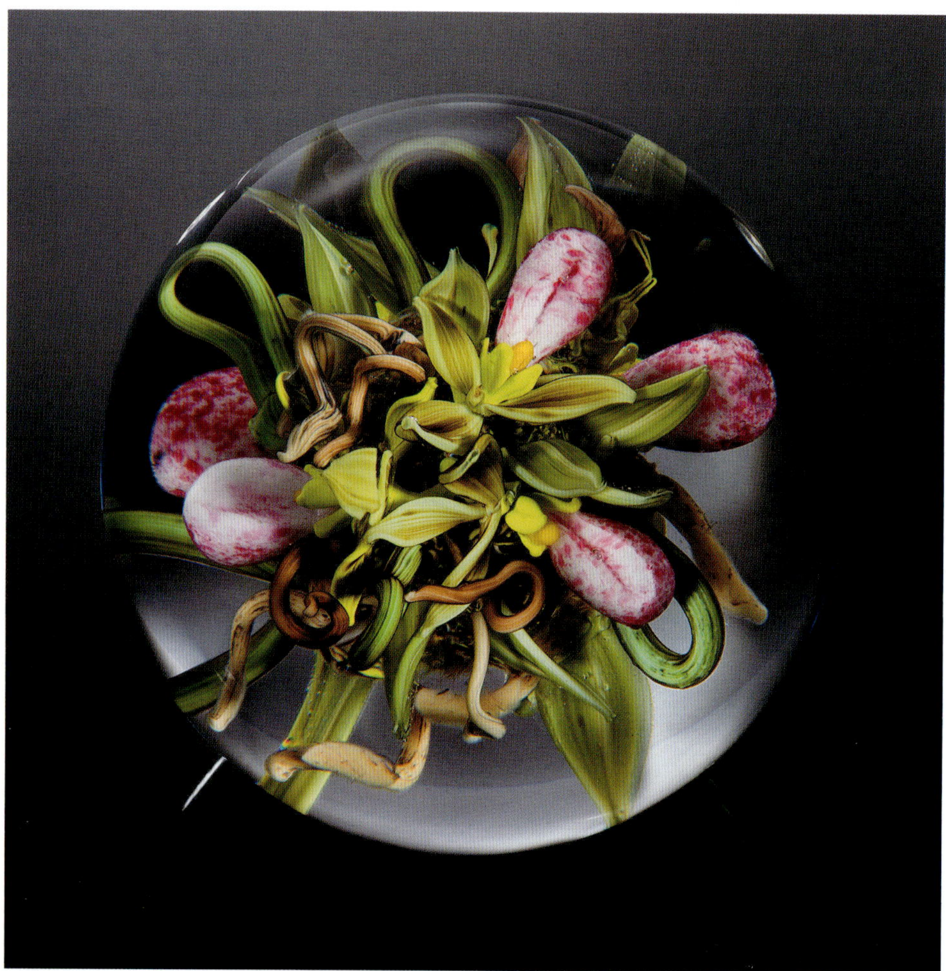

Pink Lady Slipper Cluster

This piece commemorates my bringing my mother a bouquet of Pink Lady Slippers from a morning adventure in the woods. She explained that these flowers are rare and should not be picked. As a thirteen-year-old, this struck me as odd that flowers from the woods would be too special to be picked.

A thing of beauty is a joy forever: Its loveliness increases; it will never pass into nothingness.

—John Keats

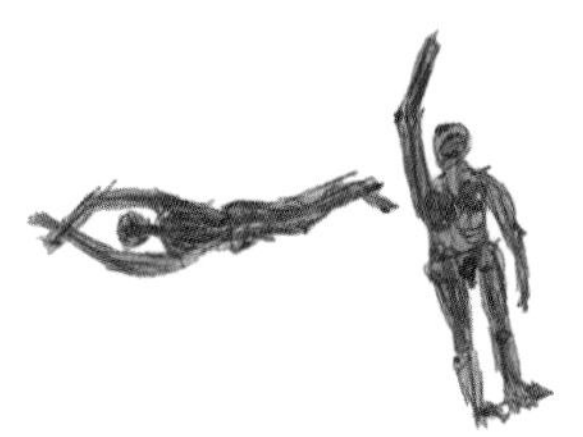

CHAPTER 8: CRAFT, DESIGN, AND ART

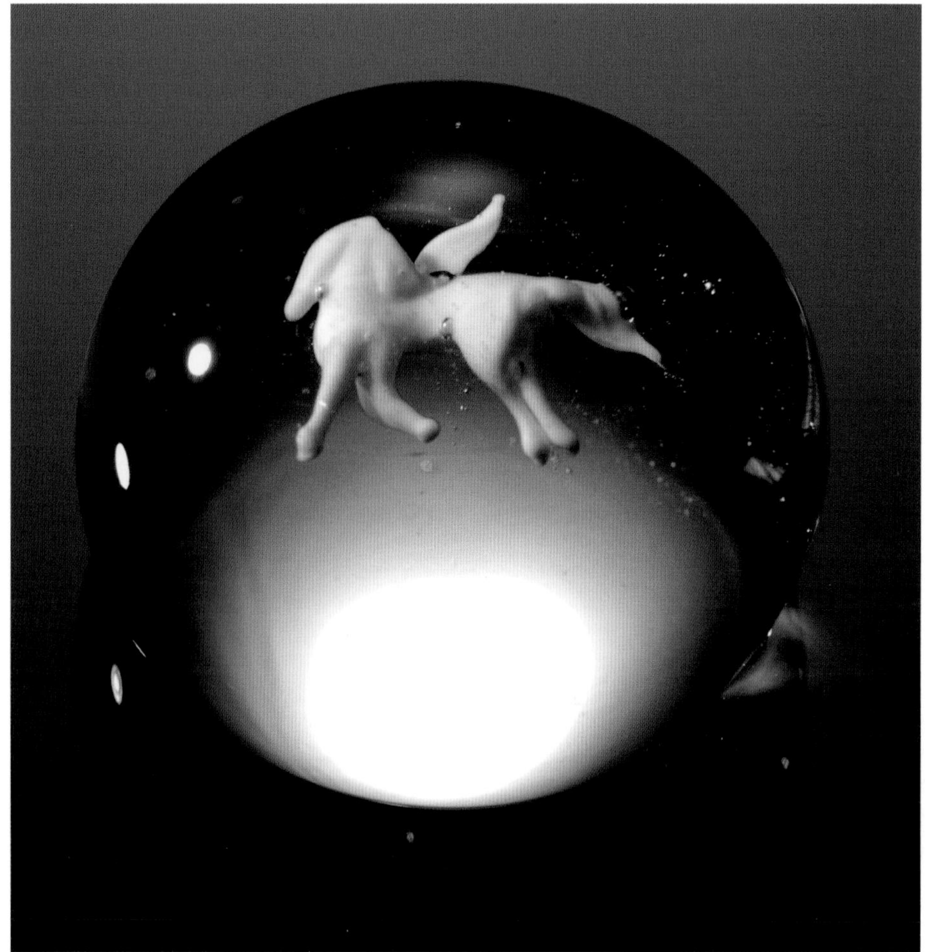

Pegasus
In 1969, I started working on the creative side in earnest. The first goal was to teach myself the art of paperweight making by flameworking soda lime glasses. Little did I know this journey would become an obsession and dominate my professional life.

Craft, *design*, and *art* are distinct categories with different objectives.

Why is this important to you? Because oftentimes you are competing with the past, and it is important to educate yourself about the heritage of your field. There are distinct differences among craft, design, and art, all of which can be entwined into the whole as fine art. It's essential, if you want to excel in any of those categories, to be familiar with the parameters and to understand what is respected within those categories.

The goal of *craft* is to master skills that enable a maker to execute fine work. One way to evaluate the success of the work is to build on and compete with historical masterworks. The aim of makers, collectors, and museum curators, and in the marketplace—at least from my perspective as an object maker—is to seek out excellence and be familiar with the history of the field in ways that celebrates truth to the material

Respected *craft* that celebrates high quality, as treasured objects are noteworthy for the skilled hands that crafted them. As an artist craftsperson, I believe that crafted objects that celebrate fine craft in the pursuit of excellence reflects both a disciplined and a spiritual journey.

I think of the design category as producing functional *objects* in multiples for the marketplace. For me, design is all about function, attractiveness, and economy of production, and at times the convergence of these virtues will elevate the work onto a fine-art realm.

Art is when you explore personal feelings and concepts in ways that gives expression a reality. Often the artist's expression builds on the new for the sake of the new. Art making is subjective, and when discussing a work of art, it often becomes philosophical. Art is about nuancing personal expressions into a visual experience. One of the paradoxes in a work of art is that one person's art can be another person's craft. For example, Grecian urns, originally a craft item used for utility, are now thought of as fine art. If your work is excellent, the excellence over time will attract an audience that elevate it into an appropriate creative and historical continuum.

Thus, it's essential to know the category and tradition you find yourself drawn to and challenged by. Without the intuitive knowledge of these categories, and being unaware of the best within the historical parameters, the work often evidences naivete.

How does one calibrate excellence in craft, design, and art? Each category has its own criteria. I tell my students to seek out creative work in all categories by visiting museums and keeping abreast of recent work through publications. When I respond to exquisite works of art or craft, I sense a halo floating above the piece that touches my soul. In general terms, craft is measured by skilled hands, design is measured by its functional success and appeal in the marketplace. But art is measured and celebrated on a personal level of originality, reflecting one's artistic maturity.

This is not to minimize the value of good craft and good design, which can rise above these generalizations into an artistic realm.

The way I use the term "art making" generally refers to an intimate process in which the artist is learning from the work, and innovative decisions are based on intuitive creative efforts—the results of risk-taking and experimentation.

When I moved beyond the representational mindset and started to present nature in a referential way, this led to more-personal interpretation of the plant kingdom. I'm both surprised and inspired by the results as the process teaches me how to be more creative.

What I mean by "referential" can be explained by unusual imagery of flowering plants, which occasionally have human references tucked into the root system.

The figures and masks suggest myth. My creative need is to evoke an unseen world. Oddly enough, as my work became more referential, it reflected stronger detail and is interpreted by many viewers as "realistic." My take on the plant kingdom evoked a depth of feeling that connects to my childhood, with an obsession that has stayed with me to this day. To my delight, the work is attracting a growing audience, with inclusions in museum collections of contemporary glass art around the world.

In 2006, I destroyed hundreds of experimental works that led me through the process of turning craft and design into art. With the initial idea of using these efforts one day, I lost interest in the dream. So in 2006 I shattered hundreds of test pieces, experiments, studies, and "failed" efforts (although "failures" are not wasted effort, something I explore in another chapter).

Now, at age seventy-eight, I'm still editing material clutter out of my studio. I realized it's not fair to burden Pat or my family with the artifacts that were always very important to me after I'm gone. These objects were largely sentimental, and without incorporating them into my grand plan, they would be a detraction to my career, so I destroyed them.

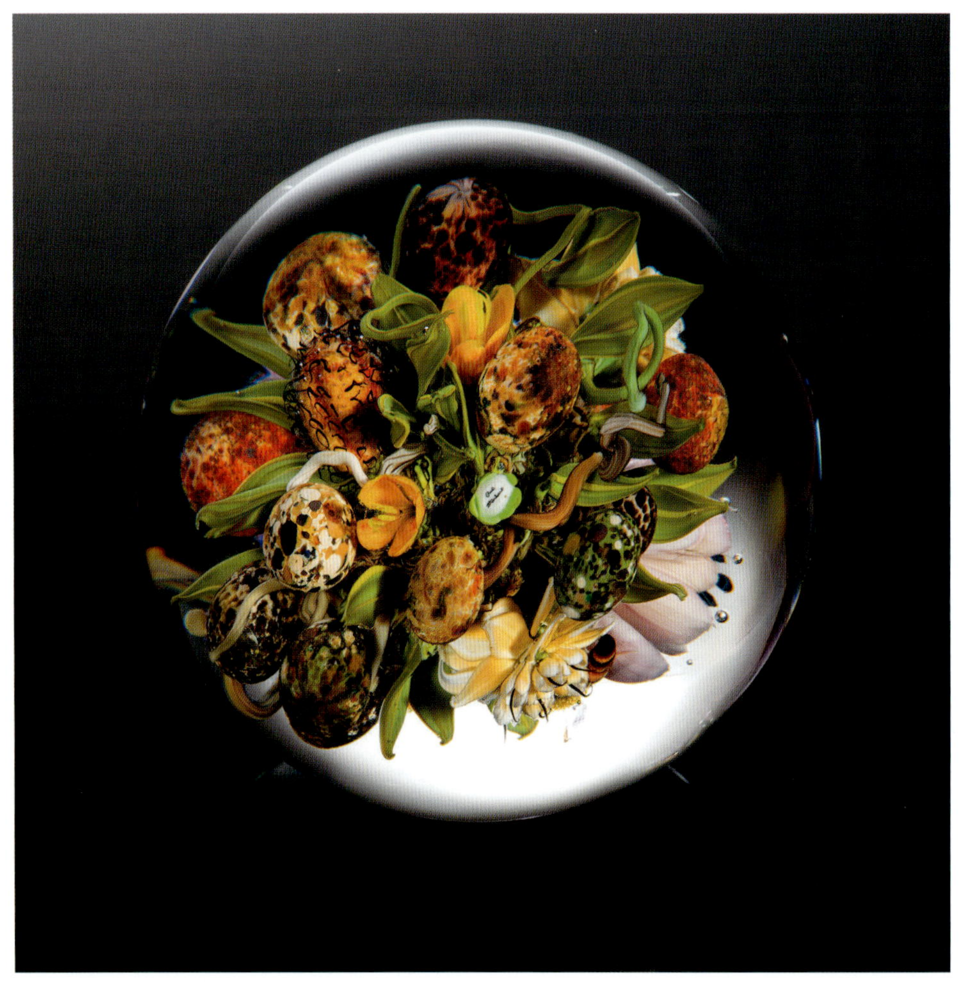

Bouquet—*Emily Dickinson's Garden*
Experimentation has made me more aware of the intricacies of nature and allowed me to express nuances on an artistic and personal level. I experiment and study to interpret the plant kingdom with a truth to the botanical characteristics of a flower. The above orb pays homage to Emily Dickinson and was inspired by her work in her conservatory, a greenhouse-like room attached to her home. The idea is to suggest the organic nature of a flowering plant that was plucked from the ground in a ball of flowers, fruit, leaves, and roots.

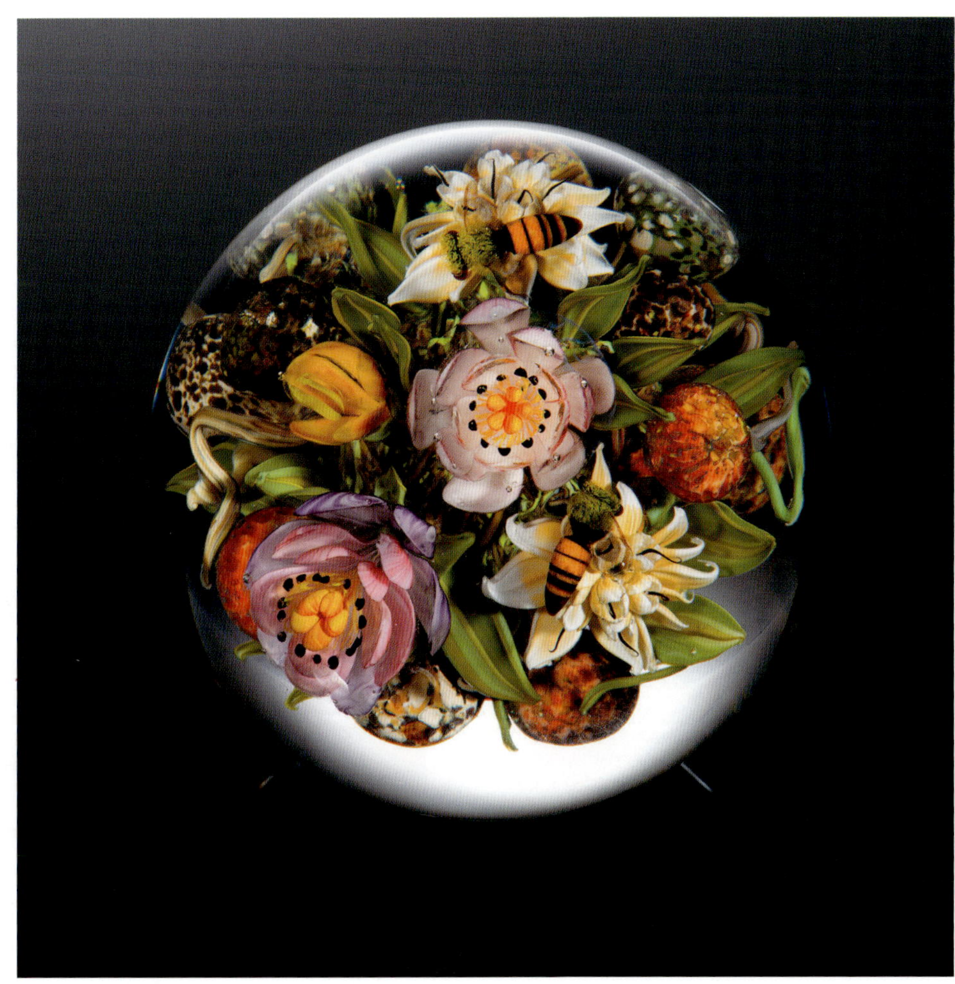

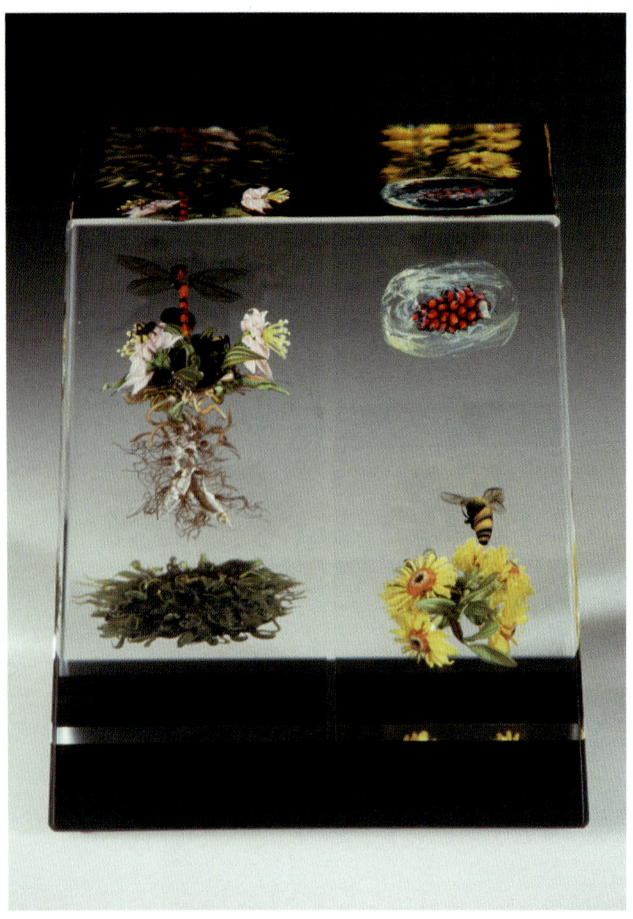

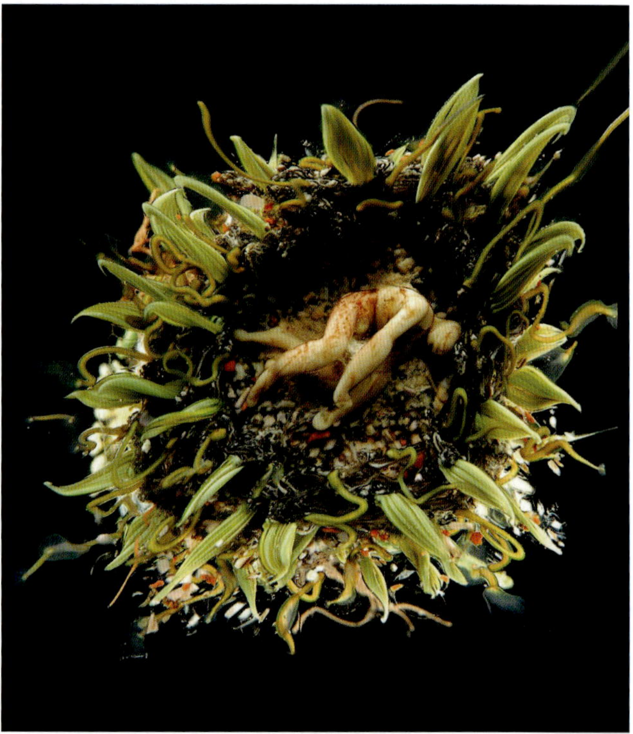

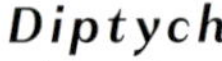

Diptych

This piece exemplifies an early example of cutting, polishing, and laminating components together into a more ambitious presentation. Under the patch of green in the lower left, I have nestled a human form in repose. I love camouflaging information into the work that provides the viewer opportunities for discoveries—perhaps much later after the first viewing of the work. I like to think that the poetry of my work continually reveals the visual information over time.

This figure in repose was tucked under the moss patch in the diptych.

Art never responds to the wish to make it democratic; it is not for everybody; it is only for those who are willing to undergo the effort needed to understand it.

—Flannery O'Connor

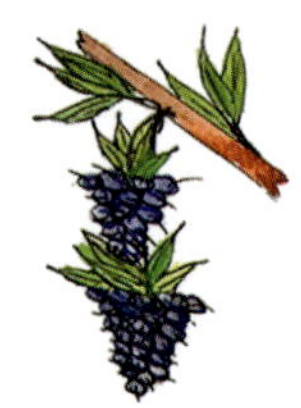

CHAPTER 9: BLEND THE PAST WITH THE PRESENT

National Gallery of Art; 1967.6.1.a; *Ginevra de' Benci*; Leonardo da Vinci (painter) Florentine, 1452–1519; c.1474/1478; oil on panel; 15 × 14 9/16 in.; Ailsa Mellon Bruce Fund

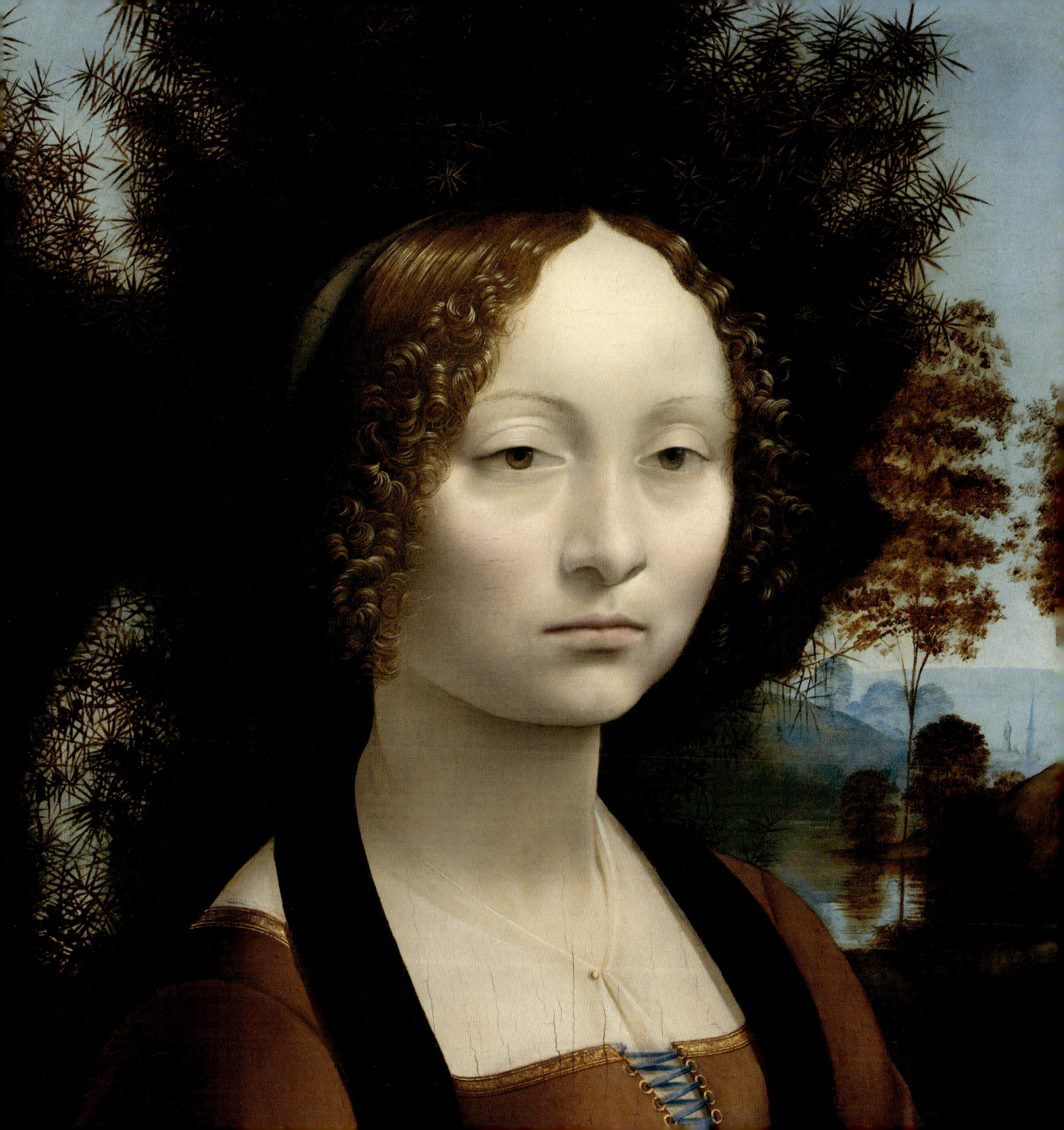

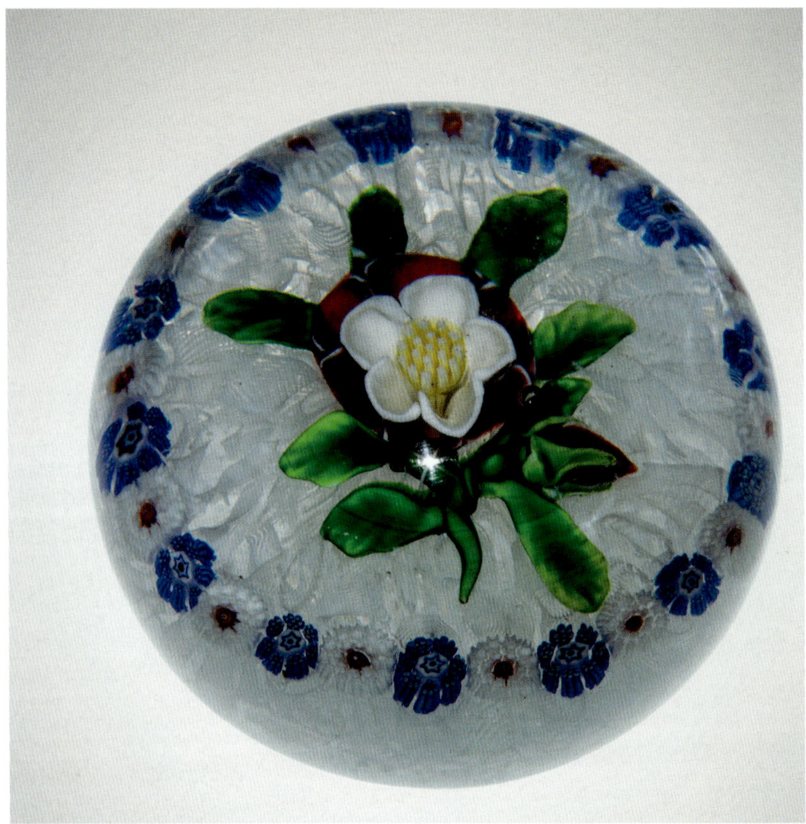

Antique French paperweight from Corning Collection
83.3.129, Collection of the Corning Museum of Glass, Corning, NY.
Bequest of Clara S. Peck.

Three major French factories in the mid-1900s produced paperweights with flameworked floral motifs and furnace-pulled millefiori canes to be cut and encapsulated in the paperweight designs. This example takes advantage both of flameworking and ornamental canes encased in clear glass as a paperweight.

Early in your career, make it a point to overview the creative landscape by visiting museums, cultural centers, and galleries. These field trips, especially when directed to your particular interest, most likely will continue throughout your professional life and will keep you informed. The more exposure you have to a wide variety of significant art, the stronger your confidence and artistic maturity will become in your own artwork.

Pay attention to the times you say, "Dear God, I wish I could be that talented." You can, and your approach and commitment to view works of art will connect you more closely to your authentic interests. As you start your journey, with persistence and diligence, you'll develop skills based on a personal depth of feeling—hence making it original.

The creative landscape is vastly varied, and by visiting cultural centers, respected galleries, and museums, as well as surveying art history in books and other publications, you will reinforce areas in art making that touch your emotional chord. You'll slowly embrace artwork that not only inspires you but lights a fire in your soul.

On a visit to the National Gallery of Art in Washington, DC, I was emotionally touched by Leonardo Da Vinci's portrait of Ginevra de' Benci. This was painted five hundred years ago but possesses an eloquent expression that is unique to this day. Viewing this for the first time was an emotional learning experience that inspired me with the hope of bringing that level of sensitivity to my creative world.

When I think of work that will endure into the future, I believe it's about being creative on a personal level. The deeper your introspection is expressed through your work, the more universal the work becomes. We are all humans—we relate to the essence of human expression.

Not all of what you encounter may seem immediately relevant, but it's important to be able to hold an intelligent conversation on the diversity and originality in the artistic landscape. The more art literate you become, the more confident you'll be with your intuitive direction and the less intimidated you'll be by others' significant accomplishments. You'll learn to appreciate the integrity and professional efforts of other artists more from an intellectual interest and less from the idea of replicating. You'll understand that being selective is not a negative stand; if you like everything, it could be you don't have a personal point of view.

As you become more knowledgeable in your area of interest, seek out galleries that represent artists whose artwork you respect. During exhibitions or gallery openings, talk to the artist about his or her work.

This advice applies to collectors as well. Travel to juried art shows that exhibit art of interest to museums building contemporary collections and attracting serious collectors. This will provide a reference to what's respected in the marketplace representing new work.

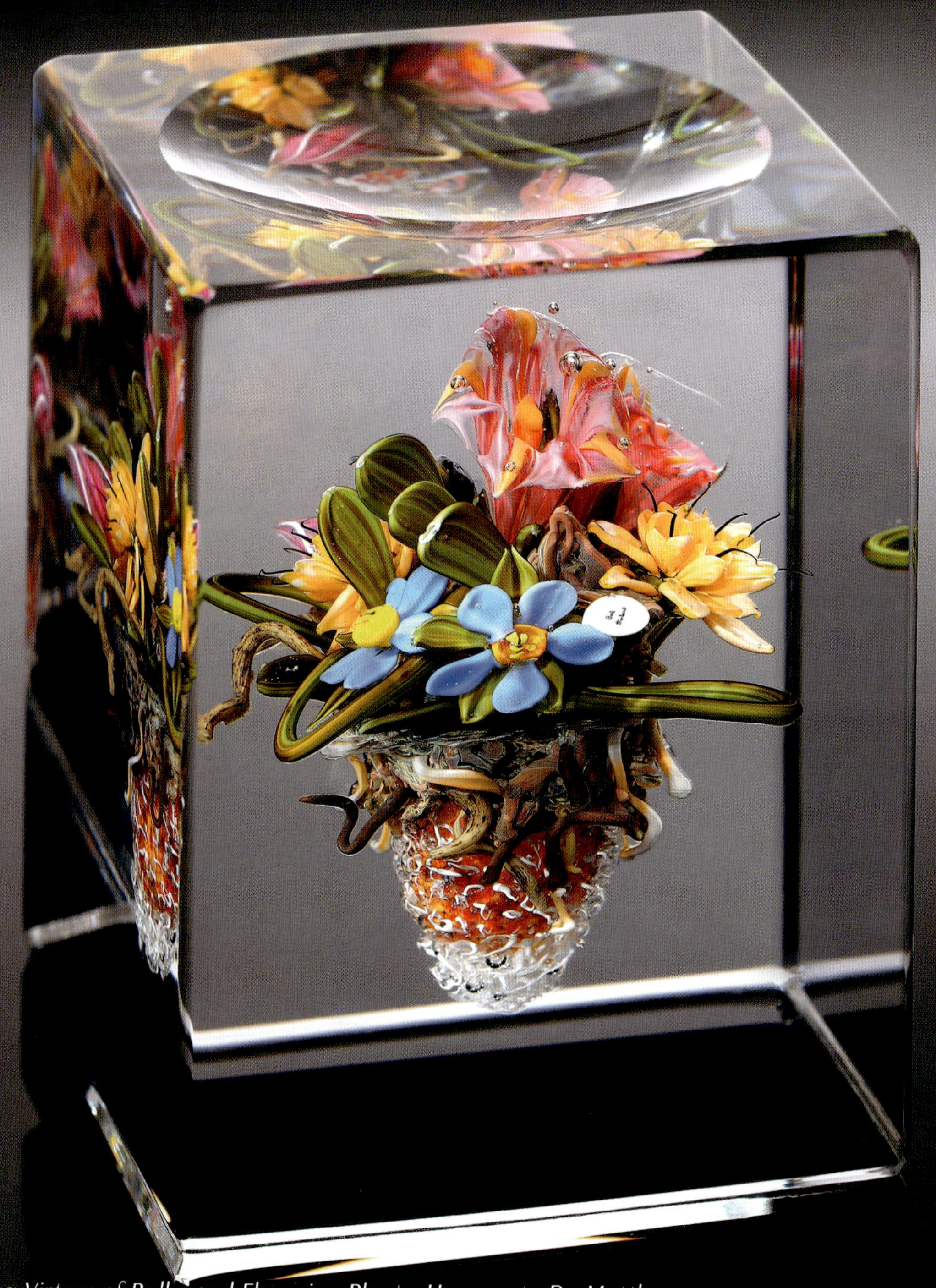

The Healing Virtues of Bulbs and Flowering Plants: Homage to Dr. Matthew Carabasi

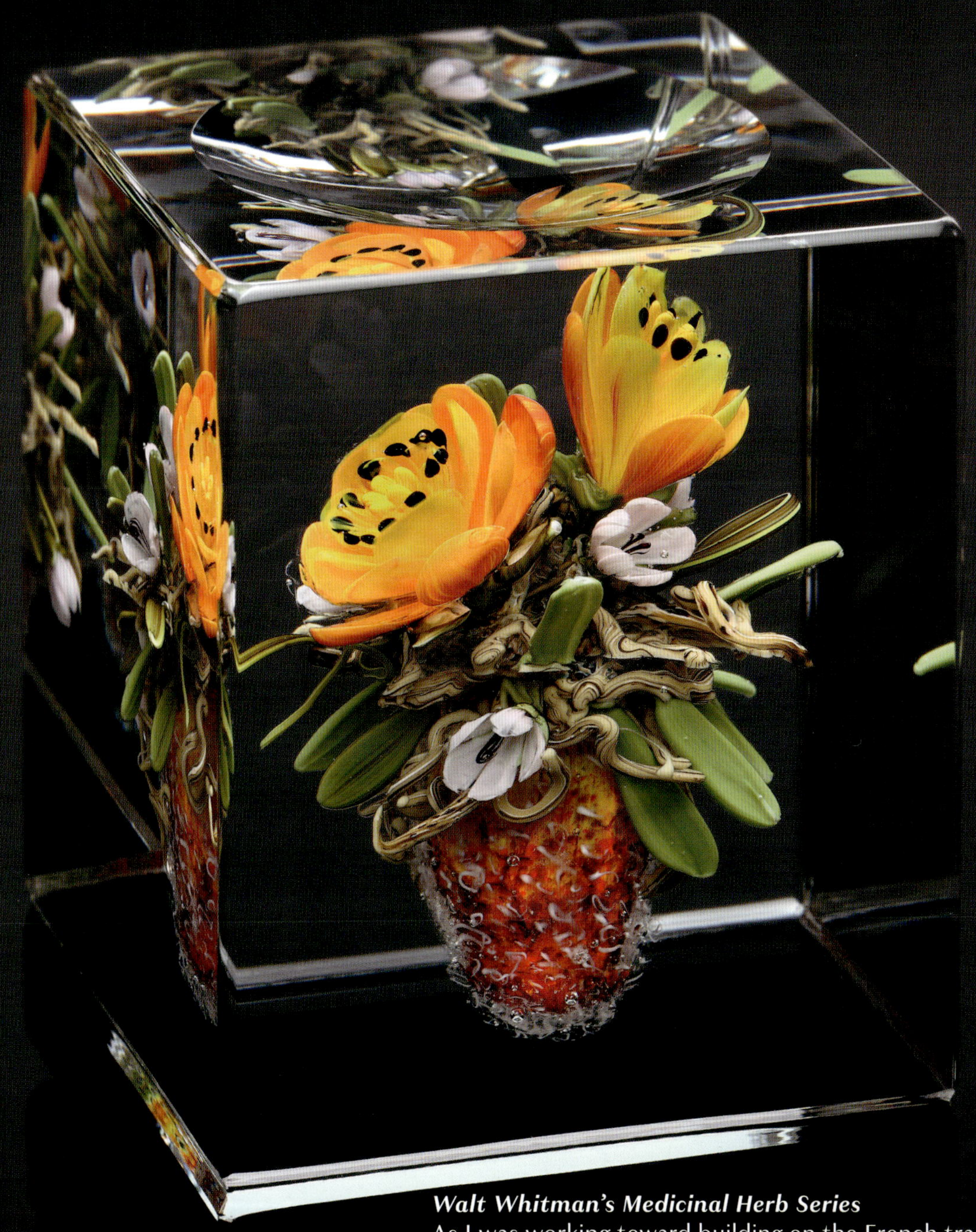

Walt Whitman's Medicinal Herb Series
As I was working toward building on the French tradition, I moved away from the stylized floral patterns to reference the native flowers of North America.

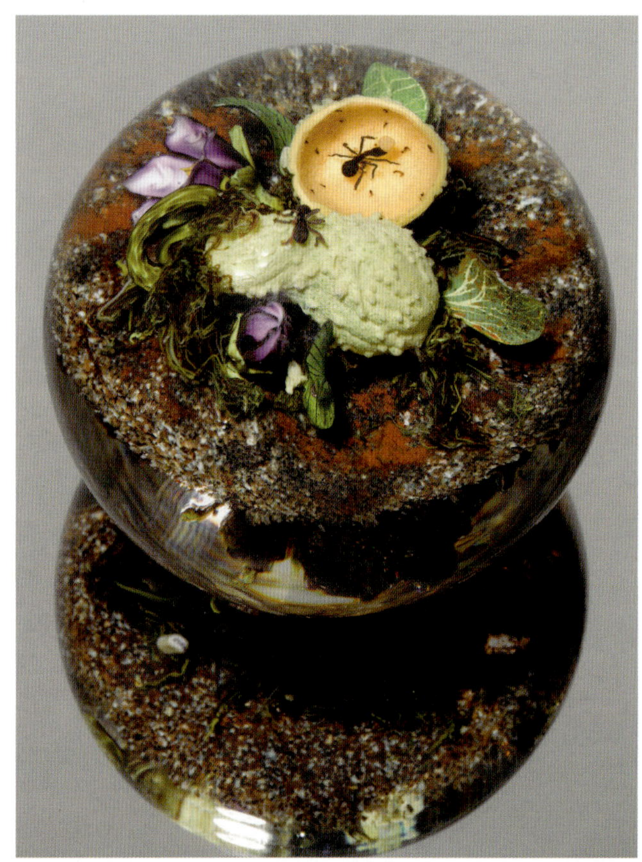

Contemporary paperweight with gourds, blossoms, and ants on crushed glass mimicking soil
The solid-glass paperweight design suggests negative space as a trompe l'oeil illusion in ways that glass is uniquely suited to.

The noblest pleasure is the joy of understanding.

—Leonardo da Vinci

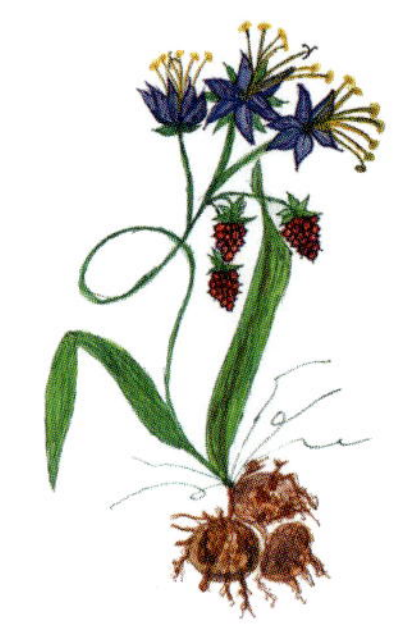

CHAPTER 10: DETAIL AND DELICACY

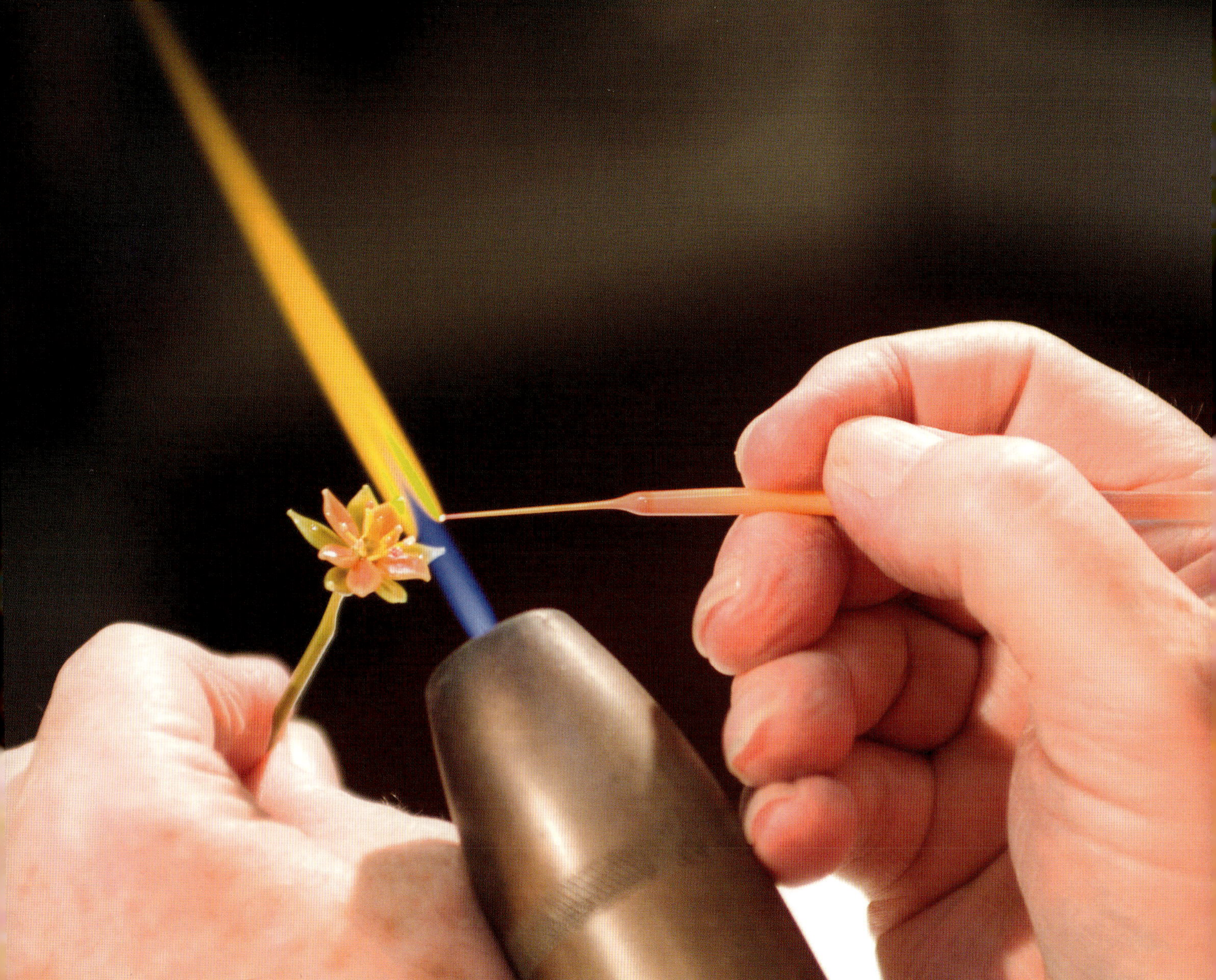

Close-up of sculpting blossom
Here, I am using an oxygen bench burner to melt the glass as I craft a flower. Being trained as a scientific glassblower to create precision glass instruments, I was able to redirect the technical process to focus on the delicacy of a blossom.

Detail and delicacy are both clearly important to artists, but there is a difference between the two.

For me, detail is generally regarded as a minor feature that contributes to the whole. Delicacy is about color, form, and grace. When I combine nuanced detail with delicacy, a poetic illusion is created, celebrating nature frozen in time.

On close inspection, once the viewer focuses on the design's detail, there's a trompe l'oeil assumption of credibility. I imagine the viewer would assume, when viewing such a high level of detail, that the work must be an accurate representation.

In fact, detail is the underpinning of my illusion, which suggests organic fidelity.

Over the course of a half century at the glassworking bench, I've invented hundreds of techniques to produce delicate illusions.

A part of my evolution into the realm of artistic detail is the labor-rich technique of layering colored glasses used in material preparation. Over my career, I developed techniques for crushing glass into powder, heating and rolling complementary-colored glass onto the powder. Illusions were developed by overlaying a selection of transparent colors over opaque glasses that suggest botanical credibility. Color has always been and remains one of my primary concentrations.

Gradually over the years, the work became less about botanical accuracy and more about a referential cluster of flowers, berries, and bulbs suspended with pollinating insects floating in clear glass. Exploring color for the sake of beauty, and becoming blissed out when the composition reads well, is a special moment when the glass is taken out of the oven.

Every artist's transition from detail to delicacy will follow a different path. In my case, my techniques evolved from working as a scientific glassblowing technologist producing custom precision instruments used for medical and organic-chemistry research. Interestingly enough, my mistakes in the scientific apparatus were less of an issue than when I am crafting art.

In my art, the visual credibility will make or break the piece.

Art making is as varied as are the artists working. You take advantage of the skill set you know, and you make it personal. You go beyond the practical, and you go beyond making a product.

You learn from your process and build on your personal vocabulary, fusing your detail into the realm of delicacy.

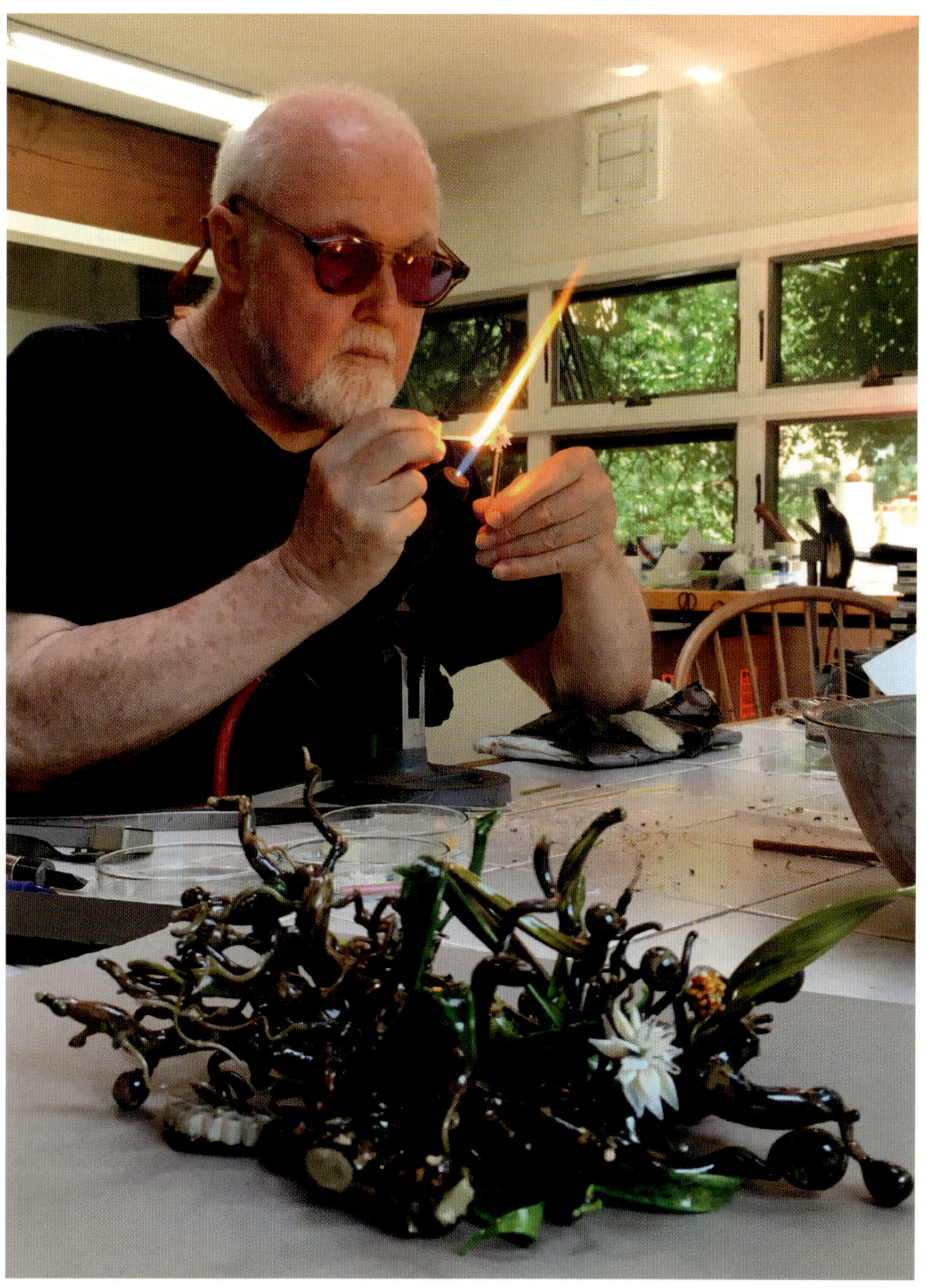

Walt Whitman's Bouquet with Honeybees, Flowers, Fruit, and Bulbous Forms

Detail fascinates me. I've noticed that the more detailed my designs are, the more believable my floral interpretations became. It's one of the interesting aspects of my work that requires experimentation and patience. The results have allowed the process to teach me how to make things more personal in a believable way. At times I worry if I am too obsessive about detail in a grouping. You reach the extremes and then you realize you had better back it up a little bit. There obviously is such a thing as too much detail, but you're never sure about that until you've had a chance to live with the object. Slowly, it will lead you to variations on the concept. Here is an example of a piece that has, in my view, just enough detail to represent my signature masterwork. This floral grouping took me to an interesting limit.

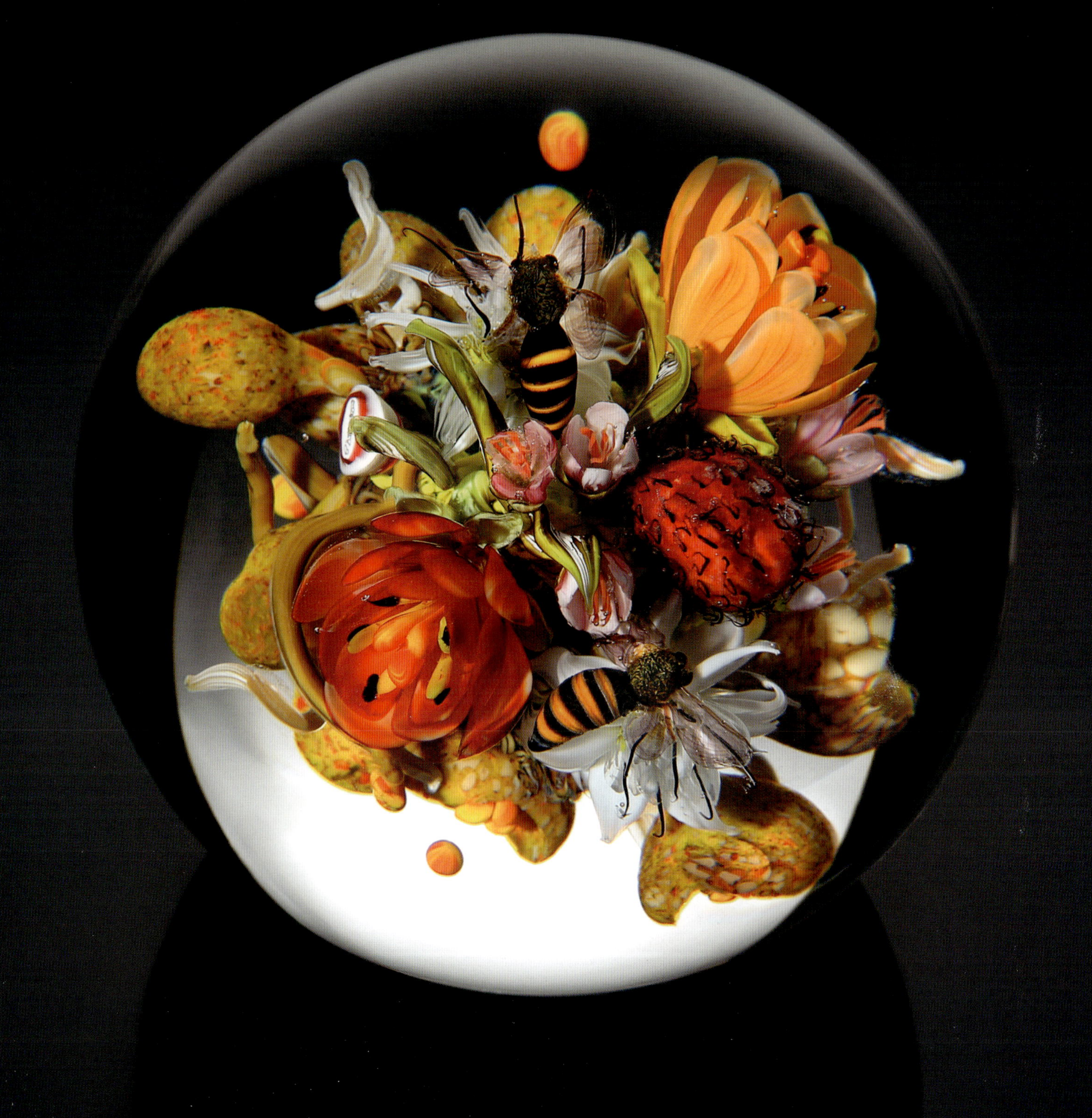

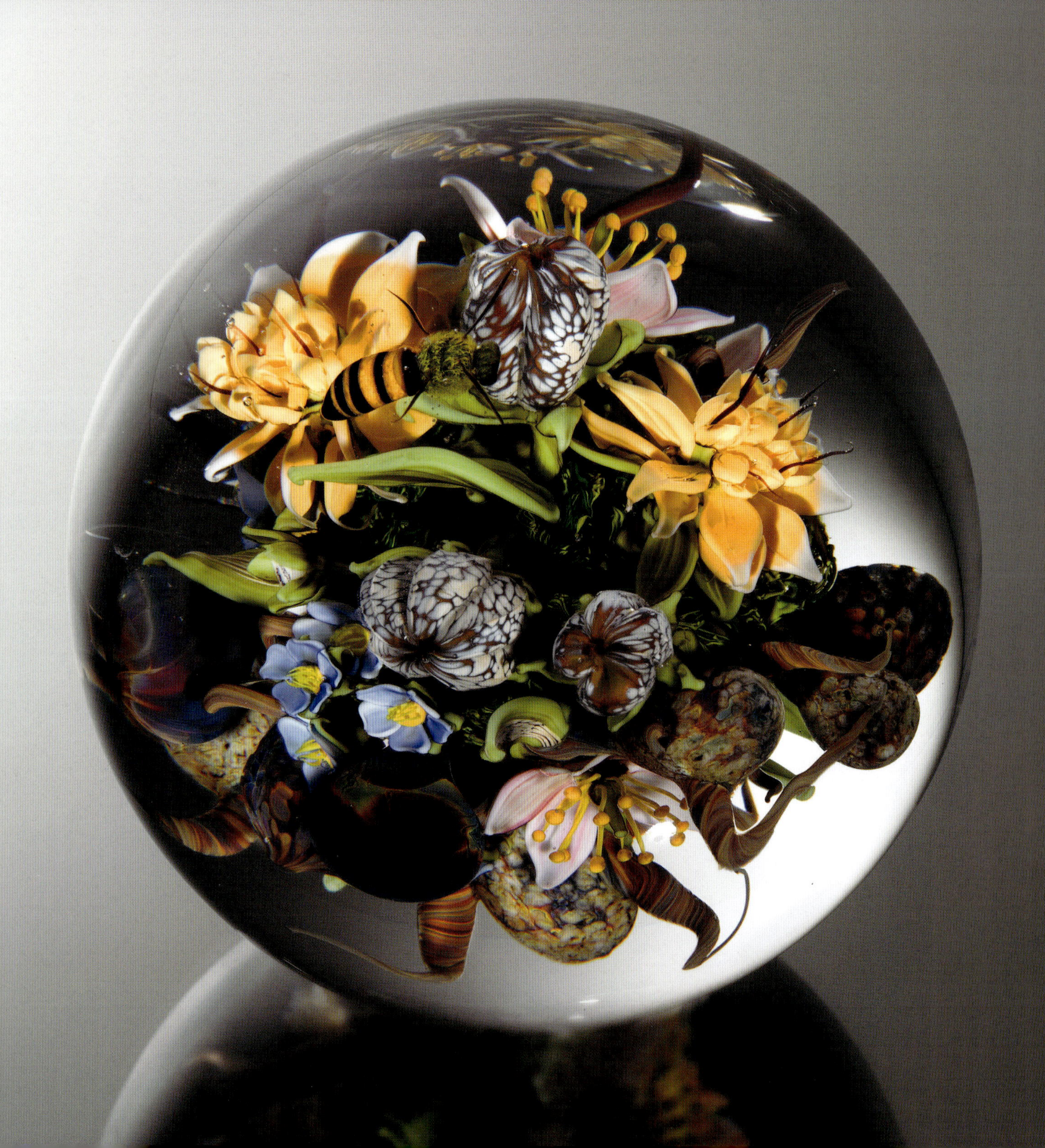

The first wild-flower of the year is like land after sea.

—Thomas Wentworth Higginson

Flowers, Honeybee and Bulbous Forms
This is an exploration into the under-earth. The brown bulbs are rolled in a variety of colored glasses to give the surface a mottled effect. This esoteric detail lends authenticity to the belief that there is more to be discovered in the plant world.

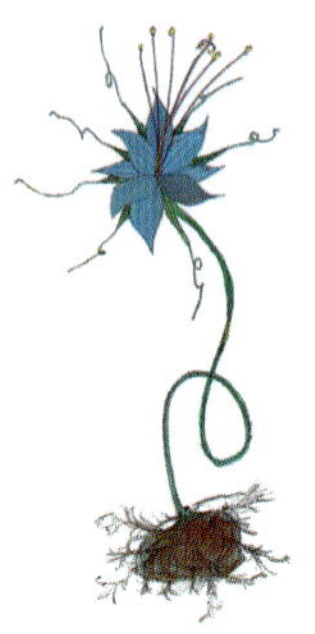

CHAPTER 11: KNOW THYSELF

Flowers, Fruit and Swarming Honeybees

The Art Institute of Chicago was interested in a major piece to complement their paperweight gallery. At the time, the curator complimented me on the honeybee swarm design that I had incorporated into other pieces. The goal to me was to bring a credibility and an intelligence to a work of art that celebrated my dedication to interpreting nature in glass. In fact, this effort was close to the limits of my ability and involved a great deal of work. Still, my goal was to ensure that it did not look overlabored. Working in glass over the years, I had learned how to work with the negative space and push the limits of the working characteristics of the material and process. My challenge is to have the labor appear invisible.

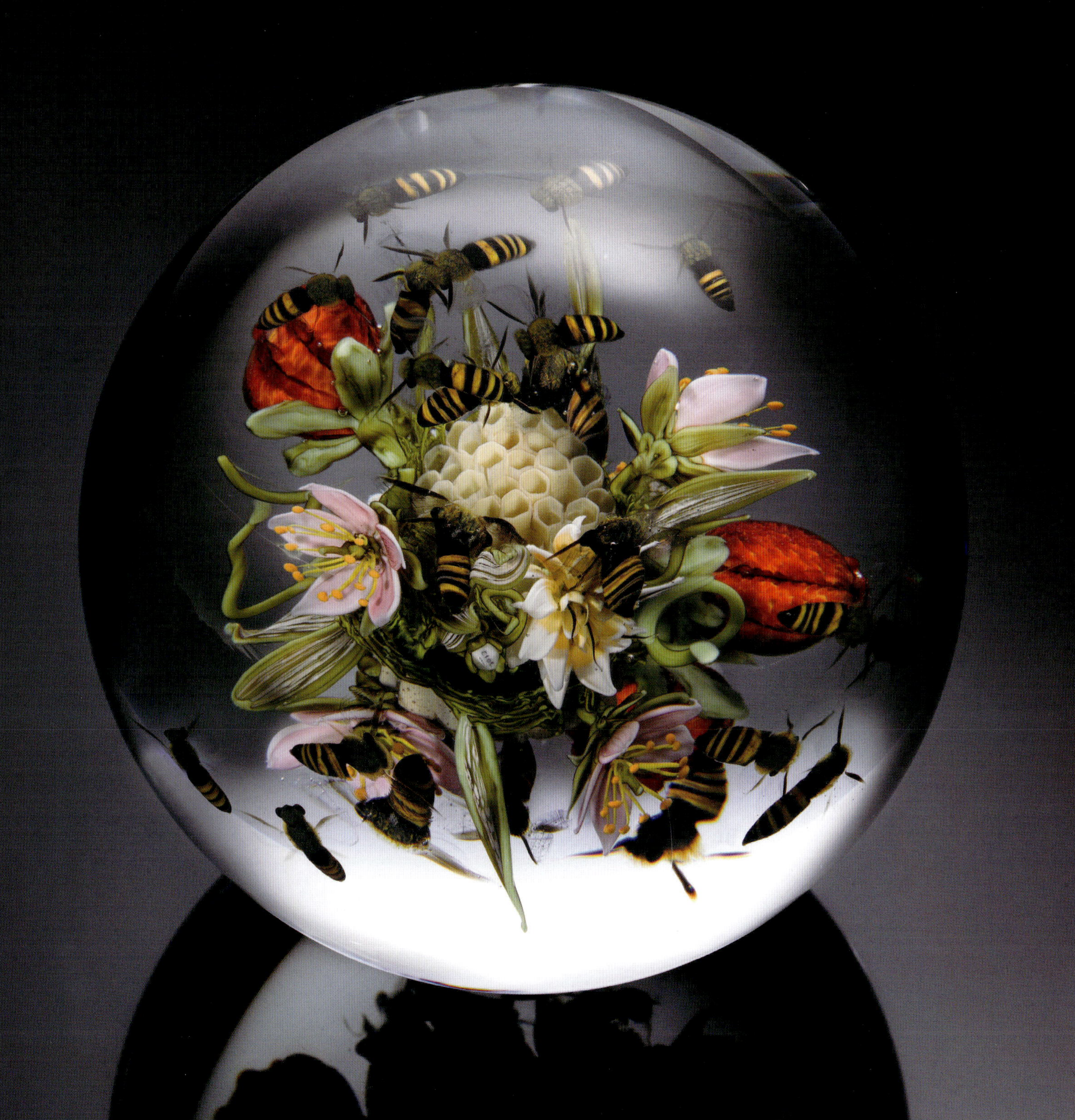

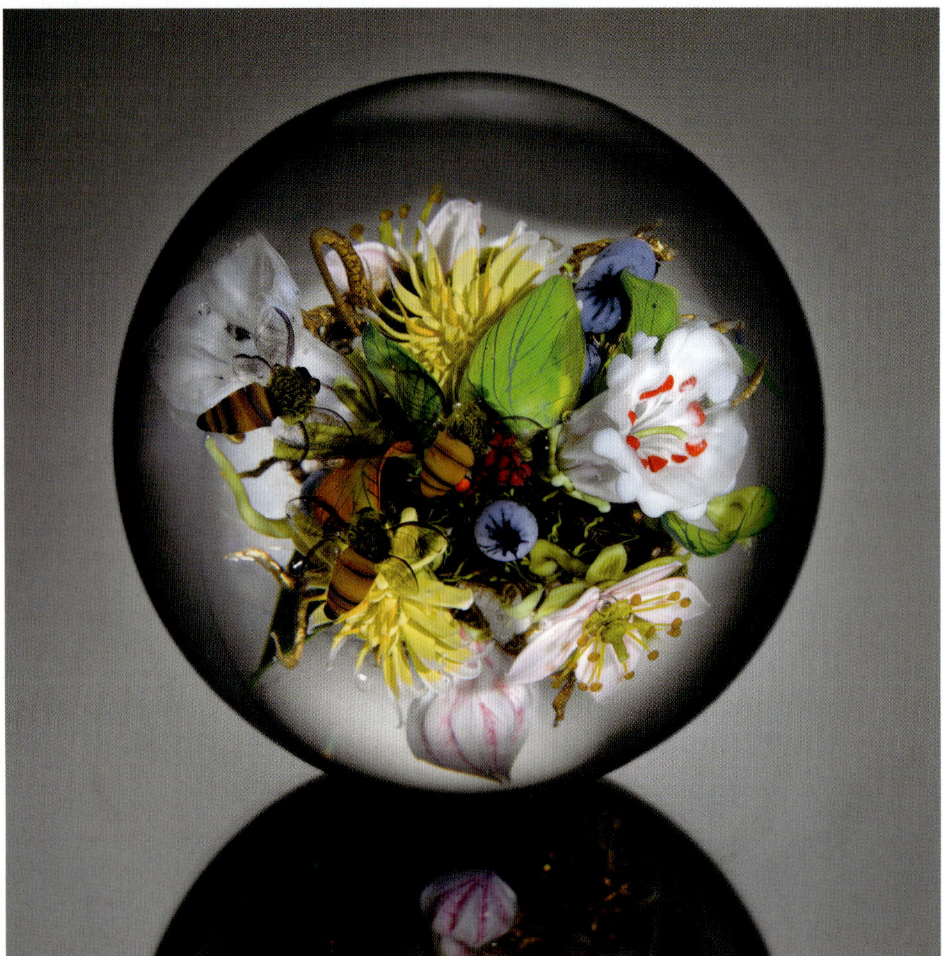

Mountain Laurel, Blueberry and Honeybee Bouquet

Growing up in Massachusetts, I lived close to what I thought was an endless forest where one summer I happened upon a field of blueberry bushes. The following seasons, I would anxiously wait for the blueberries to be ripe enough to pick. Over my glass career, I recalled that memory over many designs in my work.

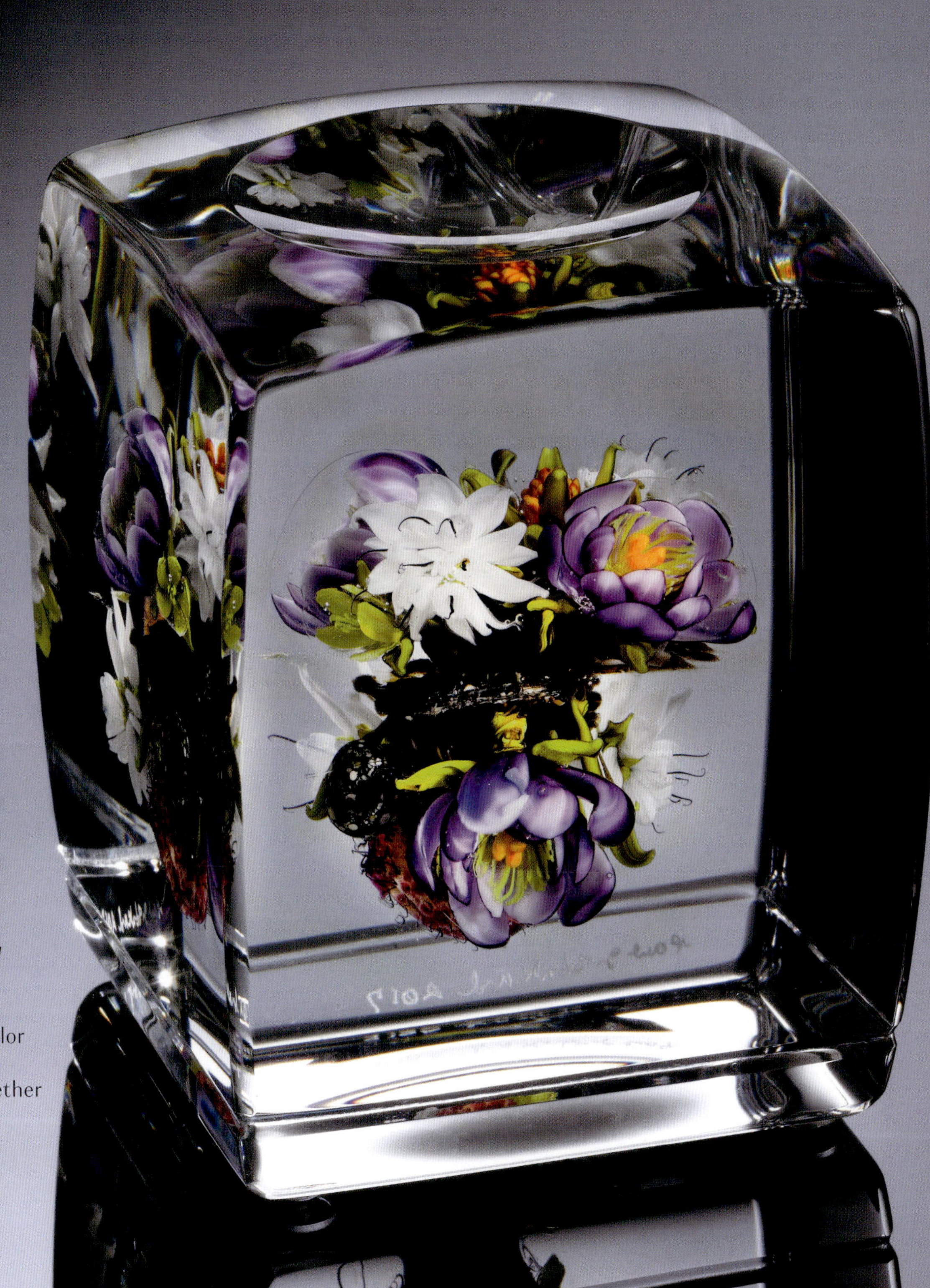

Botanical Study
The focus is nuancing color contrasts coming together with color harmony.

What I am currently focused on is nuancing flowers, fruit and bulbs with an assortment of insects and figures to reference what I call "floral clusters."

In this series, each piece represents experimental exploration. With inventive techniques, I'm addicted to the creative highs from my search for truth to nature. The "Floral Earth Clusters" series offers a sort of magical realism, evoking the imagery from the words of my current spiritual mentors, Emily Dickinson and Walt Whitman.

The experimentation has not been limited to melting glass at the bench. It's a mental game.

I recently listened to Walter Isaacson's biography of Leonardo da Vinci. It was a source of inspiration that few books have offered me. It reinforced my need to focus on experimentation.

What I gleaned from the book was that da Vinci was more interested in acquiring knowledge than finishing paintings. He dissected cadavers and made thorough studies of muscles, especially those dealing with facial expressions. His research fueled eighteen years of continual refinement on the smile of the *Mona Lisa*.

Da Vinci's labor is invisible. However, his knowledge of anatomy and his obsession with research allowed him to bring a peculiarity to his paintings that has mesmerized countless people throughout five centuries.

My study of da Vinci reinforced a commitment I had previously held: to make my labor invisible to the viewer and collector. I want the work to be poetic and even magically appear to be suspended in space. I do not want the viewer to be distracted by the complexity of my labor.

I was exhibiting at the Rosenfeld Gallery in Philadelphia when a collector seemed mesmerized by what she perceived to be unusual skill in crafting the pieces. When she left, Richard Rosenfeld said, "Stankard, your challenge is to get past the 'wow factor.'"

I immediately understood what he meant. My art was about sharing my love of nature, not showing off my hand skills.

Learning about da Vinci's dedication was humbling. It gave me a stronger commitment to my studies. I hope that somewhere down the road, my process and techniques will be singled out as a commitment to excellence and my authenticity to a vision at this new phase of my career.

My "know thyself" mind trip has moved to the forefront of my creative activities after my ongoing diagnoses of cancer. I have always felt the need to be creative, but now, near the end of my career, I feel an urgent need to continue the journey through writing, with teaching as an important part of my legacy.

Because of the medical challenges, travel is a burden. I am most comfortable close to my home and studio. I feel fortunate that I am able to work and that my restrictions have evolved into a blessing.

After an adult lifetime working with glass, in many different ways, I'm now attuned to an intuitive response to the process and how it can evolve. I couple this attitude with a heightened interest in philosophy and theology, which have allowed me to integrate core values in my art making.

Adopt the pace of nature:
her secret is patience.

—Ralph Waldo Emerson

I dwell in possibility...

—Emily Dickinson

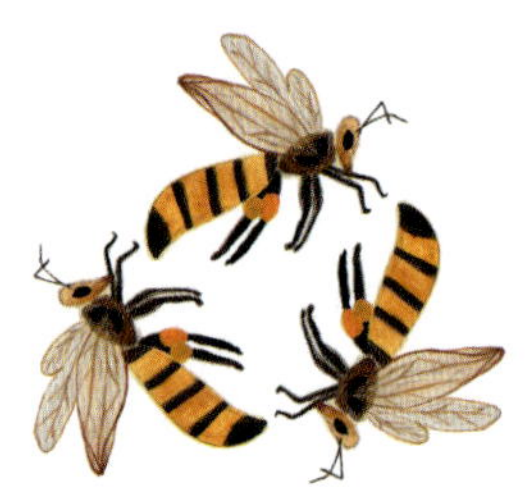

PART 3

GROWING WITH ARTISTIC MATURITY

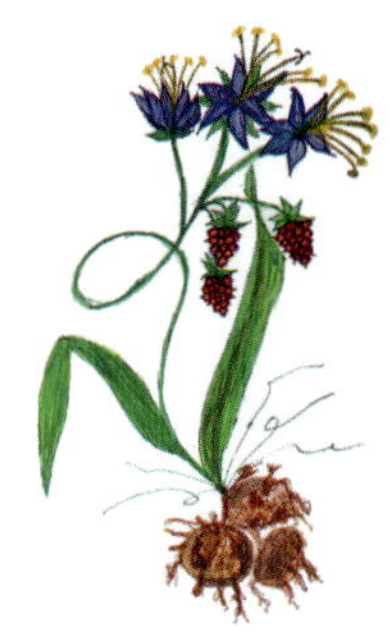

CHAPTER 12: IT'S NOT GOING TO GET EASIER

Study on Magnification and Color

What's exciting about my current work is that at this stage of the game, I am learning how the magnification of the sphere offers a new perspective. The intensification creates peculiarly intelligent and detailed information that enriches the beauty of what I feel adds magic to my work. This attribute of the work represents constant experimentation. In the case of the orb pictured above, I invested time experimenting in order to blend color harmony with detail.

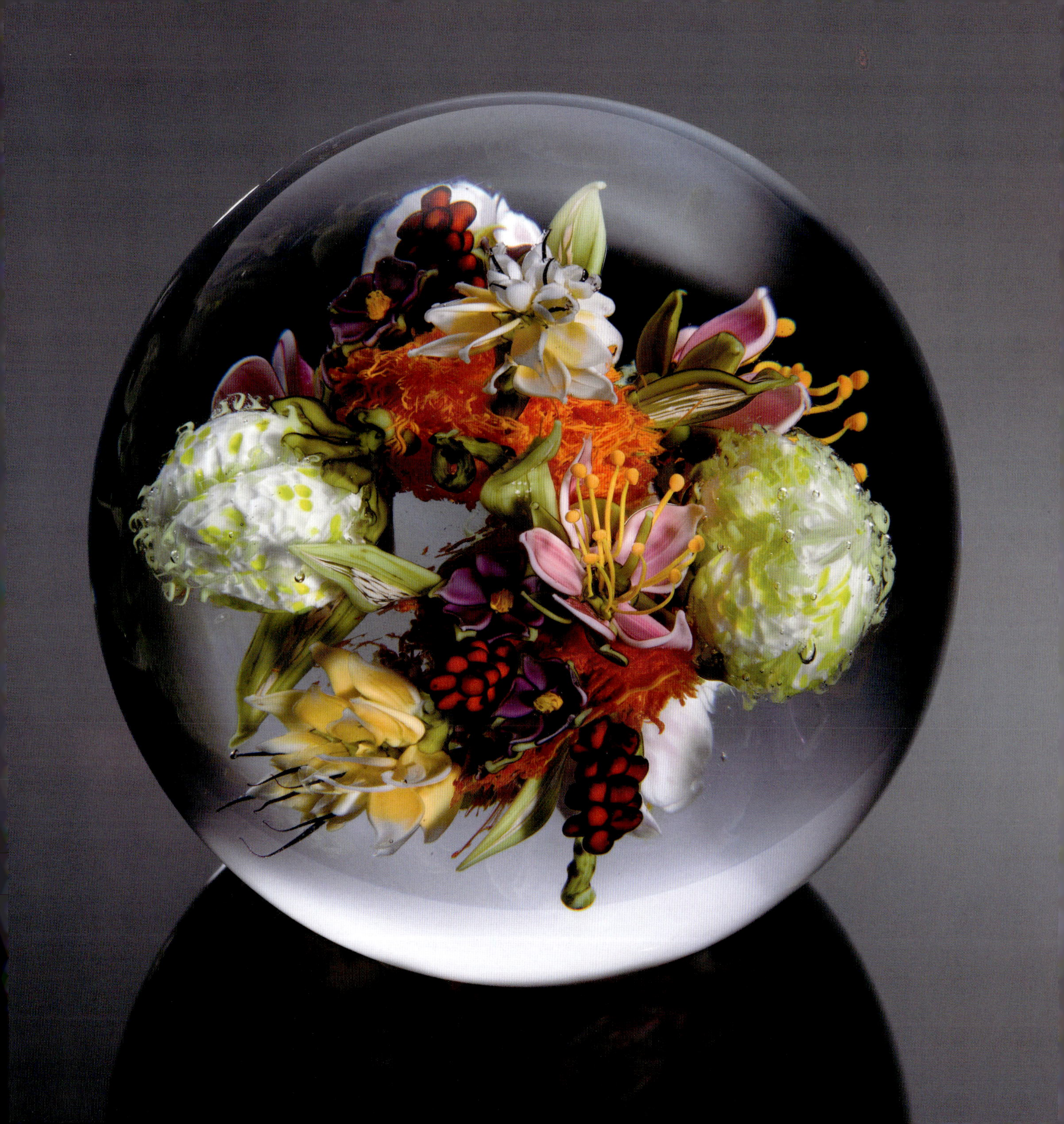

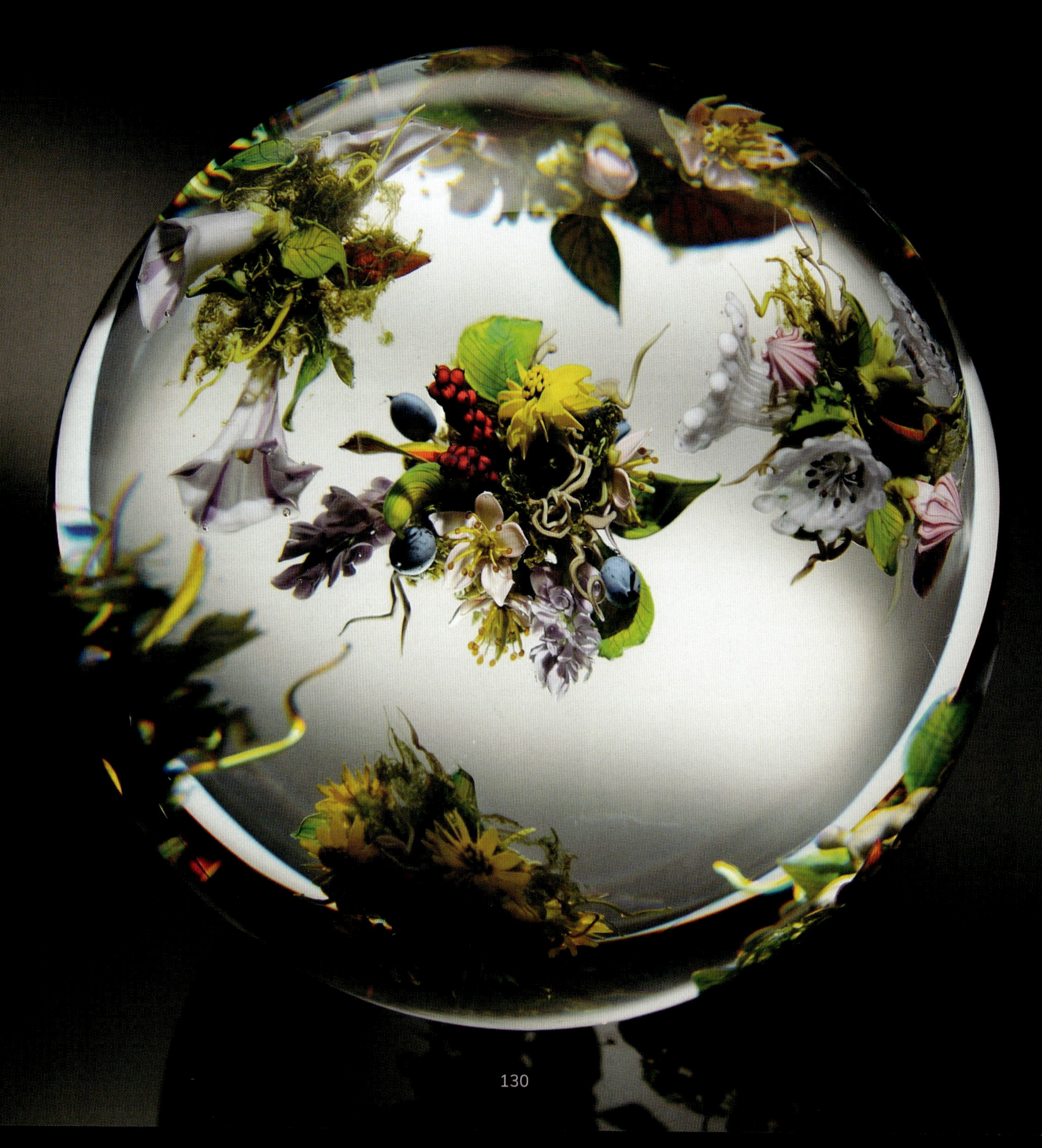

***Floating Bouquets*, 2009, 8 in.**

This 8-inch orb exploits cutting-edge glass technology and glass fabrication in ways that document current technology. It's important for artists to take advantage of current technology that will advance their work onto the contemporary landscape. In the case of the orb above, I took advantage of optical-quality glass, space-age epoxies, and high-tech spherical grinding and polishing equipment, along with computerized annealing programs. Future archeologists and historians will be able to calibrate our current glass technology through this accomplishment.

I have always been amazed when someone assumes that at this stage of my career, crafting my artwork is easier.

I seldom respond to those comments, but in truth, it's never easy. In spite of what many observers may assume, my work has progressively become *more difficult* over the years, especially during this stage of my career.

And that's the way it's always been, and I accept it. What does this mean to my art making?

There is a limit to everything, including the working limits of the material and the physical limits of a seventy-eight-year-old man. Having said that, this seventy-eight-year-old now enjoys the pleasure of finessing earlier designs. I enjoy reinterpreting certain aspects of my menu of illusions. I am not copying what I've done in the past. I am nuancing ideas with joy and artistic maturity in ways that surprise me and continually teach me about my personal aesthetic.

I am balancing the limitations of my age with designs that are original to my life's work. I am not worrying about heroic scale in the context of my crafted art making. I am currently focused on 4-inch orbs because they are the most meaningful efforts at this time.

My current focus on orbs is like going back to those early days. The anxiety I experienced in my converted utility room / studio is every bit as strong as it is today. Back then, when I was making my first paperweights, I was excited waiting for the oven to complete its annealing cycle. And here I am, fifty years later, with even more anxiety, waiting for the pyrometer to indicate that the forty-hour cycle is completed and it's OK to open the oven door.

And sometimes, just like the paperweight of fifty years ago, when I open the oven, the piece that was glowing with beauty, that I believed would be a masterpiece, is nestled in my hand as a setback. Today, however, with a labor-intensive orb, I may lose a week's work, as opposed to an evening lost on a small failed paperweight.

Despite the hard work and frustrations that plague me to this day, I don't feel disappointed by a casual observer who doesn't comprehend the arduous work that went into a piece. His or her attitude means that I have achieved one of my artistic goals: to make my labor invisible.

I don't want someone to look at a piece and say, "My God, think of all the work that went into that."

I want them to say, "That's poetic."

The beauty of an artist's career is the lifelong journey of learning as your labor progresses. You experience excitement that validates and acknowledges a life of pursuing beauty.

Don't expect it to get easier. If it does, you're coasting.

You're not growing.

A lot of hard work is hidden behind nice things.

—Ralph Lauren

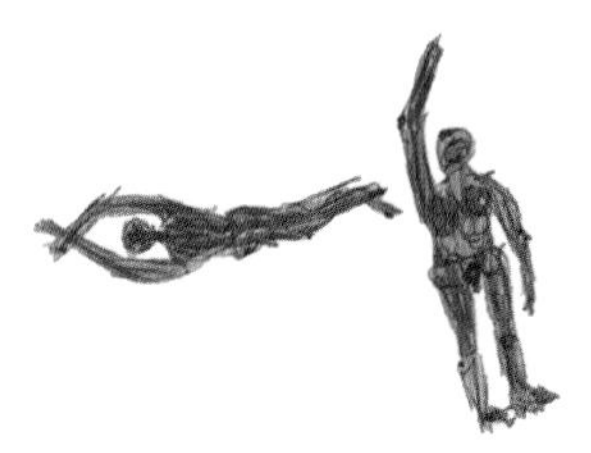

CHAPTER 13: ORIGINALITY

Learning all you can about the heritage of your craft, as well as great creative works of almost any genre, as long as they touch your soul, will allow you to evolve a signature style.

***The Fecundity of Walt Whitman's Garden*, 2021, 6 in.**
This orb celebrates fertility in glass inspired by Walt Whitman's poetic response to nature. When the core section came out of the oven, I noticed that I mistook my "seeds" word cane for my "Paul Stankard" cursive signature cane. Initially, I felt bewildered by the mistake but then realized this was a wonderful tribute to the conceptual artist, Marcel Duchamp, who inspired my word canes. I love the idea that when a viewer reads the glass word cane "seeds," it reinforces the artwork's fecundity theme.

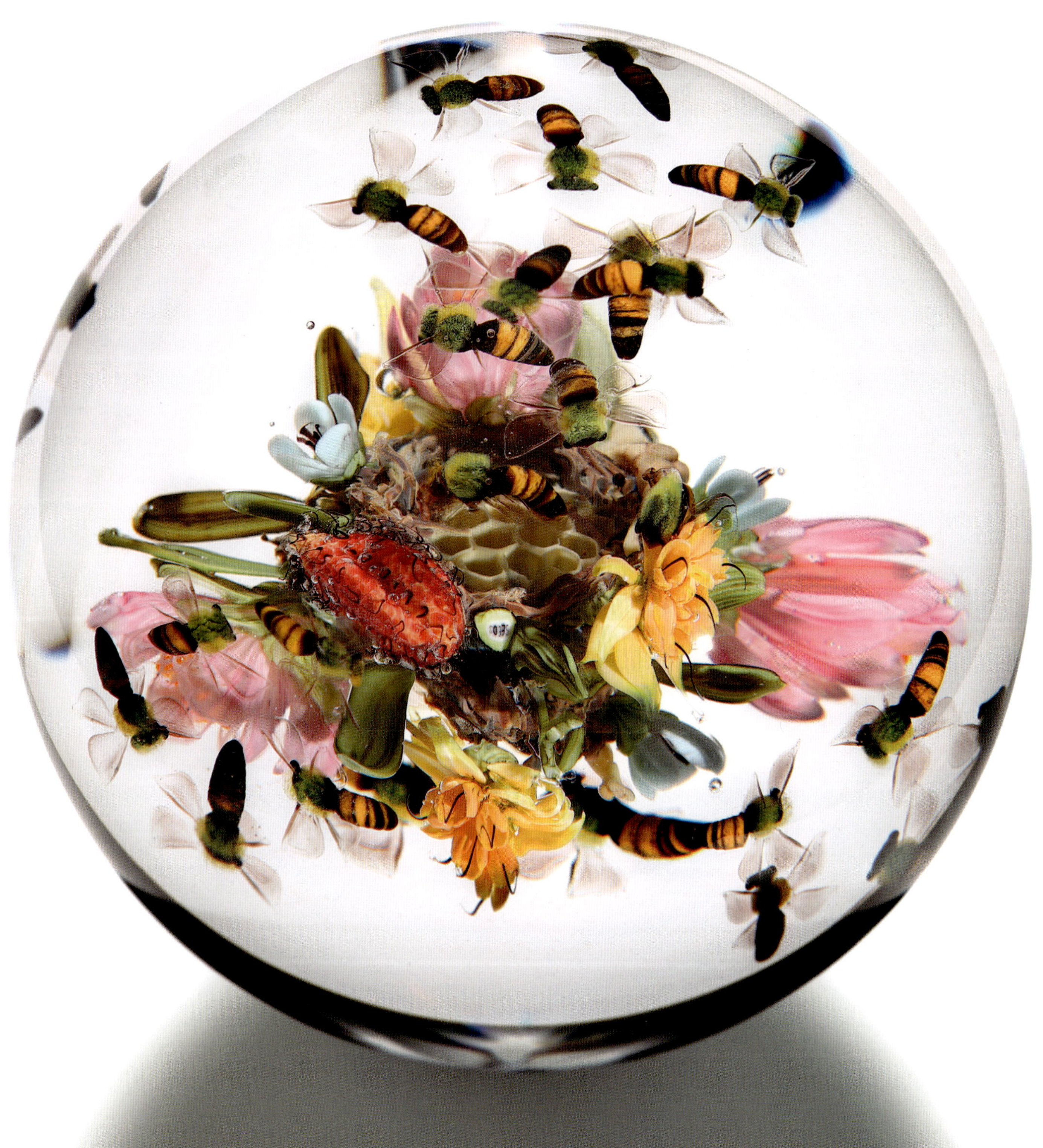

Originality is one of the hallmarks of significant work. The philosophical underpinnings of originality are broad and multifaceted, and the concept means more than simply being the first to do something.

To be original, you layer a personal point of view onto the creative experience. Your personal touch leads you into a realm of endless artistic opportunities.

How do you develop this ability? I would encourage you to study the masters whose work touches your soul. As you become familiar with these creative virtuosos, your commitment to excellence will be strengthened. Through trial, error, and perseverance, your efforts over the years will evolve into a personal realm of art making.

I've been inspired by studying myriad original creators from many eras and disciplines. My short list includes Leonardo da Vinci, Walt Whitman, James Joyce, Jackson Pollock, Morris Graves, and Glenn Gould. These talented people have redefined their various creative categories and have profoundly influenced my imaginative thinking. I will discuss their particular contributions further in this essay.

From the beginning, I intuitively understood that in order to survive on the creative side, it would take more than hard work. Being curious about art—especially how glass art built on centuries-old objects—led me to a regimented program of educating myself to great work. Over time, I sought out great work in areas related to my art making.

I learned an interesting lesson: not everyone is interested in floral art. I found how important it was for me to know my audience. Artists of all kinds will confront uninterested collectors. That is reality. But by learning which museums and galleries have serious work that is in your genre, you will gravitate toward knowledgeable and appreciative people.

The art world is so diverse that collectors are often focused on categories. It's important for the artist not to confuse lack of interest in his or her category with dismissal of the importance of the work itself.

I began to study art history and focused on the masters, and I felt an emotional connection to their struggles. Combined with walks in the woods, where I photographed plants, my learning regimen began to influence my artwork.

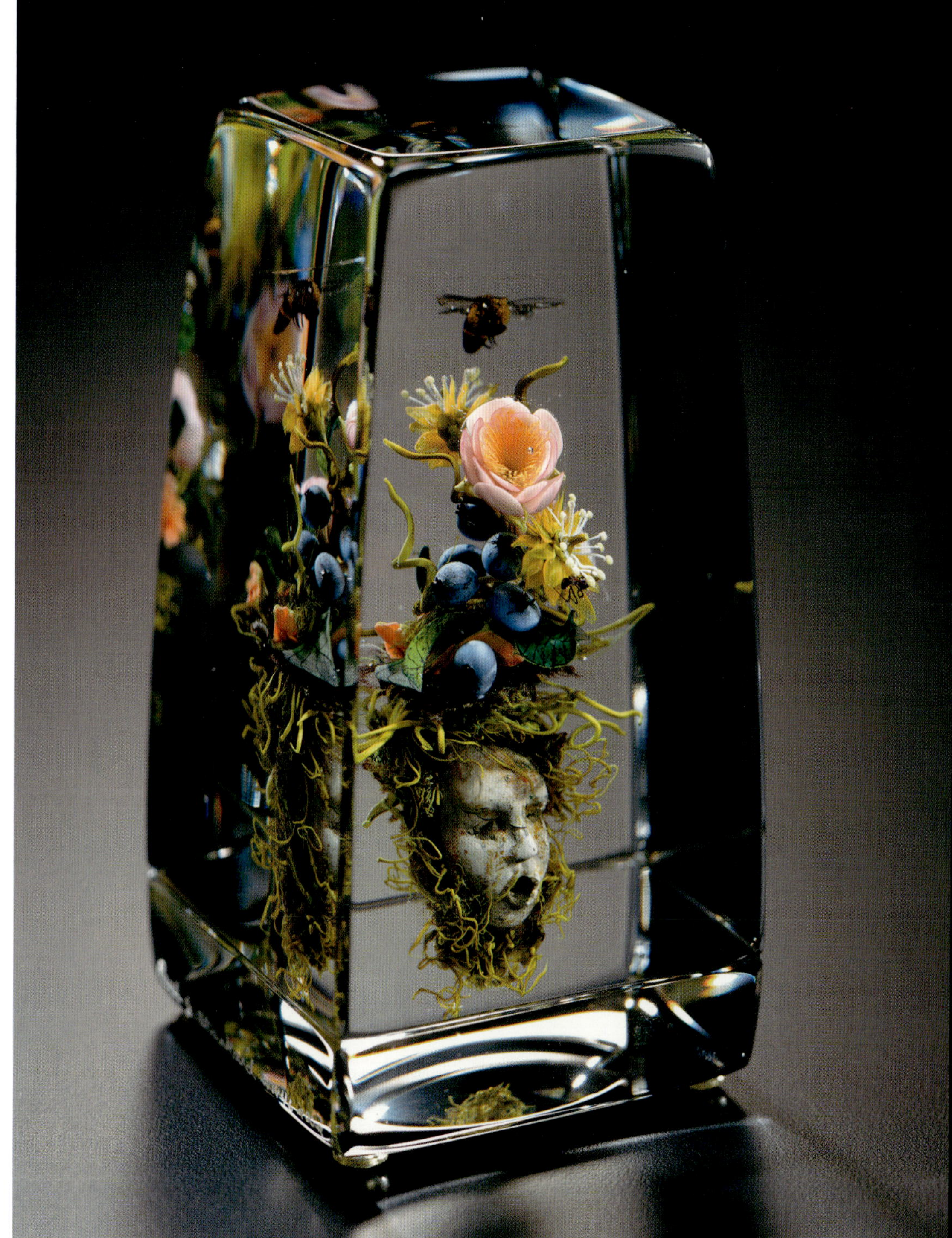

***Tea Rose Bouquet Botanical with Mask*, 2004, 5½ in.** The idea behind this design is to incorporate a symbol representing myth engulfed by the plant kingdom. This is my way of adding visual tension—not as a negative quality, but to suggest life energy under the earth.

I believe that education will lead to a personal expression, and slowly over time the work will reflect your uniqueness.

In sum, the basic formula for significant work is to make it personal, be motivated, take risk, and build on the past. Examples of originality I particularly admire include the following:

- Pianist Glenn Gould, who became legendary for his interpretation of Bach. His work is complementary to Bach, building on Bach's genius while adding a stunningly innovative interpretation based on his own genius. It was more than Bach plus Gould. It was Bach *multiplied* by Gould.
- Jackson Pollock was original, even though he may have begun his work with a novel (meaning merely "new") way of painting. He soon intuitively discovered the intelligence of his innovation, and by making it personal, he invented a visually dynamic artistic vocabulary based on his process.
- Morris Graves radiated a metaphysical respect for birds, flowers, and forms, elevating them to suggest the spiritual realm.
- Walt Whitman's words were so profound that they startled the reader with their honesty, a fresh candor imbued with a uniquely American voice.
- James Joyce respected Whitman's poetry, and, like Whitman, Joyce's Ulysses is a celebration of the ordinary as extraordinary. In Ulysses, Joyce celebrated one day in the life of Leopold Bloom. Joyce was one of the early authors to incorporate an innovative literary technique referred to as a stream of consciousness.

In fact, Whitman's words have had a profound influence not only on my work, but on generations of artists. I'm inspired by his courage to express the ordinary as extraordinary, and how he protected the integrity of the totality of his work, rejecting calls to dilute references that some found offensive.

Underside of a floral orb celebrating Walt Whitman's garden, showing figures grouped together. This is an example of taking a glass tradition from the nineteenth century and giving it a fresh point of view.

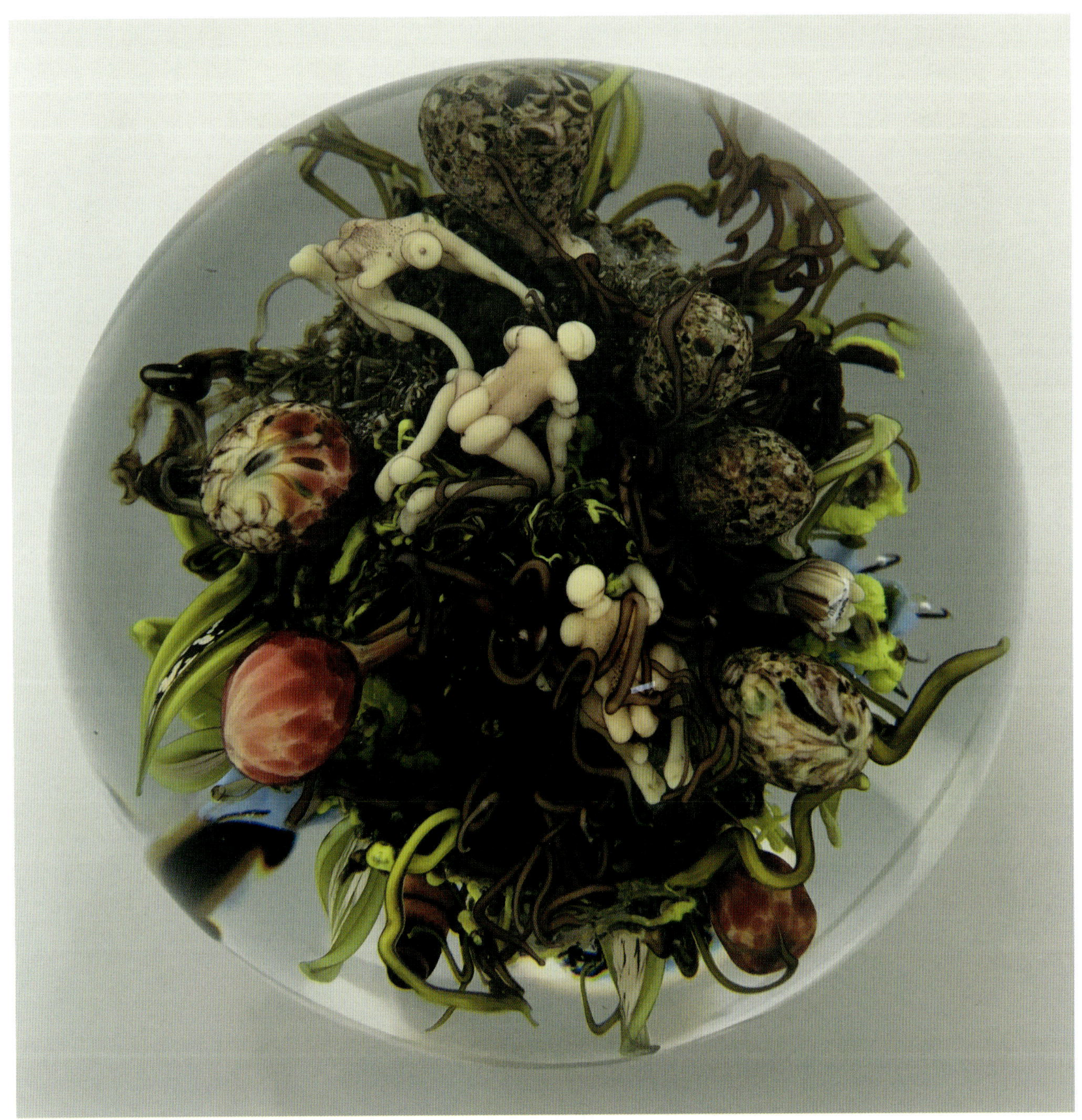

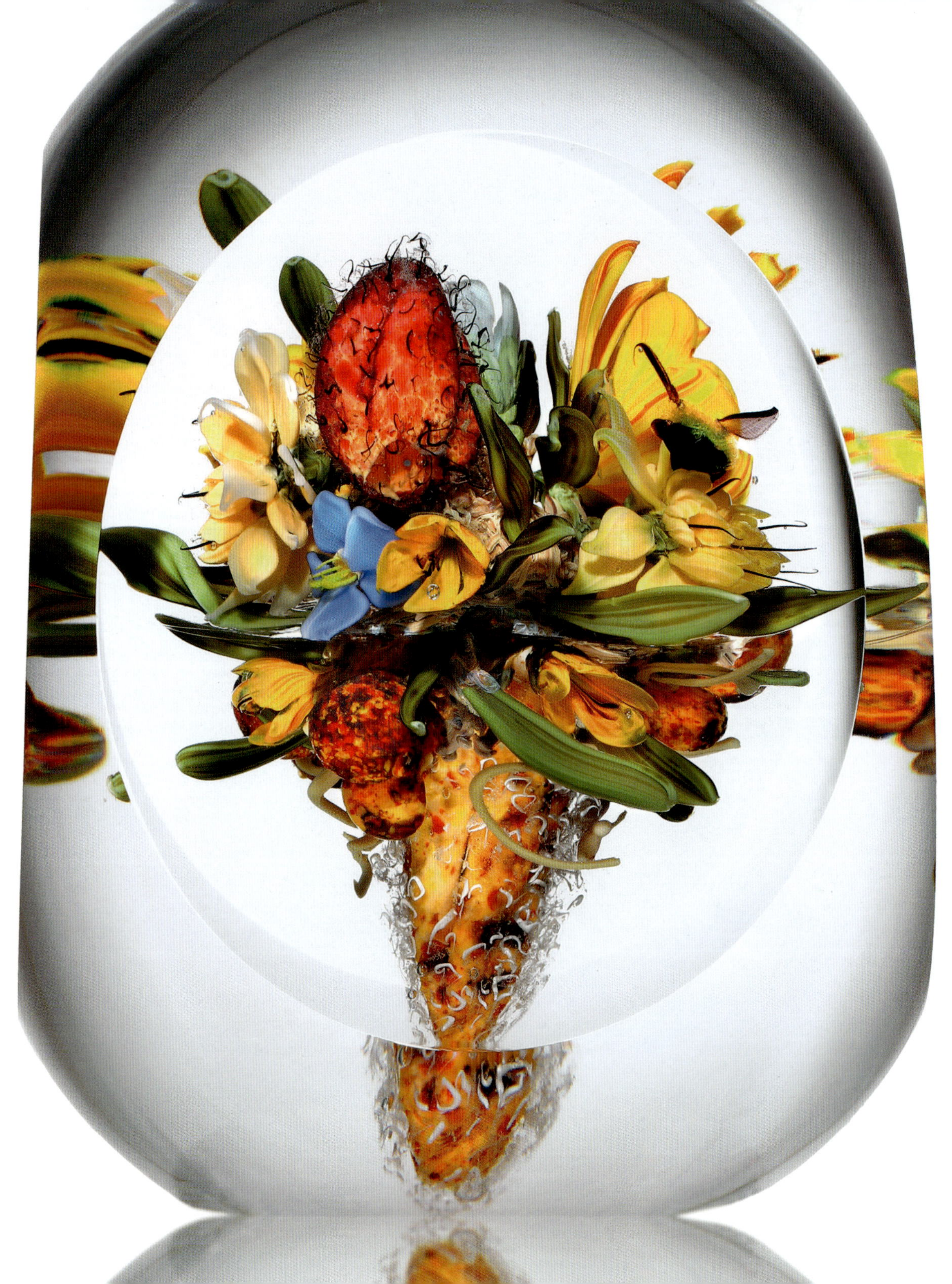

You shall not look through my eyes either, nor take things from me, You shall listen to all sides and filter them from yourself.

—Walt Whitman

Either define the moment or the moment will define you.

—Walt Whitman

***Vineland Bouquet*, 2021, 4 x 3 in.**
This piece represents a new direction for my floral designs. I felt fortunate that my experimental efforts facilitated this exciting new form.

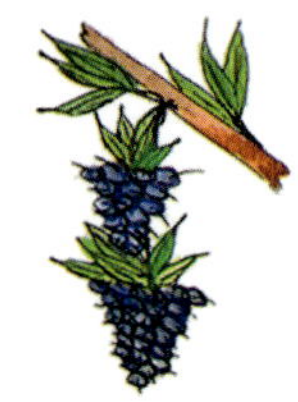

CHAPTER 14: BECOME OBSESSED

Your job is to get your audience to care about your obsessions.

—Martin Scorsese

Lilac Bouquet

Looking back over my career, being obsessed becomes apparent only in retrospect. Obsession is not good or bad—it is simply doing your work and following your torment and your bliss. This piece is an excellent example of an ambitious floral design that appears balanced, especially having the roots entwined and dangling. This grouping works because of the variations in color. You can read it—meaning that you can feel the individuality of the plants. When this came out of the oven, I was very impressed and tried to replicate it but had no success. There is a spontaneity associated with this design that made it special. This spontaneity reflected my obsession in an unusual creative need that wouldn't let me back off but pushed me into new territory.

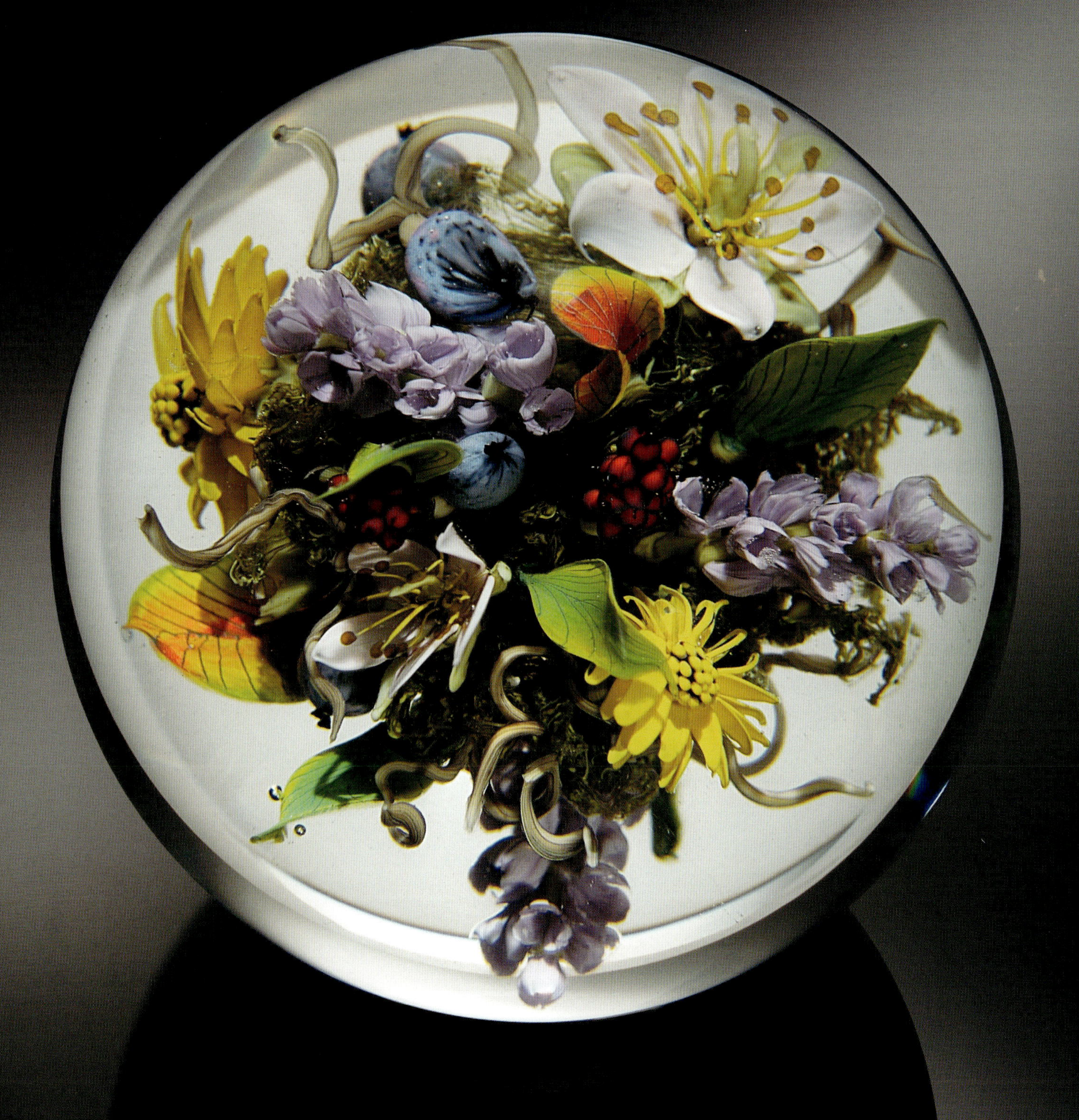

When I was in my forties, my wife, Pat, came to me one day and said, "Paul, outside of the family, all you do is work glass and talk about glass. You need a hobby."

Pat was right, but glass was my hobby and my obsession. And I was comfortable with that and still am.

The word "obsession" has a negative connotation. If you look it up, many dictionaries define it as a dominating thought that seizes the mind. The distant root of the word comes from a Latin phrase for obstructing something. While there are clearly cases where obsessive thought is an impediment to normal life, to the artist, an obsession—when internalized and expressed through the work—articulates depth of feeling, emotion, and a fresh point of view—in short, everything for which serious art is celebrated.

Being obsessed in and of itself won't contribute to significant art. You have to nurture and exploit the obsession. In industry, I reached the master's level before redirecting my skills to the creative side. As a self-employed artist-craftsperson, I've experienced a heightened sense of self-worth. By focusing my creative energy to explore and interpret the beauty and fecundity of a flowering plant, I've educated myself in a way that allows me to work toward my full potential.

This was not a passing thought: my particular emotional need has been, and still is, the motivating factor for my fifty-year journey—a career that has been propelled by wanting to be educated. My artistic goal is complemented by a spiritual desire to interpret in glass God's delicate flowering plants.

It was not an easy journey: in part because I knew I had to identify artistic excellence overall, moving beyond the boundaries of craft and sculpture. I took advantage of what I learned from studying literature and the philosophy of beauty.

Art making is a head trip first, an exercise in hand skills second. An artist beginning his or her journey might think, at first, that listening to the poetry of Walt Whitman would have little to do with my work. But in fact, I have been challenged by the depth of feeling Walt Whitman brought to his art and have been absorbed in his work and life for thirty-five years. His tools were words, fresh and significant words that broke through literary boundaries and gave America an authentic voice that influenced future writers.

Excellence, whether it's art, music, or literature, celebrates beauty, and excellence is nurtured by passion, which is another way of saying obsession.

I think my work represents an esoteric take on native flowers that speaks to my recollection of picking flowers for my mom. I believe my passion for sharing this childhood joy will become my legacy.

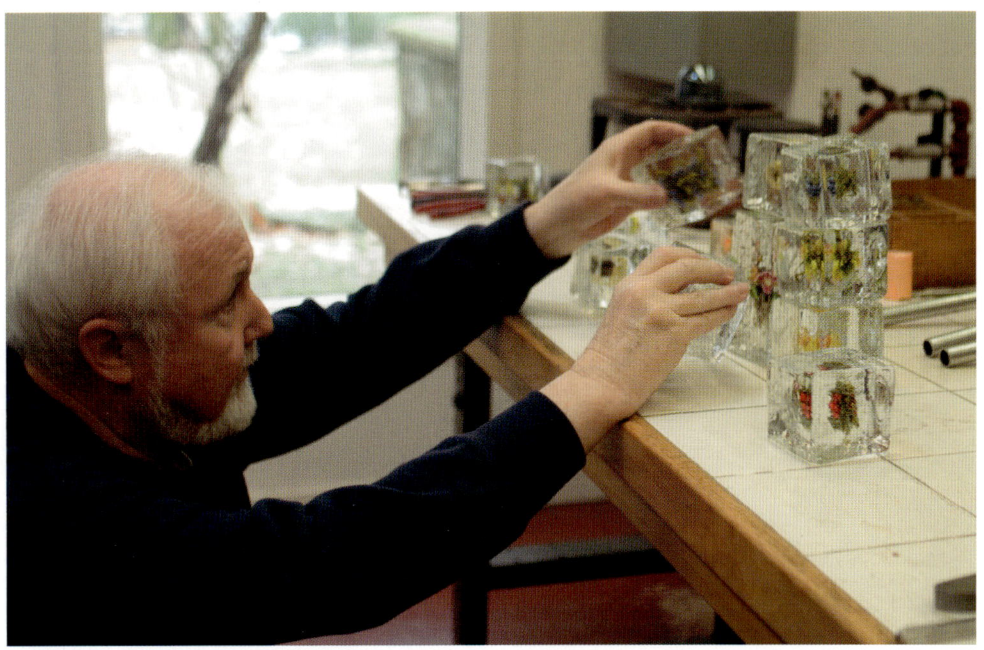

Selecting arrangement of elements for an Assemblage series

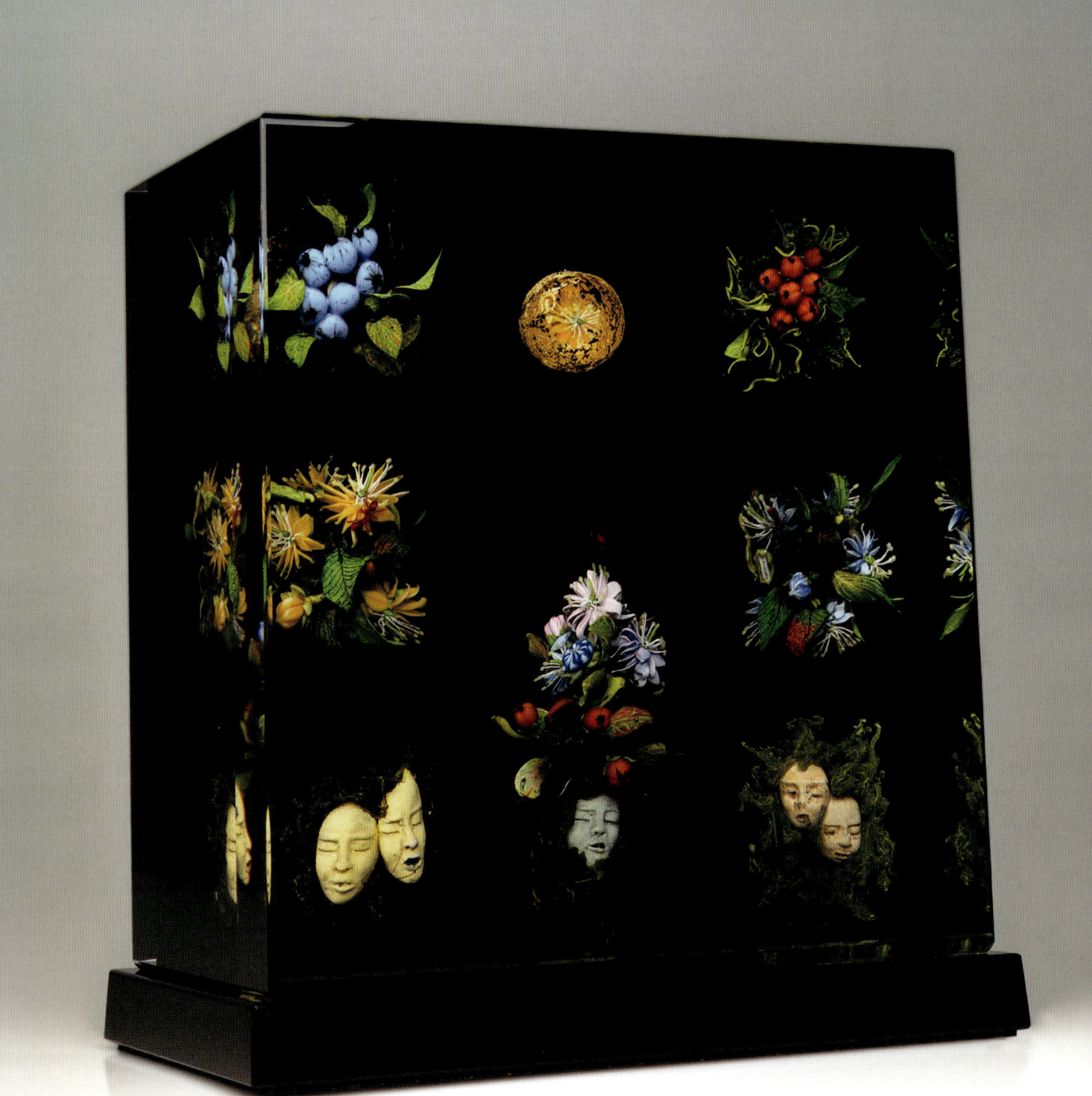

Your ability to use the principle of autosuggestion will depend, very largely, upon your capacity to concentrate upon a given desire until that desire becomes a burning obsession.

—Napoleon Hill

***Cloistered Assemblage with Native Flowers and Golden Orb*, 8.25 × 7.25 × 4.5 in., 2009, Courtesy of Fort Wayne Museum of Art, Fort Wayne, Indiana.**
In the photo at left, I am studying the groupings and relationships between the floral cubes and the whole. At right is a finished piece. My work has evolved by laminating components into a visual story celebrating the mysteries of nature. This assemblage represents an endless search for expression within the parameters of a lifelong focus.

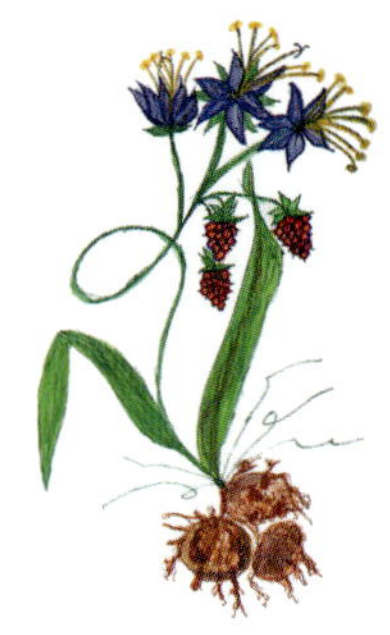

CHAPTER 15: TAKE ADVANTAGE OF ANXIETY

Anxiety is the hand maiden of creativity.

—T. S. Eliot

***Orb with Masks*, 2002, 6 in.**

This work was created to commemorate 9/11. The Heller Gallery in New York City, shortly after the 9/11 attack, challenged their artists to address the tragedy through their work. This piece was purchased by collectors Bruce and Ann Bachmann from the Chicago area, who later donated it to the Henry Ford Museum in Dearborn, Michigan, where it is now on display. Much of my work is about serenity; this represents the flip side in a direct visual dialogue.

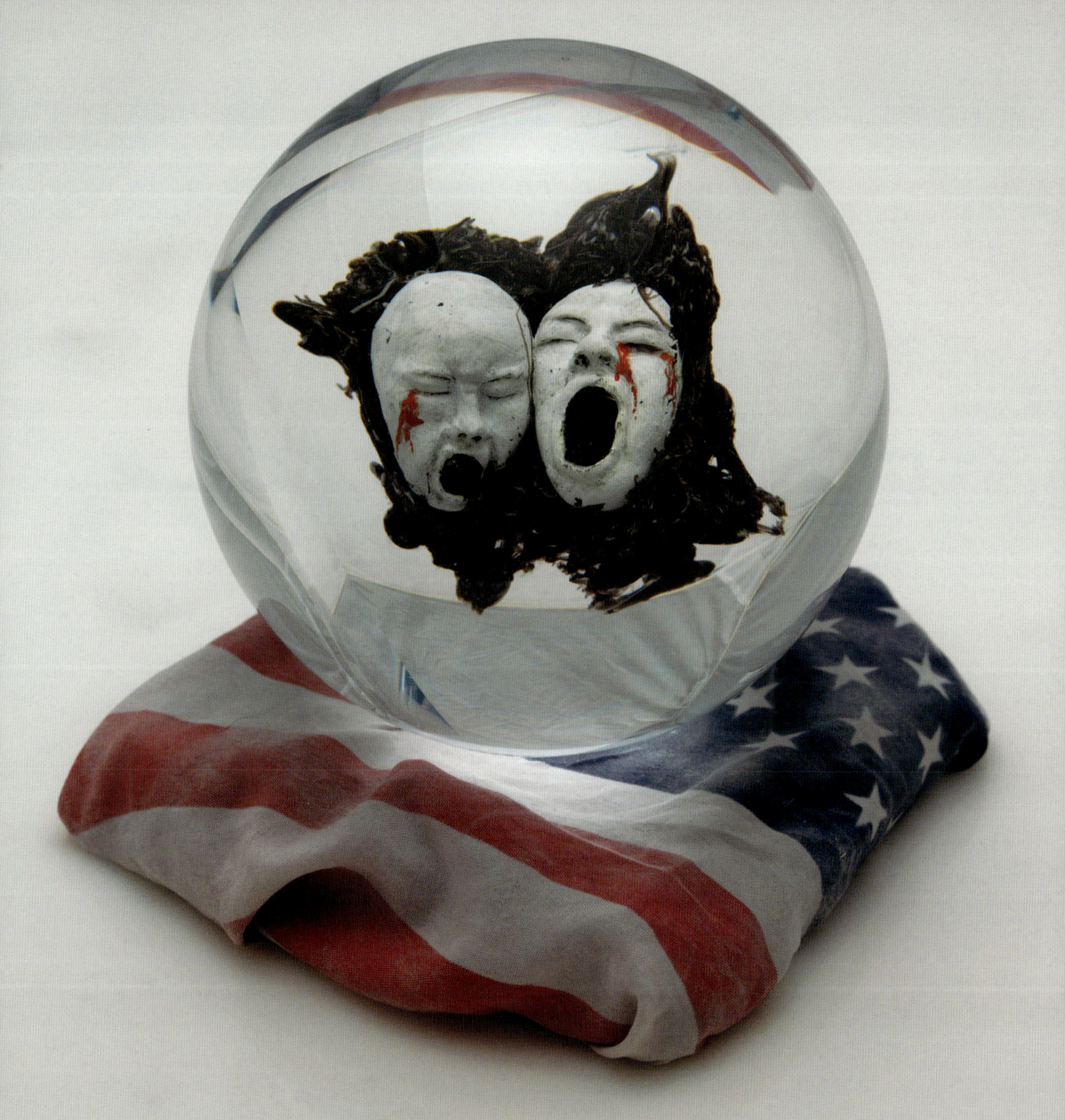

In 1972, I left industry to be on my own, working as an independent studio artist. From the beginning, I was plagued with anxiety as I was experiencing one failure after another. At one point I went to the doctors with a serious rash and was told it was stress-related hives. Thank God, during those first few years, there were enough successes to offer hope.

Just recently I was experiencing a high level of anxiety working on developing a new design with blossoms with a complex pistil-stamen structure combined with prickly fruit.

Once my experiential efforts showed promise, I spent days incorporating the new ideas into my new design to be encased in clear glass. When the work was completed at the bench, I placed the piece in the annealing oven to invisibly complete its forty-hour cycle. The anxiety was very uncomfortable.

After fifty years, my anxiety has not gone away, and in fact it is as intense as it's ever been. Ultimately, the emotional struggle has been a benefit, even though that struggle takes its toll.

For me, this is life in the studio. The process is dictated by curiosity, desire, and a spiritual celebration of beauty.

Prickly Fruit
After days of experimenting to get it right, I was confident that I had nailed it. When I put this piece in the oven on a forty-hour cycle, time seemed to stand still. The anxiety of waiting for the annealing cycle to finish was uncomfortable. I couldn't stop thinking about what I perceived to be a major breakthrough in my repertoire of illusions. On the other hand, sometimes when a work comes out of the oven it becomes apparent that the idea did not translate. You can't "read" the glass while the piece is under construction. It takes the magic of the crystal to bring out the intelligence of the piece.

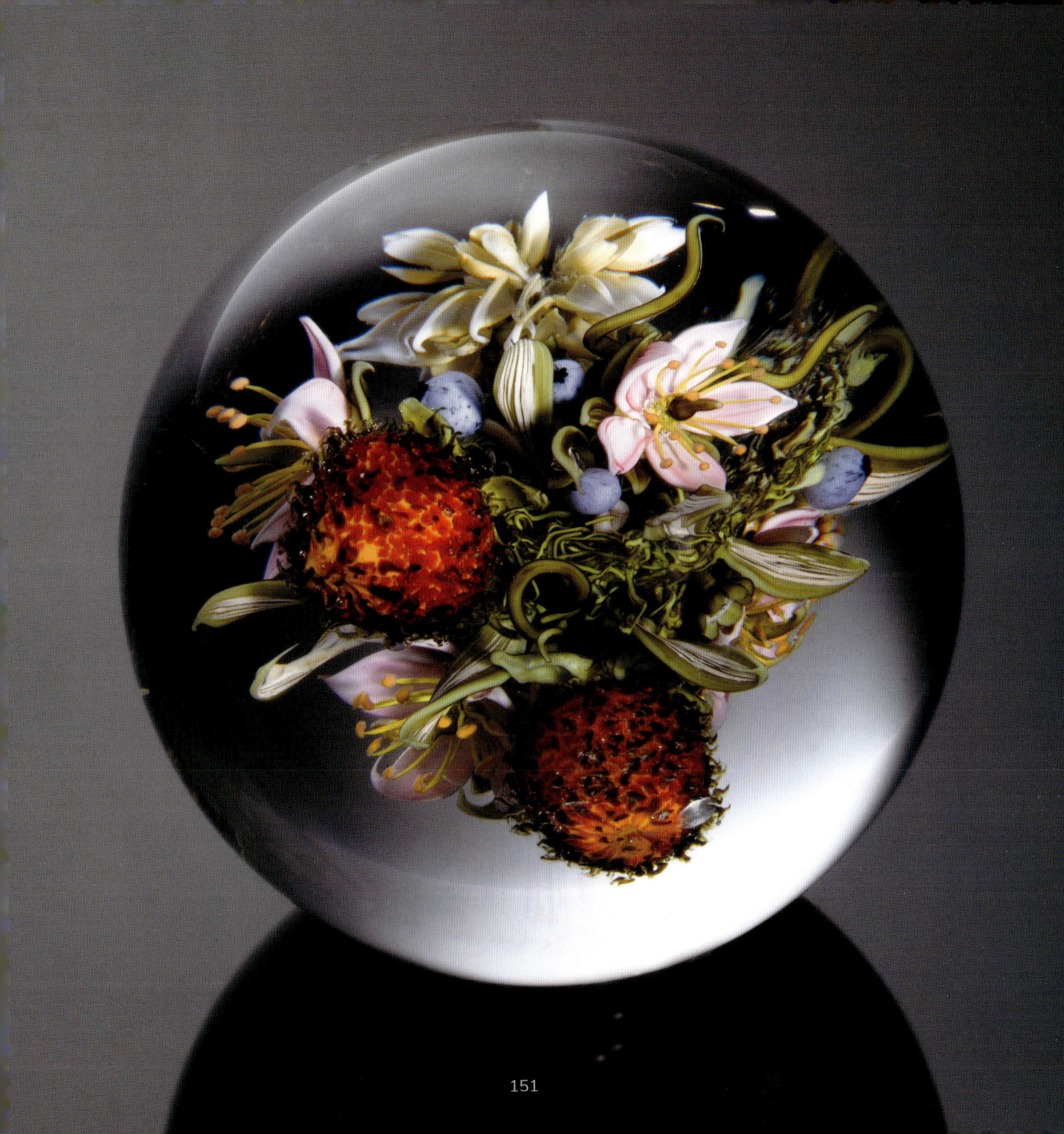

During this process, many artists, including me, pursue spontaneity that leads to a personal vision.

As uncomfortable as it may be, by embracing anxiety you are accessing the center point of your creative energy. I believe most artists are fine-tuned, and thus emotionally involved and vulnerable. Their self-worth is predicated on how they perceive their creative efforts, and to varying extents on how other people perceive their work.

Creative people are not indifferent to informed opinion about their work, regardless of how critical it is. Criticism can be a sweet blessing when it introduces the artist to new possibilities.

There are often times I am invited to speak at a museum opening or be present and available to talk about my work during the opening night for a gallery exhibit. This is a serious responsibility that often translates into art sales. It's also important to the museum or gallery, which is inviting the public into the experience, seeking to attract publicity in the community and in art news publications.

Showing your work publicly and seeking publicity in this way can be stressful. I worry about every conceivable thing, including criticism, that affects my career. If you have an unsuccessful show at a gallery, it can have serious consequences—for you and your finances. Come to terms with being uncomfortable. It comes with the territory of being an artist.

In a strange way, how artists handle anxiety separates the masters from the mediocre. Amateurs will avoid discomfort. Staying comfortable keeps you from being curious, and you may avoid taking risks that will advance the work.

Taking risks will allow you to compete with the past in an unusual way. Playing it safe can provide you some financial benefits, but you miss out on the opportunity to advance your aesthetic.

Anxiety is predicated on accomplishment and the need to do things well. Embrace it.

Tough it out. Make your anxiety an ingredient of significant work.

Creative people . . . are distinguished by the fact that they can live with anxiety, even though a high price may be paid in terms of insecurity, sensitivity, and defenselessness for the gift of "divine madness," to borrow the term used by the classical Greeks.

—Rollo May

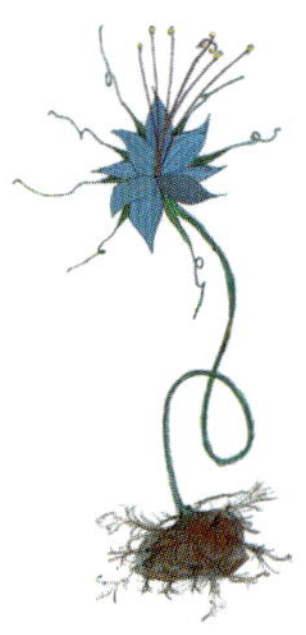

CHAPTER 16: NURTURE SPIRITUALITY AS A MYSTICAL INGREDIENT

Cloistered Botanical
The blue glass laminated on three sides of the clear suggests that the internal design is suspended in space. There are two aspects to this design. Above the earth line are cacti and blossoms suggesting the seen. The figures, under the earth, suggest the unseen. The spiritual attitude is that there is just as much energy under the earth as above, and the fact that we don't see it doesn't mean that it doesn't exist. The reclining figure is ambiguous and passive. The other figures are actively nurturing Mother Earth's plants.

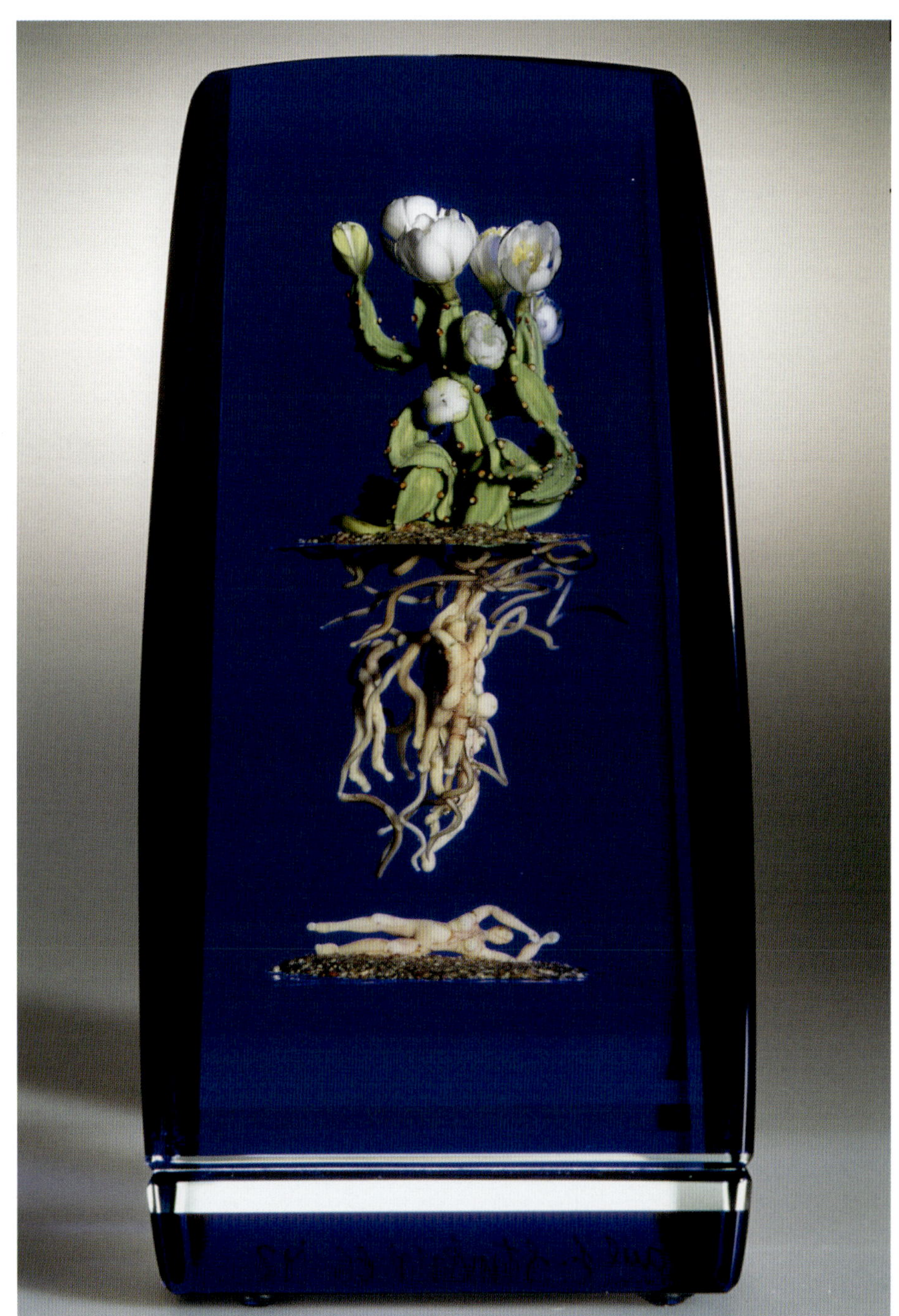

Spirituality is an ingredient in significant art. It radiates a poetic glow often thought of as "beauty." Why do we sense this experience when confronting a beautiful work of art? The fathers of Greek philosophy—Socrates and Plato—believed that the soul had experienced beauty in a previous higher realm, and when confronting beauty on earth, the soul recognized this quality from its past and would flutter.

That is a romantic explanation for why we have this hard-to-describe pleasing feeling when we experience beauty, and it works for me. One senses truth, balance, and well-being when cultured and open to visually connecting with a thing of beauty.

In essence, the Greeks were describing a philosophy that serious artists hope to evidence through their work. From my perspective as a Christian, spirituality is a concept touched through contemplation as prayer.

Spirituality has pervaded every aspect of my life, from childhood to the present. The Good Sisters of Mercy in the parochial school I attended in North Attleboro, Massachusetts, laid the groundwork for a belief system that celebrates the mystical qualities of the unseen.

When I made a career change, crossing over from fabricating scientific glass to creating decorative objects, my prayer evolved to more than mastering a craft, but to a need to understand beauty. From my first moment at the torch in my small space, I placed a crucifix where I could see it as I worked throughout the day. It has been in my view at the bench for fifty years—an ever-present visual mantra guiding the seriousness of my labor.

My belief system afforded an added tension to my artwork, because the process became more about beauty than production. This was not to say that the marketplace is not important; it is, especially when making a living. But it's a delicate compromise that will challenge your artistic maturity.

My focus has been, and continues to this day to be, to make work personal, with the goal to sculpt the essence of the plant kingdom as poetry in glass. I see God evidenced in native flowers, and I don't believe he reserved his most complex efforts exclusively for humans.

Being dedicated to significant works is a way to celebrate God's gift to humanity, and it aligns, in my mind, with the heavenly ideals the ancient Greeks believed in.

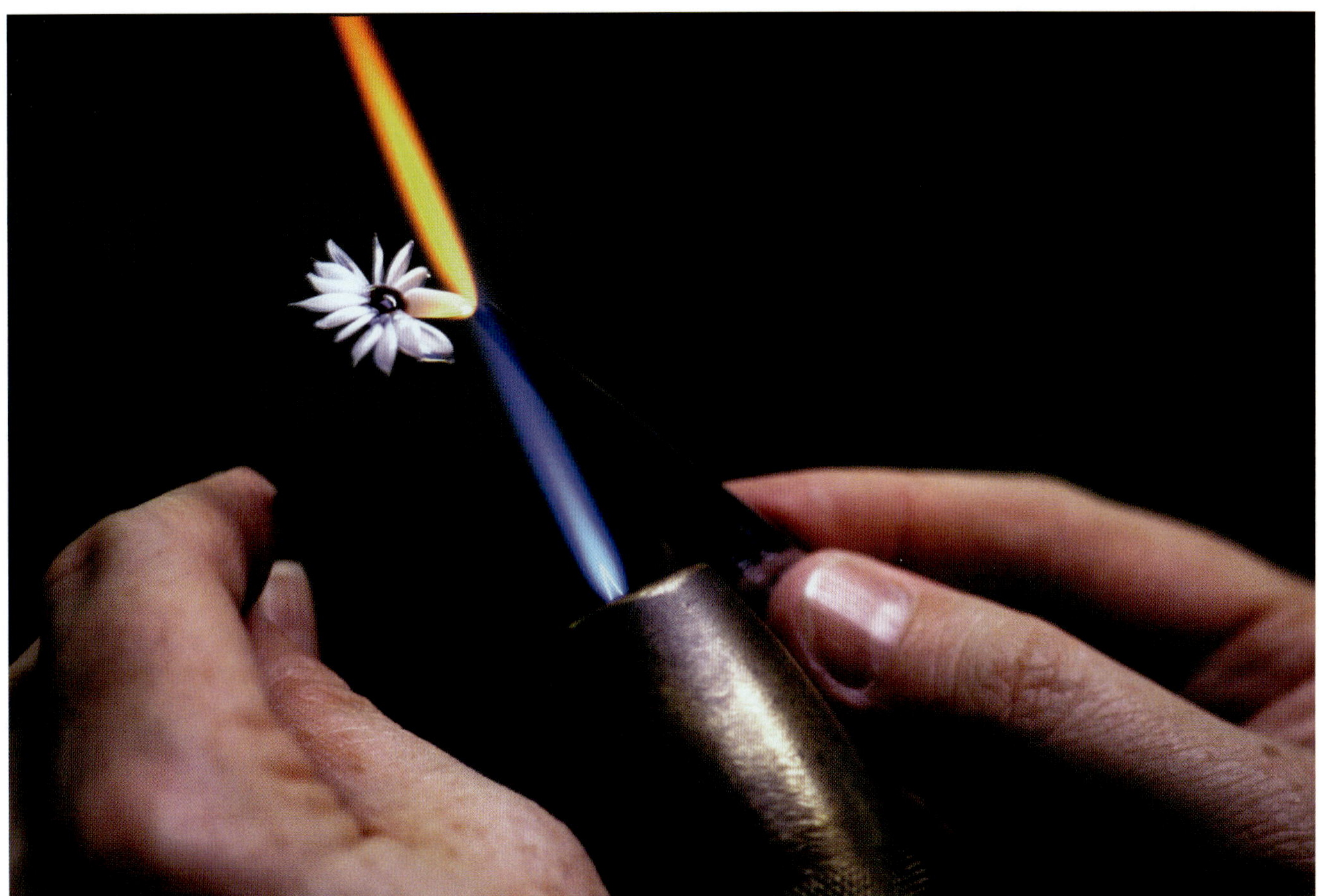

Torch and Flower
This image illustrates the basic process that has occupied my life for over sixty years. What may seem to be a repetitive activity offers a meditative depth of consciousness that occasionally is an outside-of-time experience.

The studio became and still is a sacred space, as I labor to express beauty. I'm personally inspired by the Benedictines, a monastic order whose motto, *laborare est orare*, means "to labor is to pray," and at times I think of myself as a monk in my studio.

Spirituality in the service of beauty is overlaid with labor and prayers. The work is sometimes uncomfortable; sitting over a torch for hours at a time can be challenging. Being an artist is about expressing one's values and sharing one's passion. It is about a visual dialogue regardless of the sacrifice it demands.

There are as many ways to celebrate spirituality as there are artists—it's about doing something well because it's your career. You need to create a belief that a significant effort will transcend the object, please the eye, touch the soul, and radiate a meaningful glow.

When the work is completed, I think of it as my prayer traveling into the future, my eternal connection with time, space, and beauty.

Artistic talent is a gift from God, and whoever discovers it in himself has a certain obligation: to know that he cannot waste this talent but must develop it.

—*Pope John Paul II*

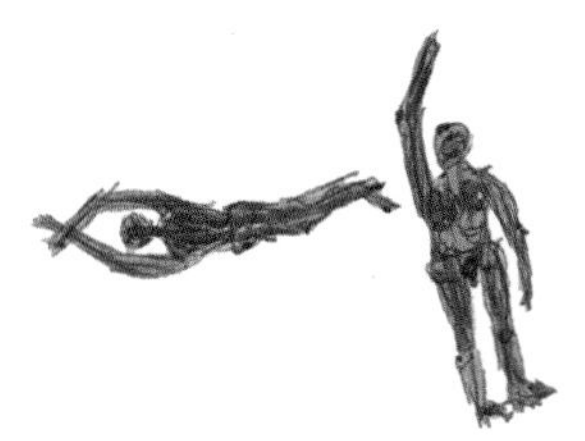

CHAPTER 17: GRATITUDE WITH ATTITUDE

Keep your values positive because your values become your destiny.

—Mahatma Gandhi

Morning Glory Bouquet with Honeybee and Golden Orb
This floral bouquet suspended in a rectangular form has a gold orb floating above. The gold orb is intended to suggest the mysteries of the spiritual. For me, the spiritual equates to gratitude for an adult life of creative exploration.

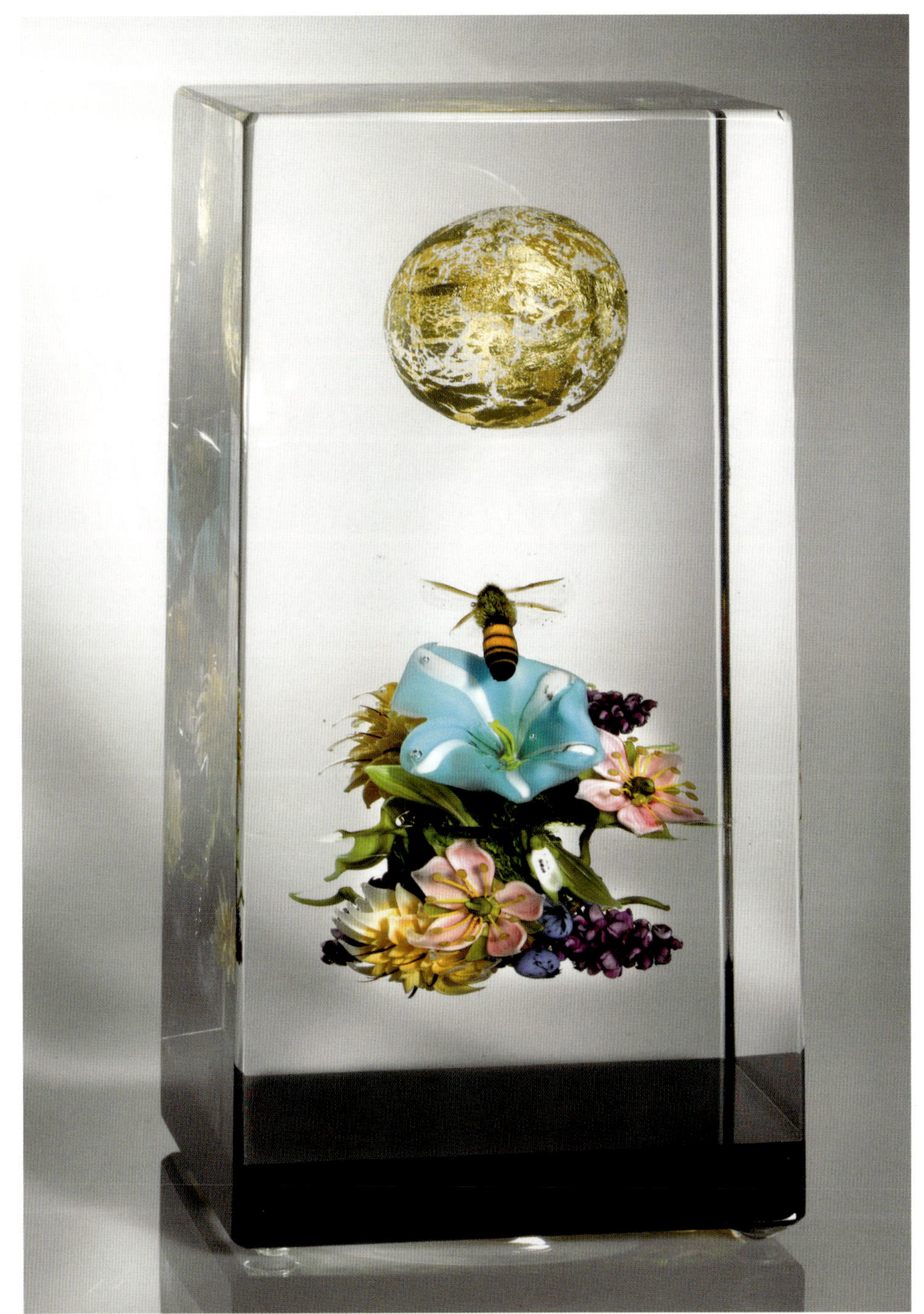

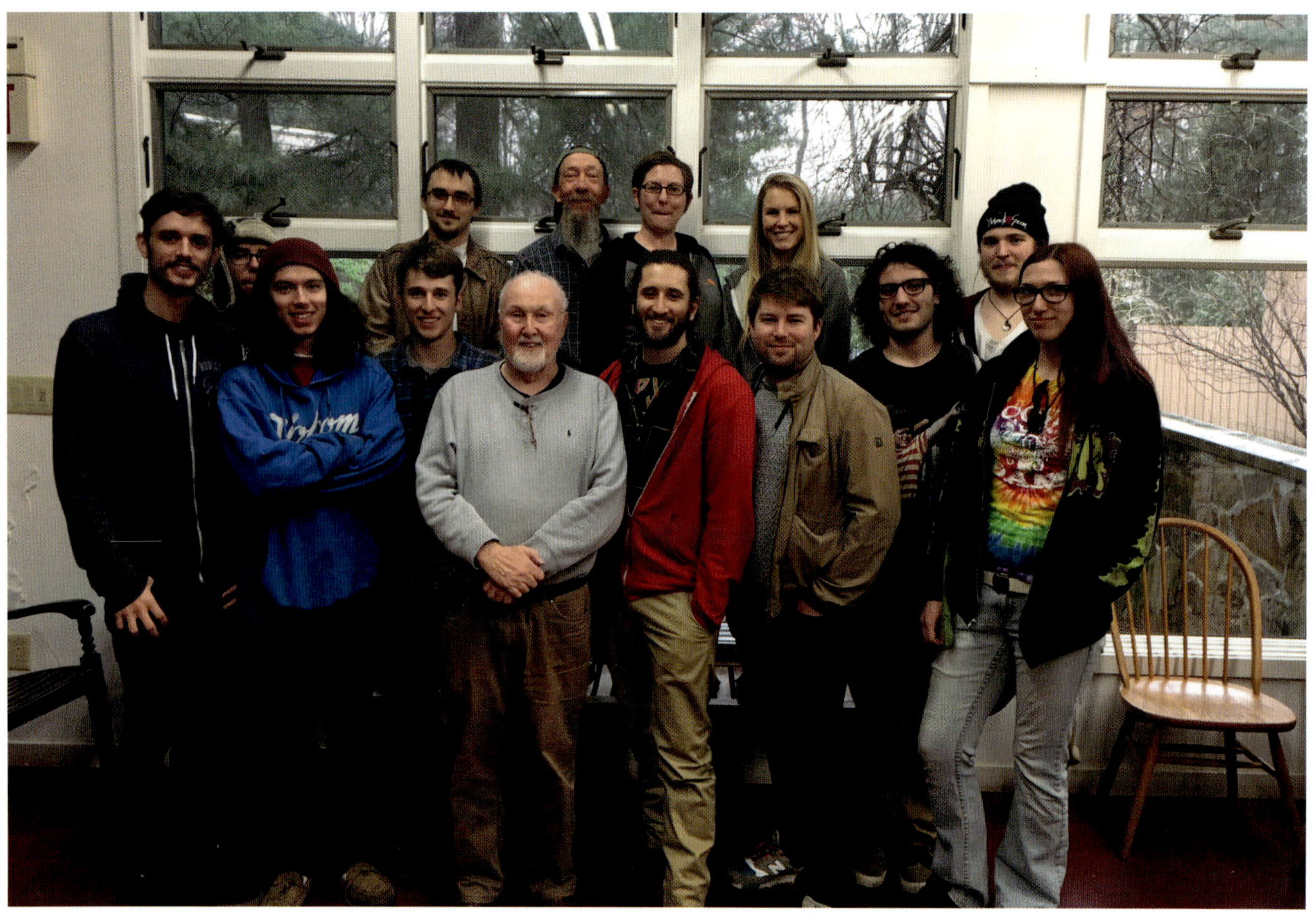

Salem Community College glass students visiting my studio
Over the years I taught at cultural centers around the world. In 1998 I was invited to teach a three-credit course at my alma mater, Salem Community College. As a student—about forty years earlier—I was an underachiever. Occasionally, when I met with students who were experiencing difficulty, I would speak about my background, and I feel I was able to connect. I earned this ability through a lot of sweat and tears. The attitudes that I have nurtured over the years have served me well, and sharing my experiences with students was an honor for which I am deeply grateful. This book is an outgrowth of the strong feelings internalized while working in the studio and teaching. My hope is that readers, like students, will seriously consider my attitudes. Even if they don't relate to my teaching, they should know that this book represents my time-tested observations and personal experiences related to art making.

Combine gratitude and attitude and you are inviting a sense of well-being into your work and life as you discover and refine your creative journey.

First, the importance of attitude: this is a quality that is not hard-wired into your brain. You can control it by bringing an upbeat desire and commitment to the work that you are engaged in.

You can be critical of your work, but you should not allow your first response to disappoint you and sour your attitude on the basis of the natural inclination to doubt your worth. Almost everyone—including me, and perhaps especially me—looks at their first effort and feels it could be better.

Often, the only people who think their first effort is special are amateurs. They lack a frame of reference. Over time, the newness of your work and your doubts about its quality will fade. This is a good thing, because when your work is new, your response is the most critical.

Everyone can do better, and once you have established a baseline you can see how your work can be improved. You are emotionally involved during this time, but if you maintain a good attitude, you are not brooding or despairing. You are benefiting from experimentation, keeping an open mind about eventually getting it right.

You don't know what right is until you get it right, which is usually an intuitive judgment based on a professional attitude.

In sum: a good attitude for a creative professional is self-imposed critique coupled with the positive view of standing back and living with your creation, giving yourself time to let the work show you how it can be advanced.

Regardless of what medium in which you create, you need to be patient and not despair or abandon the project. Have faith, through your positive attitude, that this is eventually going to reflect the quality you are seeking.

Not every piece will be a masterwork. But don't write it off as a loss, because you can learn from it and grow with it.

How does gratitude play into the equation? Gratitude is the power source you plug in to so you can sustain your positive attitude. It heightens your appreciation for everything you have in your life.

Gratitude will strengthen your resolve to appreciate and revere your life's journey. In the long run, if you focus your gratitude on creative endeavors, it will help you tap into your deepest abilities and reinforce the positive energy of that all-important attitude.

The dual power of gratitude and attitude can be profound. Many people believe that the connection evidences itself as a thank-you prayer and becomes a mindset that not only encourages success but draws success to you. Perhaps this metaphysical law of attraction will open your soul to new vistas and personal feelings. And that is what creative expression is all about.

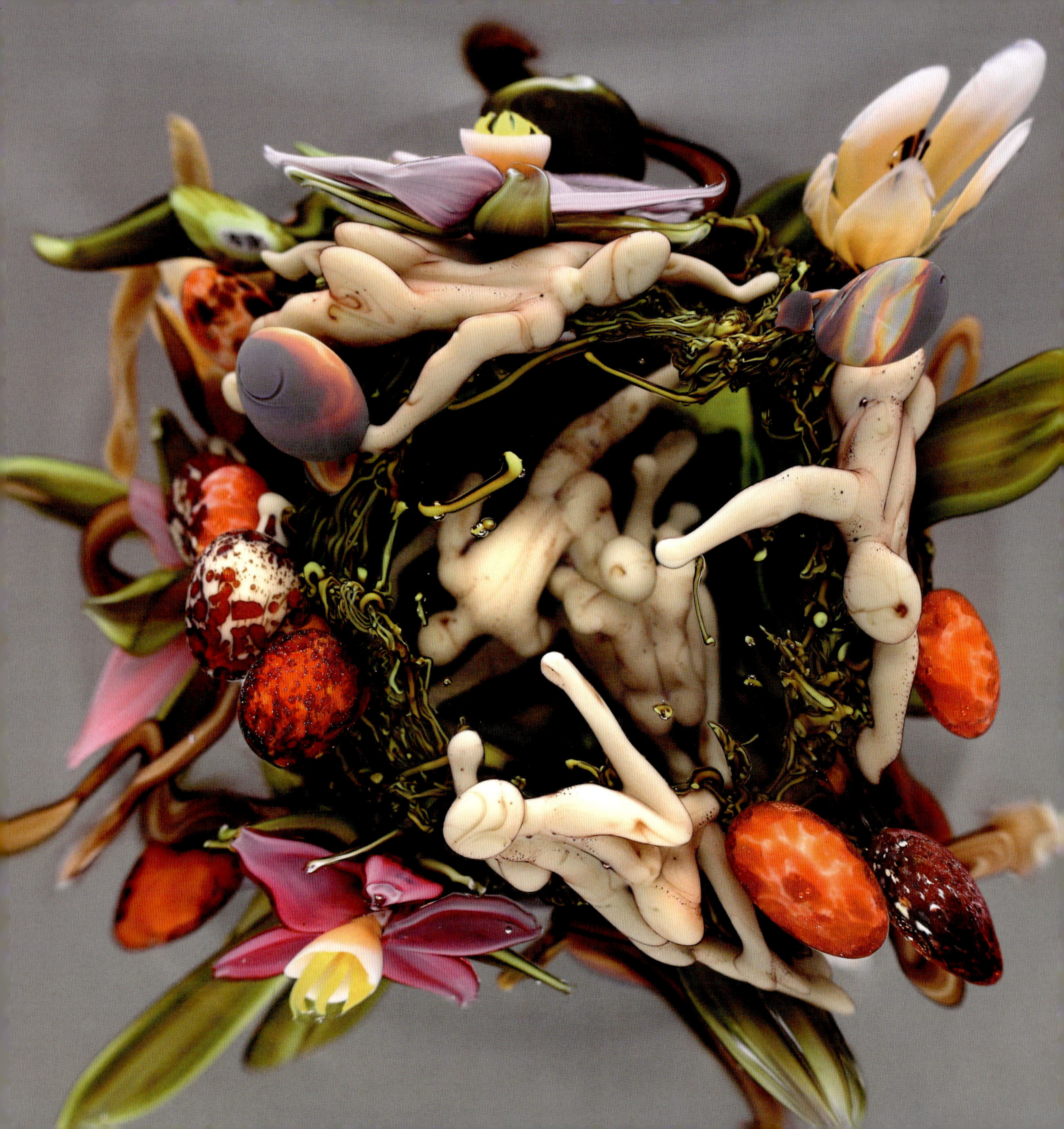

Gratitude is the healthiest of all human emotions. The more you express gratitude for what you have, the more likely you will have even more to express gratitude for.

—Zig Ziglar

Figures entwined in moss and fruit.

EPILOGUE

This book centers on making and appreciating art. You can appreciate art without being a maker; you cannot, in my view, be a serious maker without understanding serious work and the artistic impulse.

There is a commonality in creativity that transcends categories. Throughout this book, I was aware of my bias as an object maker and took pains to be open to the various ingredients and expectations that go into creativity in general. These chapters are a philosophical overview of one's search for expression, strengthened by a half century of introspection.

I am aware that there are two audiences for this book: creative people in all genres who may be curious about a self-taught approach to expressing one's feelings, and appreciators and collectors who value beautiful objects to live with, works that will enhance one's civility and sense of well-being.

Most artistic careers result in an emotional rollercoaster. There is a commitment to a lifestyle that searches for expression in ways that are outside commercial consideration. The business end obviously exists, but for the serious artist, it is not the main point.

I've woven my attitudes through the book but never stated explicitly until now how your passion can evolve into a rewarding lifestyle. You may become a celebrity, or you may not—but regardless, you will be respected in society and have the opportunity to enrich your community.

It is a blessing to realize that people enjoy your work from a variety of viewpoints that are filtered through their personal emotional prisms.

If creators are dedicated to their artistic vision, over the years the informed community will become aware of the accomplishments and will applaud your cumulative efforts. You must be focused and patient. You must possess heroic perseverance and a belief in your worth to become an "overnight success," even if it takes twenty years of struggle.

Let me close with a poem to the future. I wrote it in the late '80s, and it expresses my desire to share my vision with you today and into the future.

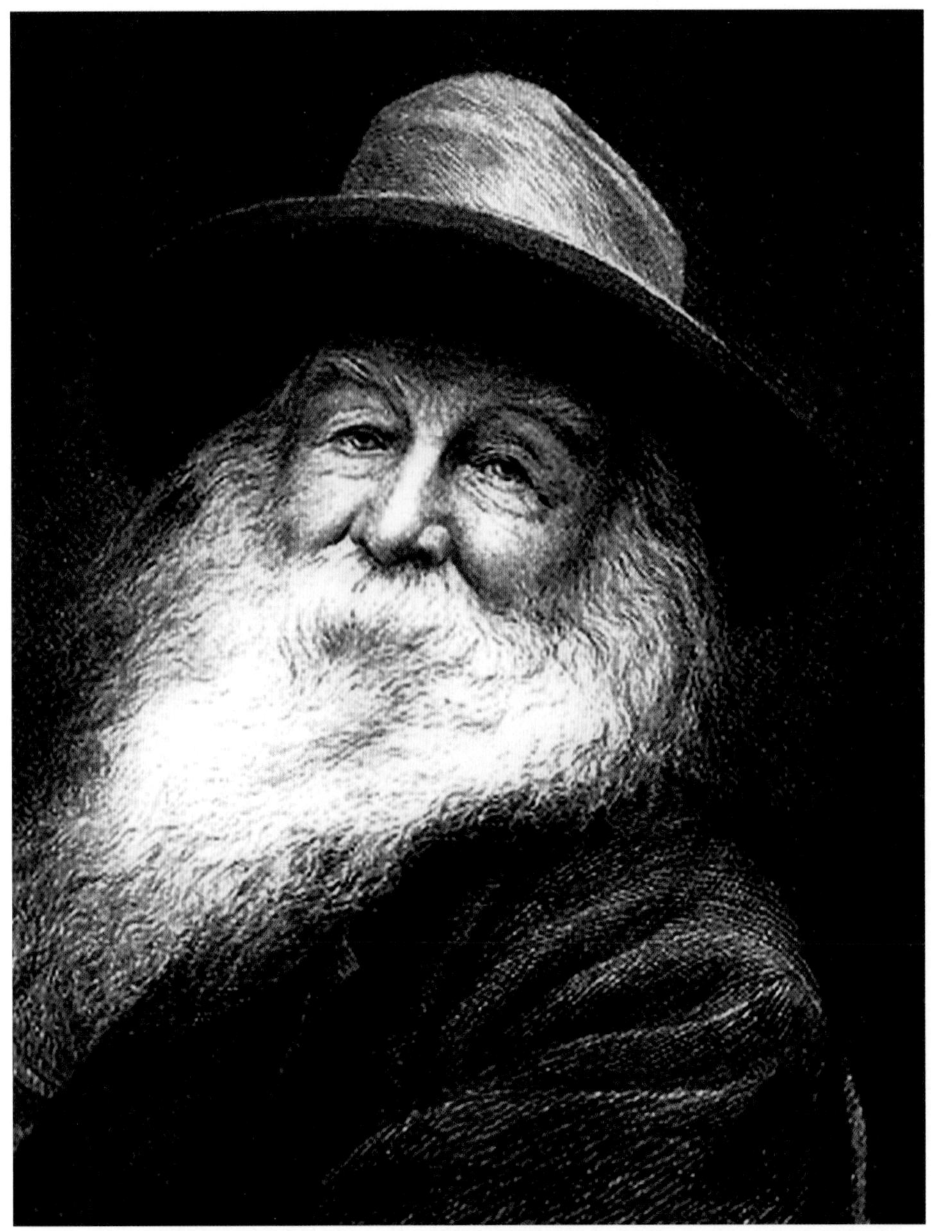

Walt Whitman's poetry was a source of inspiration to me and motivated me to take risks and work toward my full potential. Not everyone would necessarily have the same takeaway from Whitman, but that's what he meant to me.

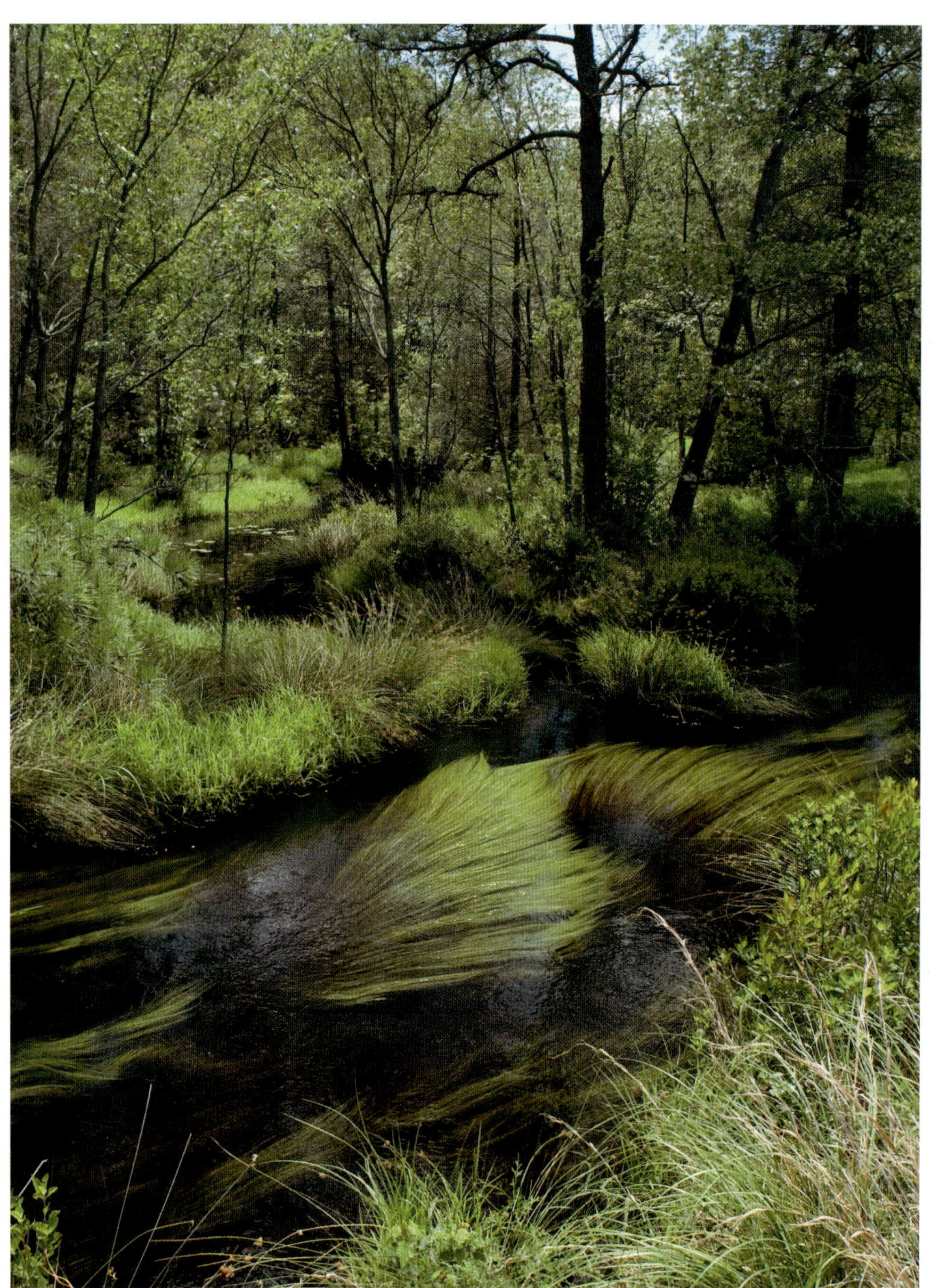

Pine Barren scenic view
Nature is perfect. The artist strives to capture the spiritual and emotional energy of the world.

Receive this glass
it holds my memories
crafted blossoms
suspended
in stillness
to be pollinated
by your sight
anticipating
your touch
through time.

—Paul J. Stankard,
Mantua, New Jersey

ACKNOWLEDGMENTS

I wish to thank Carl D. Hausman, PhD, professor of journalism at Rowan University, who assisted me in all aspects of editing these pages. His experienced counsel gave me a solid platform to stand on while sharing my experience as an object maker.

I want to acknowledge my past and present assistants: David Graeber, Pauline Stankard Iacovino, Patricia Christine Kressley, Katherine Stankard Campbell, Jim Shaw, Robert Stephan, Joseph Paul Stankard, and Patricia Clune.

These people have offered valuable insight and assisted me at various levels: Hank Murta Adams, Shane Fero, and Barry Zuckerman.

Thanks to the research library at the Corning Museum of Glass, and to Susan Gogan, president of Wheaton Arts and Cultural Center.

I would like to acknowledge publisher Pete Schiffer from Schiffer Publishing, along with editors Helena Neufeld and Sandra Korinchak.

Special thanks to Robert Minkoff and the R. M. Minkoff Foundation.

My gratitude to the following talented photographers: James Amos, Kayla Dawn, Kristin Deady, Jeff DiMarco, Dr. Michael Diorio, Ron Farina, Lauren Garcia, Michael Hogan, Pauline Stankard Iacovino and Douglas Schaible. Thanks, too, to the Corning Museum of Glass and the Seattle Art Museum for providing images.

In loving memory of Dr. Michael Diorio, Mike Belkin, and Robert M. Minkoff.

Special thanks to Dr. Michael Gorman, president of Salem Community College, and assistant dean Kristin Deady, as well as Salem Community College's past presidents: Dr. Peter Contini and Joan M. Baillie.

A heartfelt acknowledgment to Jefferson University Hospitals physician and professor Matthew H. Carabasi, MD. Dr. Carabasi has enhanced the quality of my life through his healing gifts managing my chronic lymphocytic leukemia.

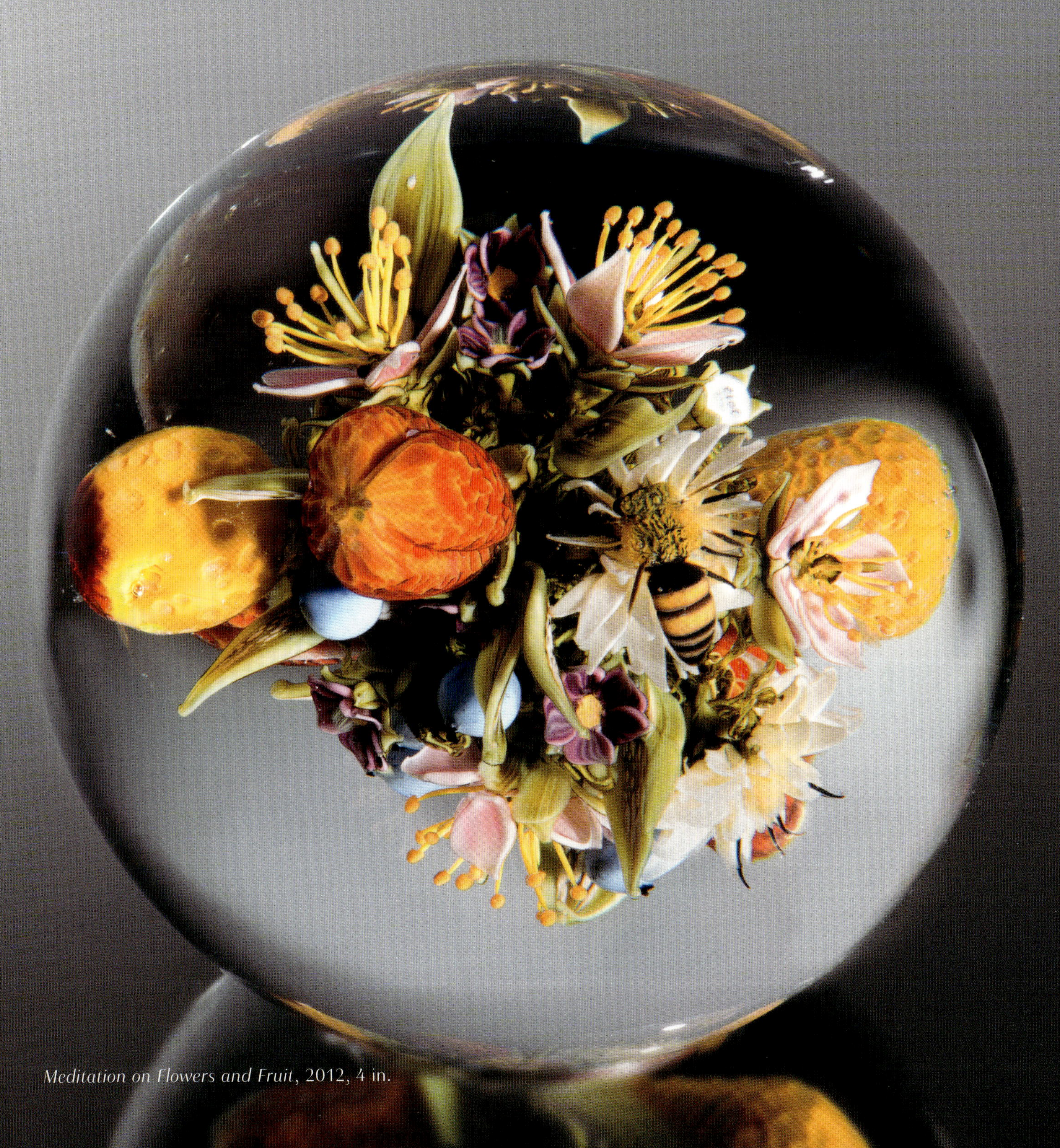

Meditation on Flowers and Fruit, 2012, 4 in.

Public Collections

The Mike and Annie Belkin Retrospective Collection, Akron Art Museum, Akron, OH *
Art Institute of Chicago, Chicago, IL *
Barry Art Museum at Old Dominion University, Norfolk, VA
Bergstrom-Mahler Museum, Neenah, WI *
Birks Museum, Milliken University, IL
Birmingham Art Museum, Birmingham, AL
Boston Museum of Fine Arts, Boston, MA
Brooklyn Museum, Brooklyn, NY
Chrysler Museum of Art, Norfolk, VA
Cincinnati Art Museum, Cincinnati, OH
Cleveland Museum of Art, Cleveland, OH
Columbus Museum, Columbus, GA
Corning Museum of Glass, Corning, NY *
Currier Gallery of Art, Manchester, NH
de Young Fine Arts Museum, San Francisco, CA
Flint Institute of Arts, Flint, MI
Fort Wayne Museum of Art, Fort Wayne, IN
GlasMuseum, Ebeltoft, Denmark
Henry Ford Museum of American Innovation, Dearborn, MI *
Heritage Glass Museum, Glassboro, NJ
Hokkaido Museum of Modern Art, Sapporo, Japan
Hunter Museum of American Art, Chattanooga, TN
Huntington Museum of Art, Huntington, WV
Hsinchu Cultural Center, Hsinchu, Taiwan
Indianapolis Museum of Art, Indianapolis, IN
Imagine Museum of Glass, St. Petersburg, FL *
Karnnert Art Museum, University of Illinois, Urbana, IL
Kobe Lampwork Glass Museum, Hyogo, Japan
Lowe Art Museum, University of Miami, Coral Gables, FL
Metropolitan Museum of Art, New York, NY
Milwaukee Art Museum, Milwaukee, WI
Milwaukee Public Museum, Milwaukee, WI
Mint Museum Randolph, Charlotte, NC
Missouri Botanical Gardens, St. Louis, MO
Mobile Museum of Art, Mobile, AL
Montgomery Museum of Fine Art, Montgomery, AL
Morris Museum of Arts and Sciences, Morristown, NJ
Musee des Arts Decoratif, Palais du Louvre, Paris, France
Musee des Beaux-Arts de Montreal, Montreal, Canada
Musee Du Verre, Conches-en-Ouche, France
Museum of Arts and Design, New York, NY
Museum of American Glass, Wheaton Arts and Cultural Center, Millville, NJ *
Museum of Glass: International Center for Contemporary Art,
The Robert M. Minkoff Foundation Collection, Tacoma, WA
Muskingum University, New Concord, OH
National Museum of American History–Smithsonian Institution, Washington, DC
National Museums of Scotland, Edinburgh, Scotland
Newark Public Museum, Newark, NJ *
New Jersey State Museum, Trenton, NJ
New Orleans Museum of Art, New Orleans, LA
Philadelphia Museum of Art, Philadelphia, PA
Racine Art Museum–Charles A. Wustum Museum of Fine Arts, Racine, WI *
Renwick Gallery of the National Museum of American Art –Smithsonian Institution, Washington, DC
Rockford Art Museum, Rockford, IL
Rowan College at Gloucester County, Sewell, NJ
Rowan University, Glassboro, NJ
Royal Ontario Museum, Toronto, Canada *
Salem Community College, Carney's Point, NJ*
Sandwich Glass Museum, Sandwich, MA
Seattle Art Museum, Seattle, WA
Southern Alleghenies Museum of Art, Lorretto, PA
Suwa Museum, Toyoda, Japan
The Dayton Art Institute, Dayton, OH
The JB Speed Art Museum, Louisville, KY
The Works, Ohio Center for History, Art & Technology, Newark, OH
The Pilchuck Glass School Museum Collection, Seattle, WA
Tittot Glass Art Museum, Taipei, Taiwan
Toledo Museum of Art, Toledo, OH
University of Michigan–Dearborn, Dearborn, MI

Victoria & Albert Museum, London, England
Washington County Museum of Fine Arts, Hagerstown, MD
Wiener Museum of Decorative Arts, Dania Beach, FL*
Zanesville Museum of Art, Zanesville, OH

*large collection

Public Exhibitions

Making It In Crafts III
The Art Museum of Greater Lafayette, Lafayette, Indiana, 2017

Glass At Pilchuck: Making History
Seattle Art Museum, Seattle, Washington, 2014

Beauty beyond Nature: The Glass Art of Paul Stankard (Traveling Exhibition)
Museum of Glass, Tacoma, Washington, 2012

Paul Stankard – Glass Flowers and Walt Whitman
James Renwick Alliance Distinguished Artist Lecture
Renwick Gallery, Smithsonian American Art Museum, Washington DC, 2006

Floating World: Exhibition of Paul J. Stankard (Traveling Exhibition)
Museum of Arts and Design, New York, NY, 2004

Poetic Vision of Nature: The Solo Exhibition of Paul Stankard
Tittot Glass Art Museum, Taipei, Taiwan, 2003

2001 Contemporary Glass Exhibition
Beijing to Shanghai, China, 2001

Paul J. Stankard
Brooklyn Botanical Garden, Brooklyn, New York, 2000

Venezia Aperto Vetro
Venice, Italy, 1998 (catalog)

International Exhibition of Glass
Kanazawa '98 Design Center Ishikawa, Kanazawa, Japan, 1998 (catalog)

Glass Today by American Studio Artists
Museum of Fine Arts, Boston, Massachusetts, 1997 (catalog)

Glass Today: American Studio Glass from Cleveland Collections
The Cleveland Museum of Art, Cleveland, Ohio, 1997 (catalog)

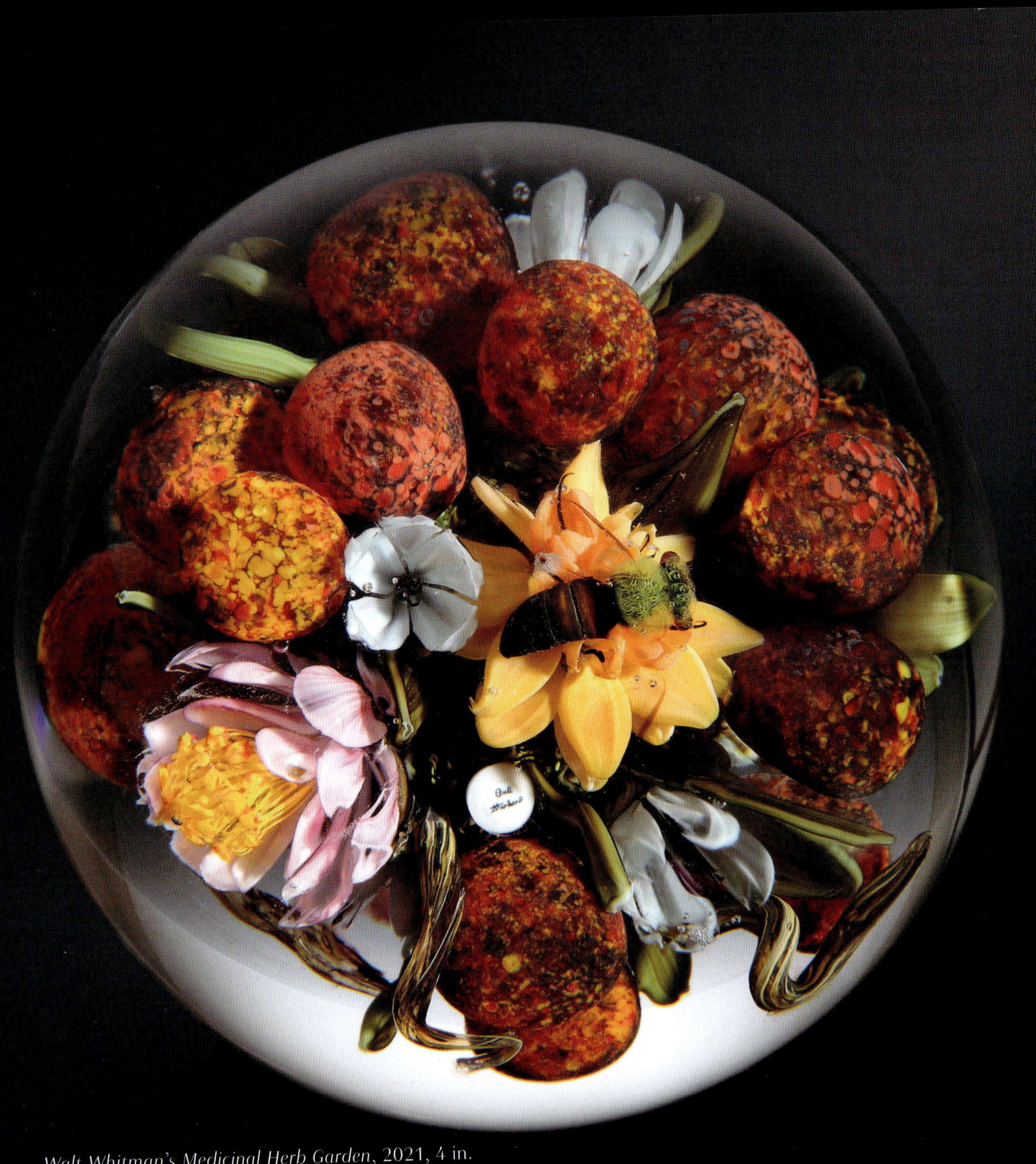

Walt Whitman's Medicinal Herb Garden, 2021, 4 in.

Photo Credits

James L. Amos Photography: Pages 47, 54, 55, 56, 80, 102, 110, 113, 155, 157

Courtesy of Corning Museum of Glass: Page 23

Kayla Dawn Photography: Pages 6, 31

Jeff DiMarco, Glass Art Photographer: Front cover, pages 19, 34, 35, 39, 62, 68, 78, 79, 100, 101, 108, 109, 117, 123, 135, 139, 140, 164, 171, 174

Ron Farina Photography: Back cover, pages 2, 8, 9, 33, 45, 50, 51, 52, 77, 82, 83, 86, 87, 88, 90, 91, 94, 118, 121, 122, 129, 143, 149, 151, 161

John Healey Photography: Page 146

Michael Hogan Photography: Pages 14, 15, 16, 17, 168

Douglas Schaible Photography: Pages 5, 24, 25, 32, 75, 84, 85, 89, 97, 130, 137

Schiffer Publishing: Page 176

Studio Achieves: Pages 10, 12, 29, 30, 40, 48, 53, 69, 70, 115, 145, 162, 167

Courtesy of WheatonArts: Pages 60, 61

An internationally acclaimed artist whose work is represented in over 70 museums, Paul J. Stankard is the recipient of numerous awards and two honorary doctorate degrees. He is a member of the American Craft Council of Fellows and received the Masters of the Medium Award from the James Renwick Alliance, Smithsonian Institution. He received a lifetime achievement award from the Glass Art Society. He is an artist in residence and honorary professor at Salem Community College, southern New Jersey. Stankard's previous books include *No Green Berries or Leaves: A Creative Journey of an Artist in Glass* and *Studio Craft as Career: The Guide to Achieving Excellence in Art-Making*.

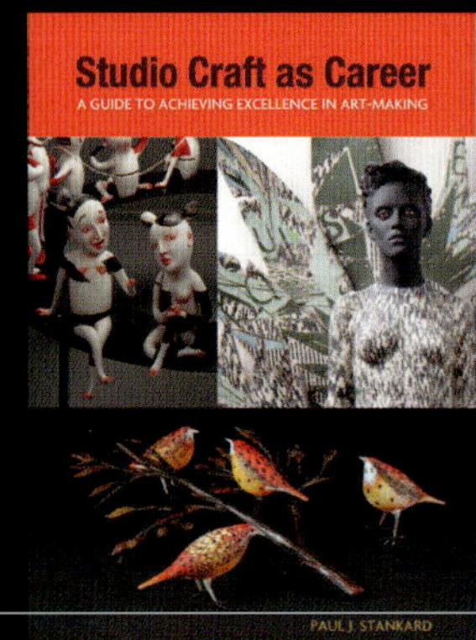

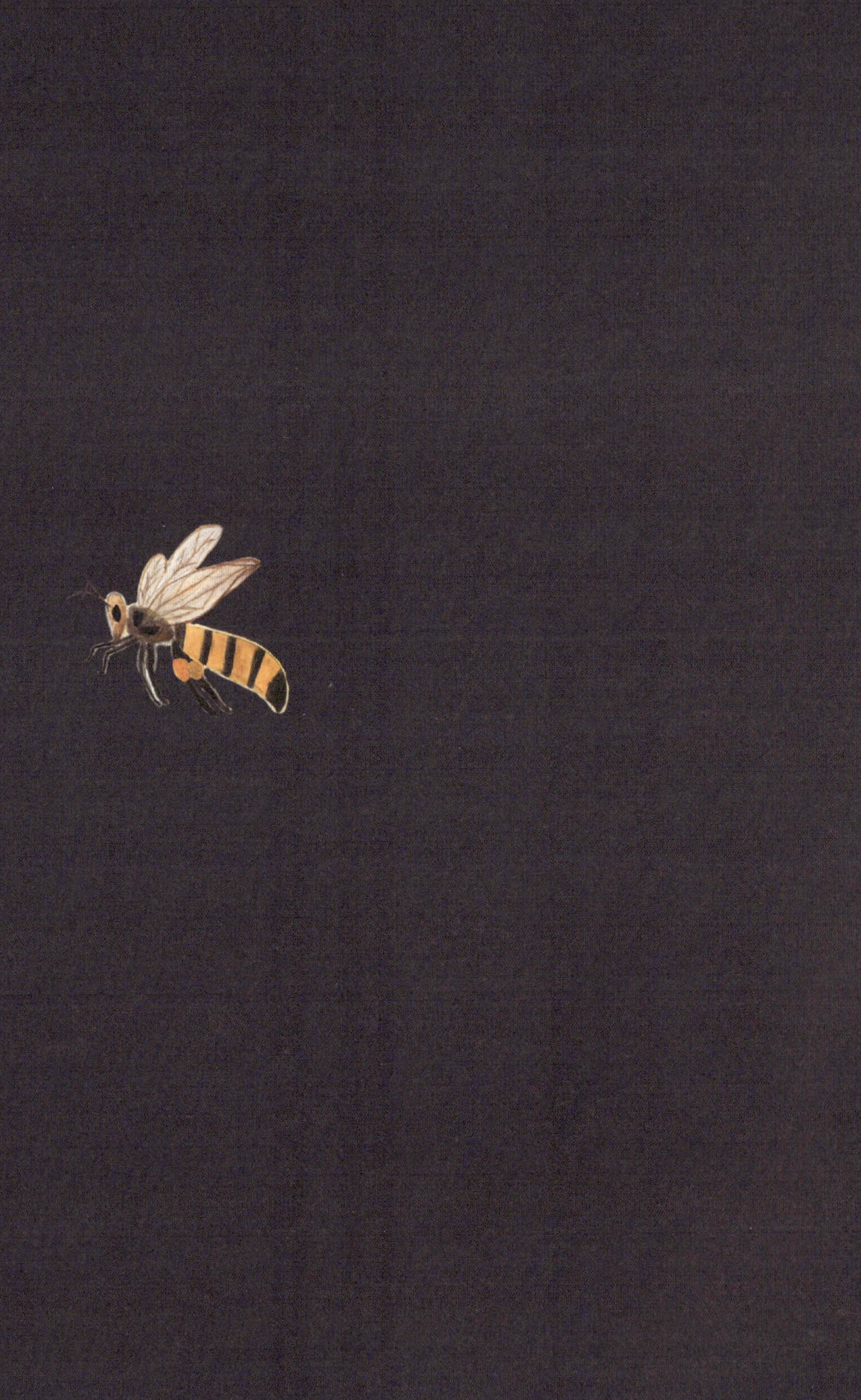

PART 2

THE ELEMENTS OF ART

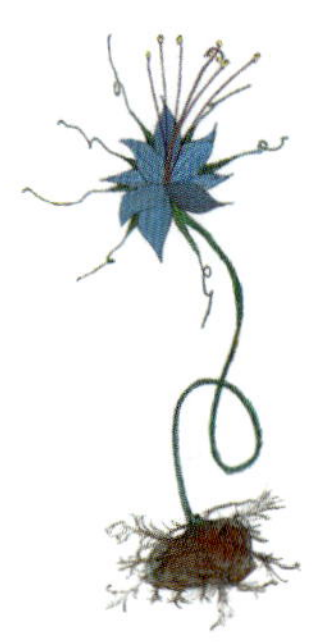

CHAPTER 7: HOW I DEFINE BEAUTY

Never lose an opportunity of seeing anything beautiful, for beauty is God's handwriting.

—Ralph Waldo Emerson

Mid-1970s paperweights

Each effort, regardless of the series—from the early days of the paperweights, to cubes, to botanicals, to assemblages, including triptychs and diptychs, to the more recent orbs—it's mostly about crafting a personal response to the beauty all around in ways that offer the viewer a fresh take on nature. Throughout my studio glass history, the intricacies of the interpretation of flowers have held a consistent and strong focus.

Above, from left to right: *Native Flower Bouquet*, *Bunchberry Blossom and Berries*, and *Blackberries and Buds*. These works are the forerunners to a search for personal expression of beauty—a means of expression that has evolved to this day.